How to
Be a
Better
Boss

How to
Be a
Better
Boss

A Leader's **Three** Perspectives

Jim Delia

ISBN: 978-1-7379284-0-9 (Hardcover)
ISBN: 978-1-7379284-2-3 (Paperback)
ISBN: 978-1-7379284-1-6 (ebook)

Printed in the United States of America.

FIRST EDITION 2022.

Delia and Associates
2055 Lombard Street, #470202
San Francisco CA 94147
www.deliaconsulting.com

Designed by Michele Delia and The Book Designers.

*To my mother, who unconditionally supported
me and my dreams, no matter what they were.*

Table of **Contents**

The **Introduction**

I'm fortunate that I still remember what it felt like when work sucked. I wish I could say that I've had so many positive work experiences that I *had* to share them. I can't.

When I had a job, I always tried my best. Even when I produced some excellent work, I often felt uninspired at the end of the day— or worse. With few exceptions, I trace much of my work dissatisfaction back to my bosses.

When I had a bad boss, my workdays dragged for me. I remember feeling de-skilled, de-motivated, discouraged, disengaged, dejected, and even depressed. I often *dreaded* showing up. Looking back, I honestly don't blame my bosses or feel victimized by them. I just expected more from a boss. Did I expect too much? Or was I simply unlucky?

Do you know what it feels like to dread going to work? As a boss, *you* are often the most significant factor in determining how work feels for the *people* you are responsible for. The people I mean are your team members, employees, staff, workers, or direct reports. (By the way, I intend to use all these terms interchangeably throughout the book. Am I leaving anyone out?)

Most of us spend about half our waking hours at work, so what we do there and how we feel when we are there matters enormously. Among the most common reasons why people leave organizations, "not feeling valued by my manager" almost always appears near the top of their list. A Gallup poll of over 1 million employed U.S. workers found that among those who eventually left their jobs voluntarily, 75% did so because of their bosses. Had I been polled years ago, I would have been one of those workers who left a job (more than once) because of their boss.

I've learned a great deal about good leadership and management directly through my own experiences, as well as indirectly through years of observation and listening to my clients' stories. Many of the most important lessons that I've learned and shared over the years as a consultant, coach, and trainer result from seeing and experiencing what *not* to do as a boss. This is one of the primary reasons I do what I do: I help people in organizations work better, work smarter, and hopefully be more satisfied doing their jobs. The information, tools, and approaches you'll find in this book are based on what I've seen work—and *not* work—in the private, public, and even nonprofit sectors.

It's clear that we need more leaders, not merely managers. "Manager" implies a role or position that typically comes with some level of authority given by the organization or the company's ownership. Anyone can be given the title of manager. However, no one can make you, or anyone else, a leader. "Leader" is a distinction that is only given by followers. Even a single follower can make you a leader!

The theories of "how-to" leadership are not new. As early as 700 B.C.E., the Greeks understood what good leadership was. In his epic work *The Odyssey*, Homer described his main character, Odysseus, as an unselfish leader who was loyal and supportive of his followers. Most successful leaders today also possess similar qualities. I've found that being a leader is a choice you make. It's something you have to decide that you want to do, in whatever role or position you're in.

I have been driven to develop and share practical tools and "how-to" guides in countless training and coaching sessions that I've led. I've worked to help thousands of people create teams and organizations that can be both effective and "healthy" places. This book is for those of you who genuinely want to be good at being a boss. That means being both a good manager *and* a good leader. For those who value simplicity and are looking for straightforward approaches and methods for how to excel as a boss, I think you'll find what you're looking for within these pages.

I did my best to avoid buzzwords and consultant-speak. There are other related books to read with more complex-sounding terminology or data from recent surveys and studies. And if you have the time and interest, I encourage you to read them. Although I have much respect for research, theory, and some theoretical constructs, I wanted to keep things simple in this book because what you need to *do* is simple. Be clear, however, that "simple" does not mean "easy."

I'm a practitioner, not an academic. So, consider this book to be a field guide rather than a comprehensive reference for management and leadership topics. The focus is on the best "practice" of management and leadership when you are the boss. You'll also find many practical tips on coaching because I've found that the best bosses are good coaches.

If you're already in a management role, and especially if you're still considering whether or not to be a manager, do everything you can to remember that "nobody wants to have a lousy time at work." This is a fundamental principle that motivates me to do what I do. I hope that you, too, will always remember this in the work you do.

The sad reality is that many people will not always, or maybe never, have a job they truly love. The least you can do as their boss, then, is to do your best to make each person's job as enjoyable and productive as it can be. Make a real effort to be an effective manager *and* a leader.

I firmly believe that you change the world one room at a time. With your help, let's create a better world of work one person at a time! You can start by being a better boss.

Chapter **1**

It Starts at the Core

When you throw a pebble into a smooth pond, concentric rings or circles form, and ripples flow outward from the point of contact— from the center or core. Each ripple, beginning with the first, will affect the shape and velocity of each of the following concentric rings. The impact starts at the center, and the ripples flow from it.

When I think about how people in organizations connect, I don't visualize top-down, hierarchical organizational charts. Instead, I see concentric circles, like ripples on a pond, as illustrated in *Figure 1.1*.

The Core

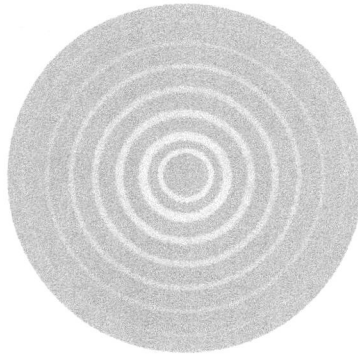

Figure 1.1

The manager–employee relationship is the fundamental unit of any organization. Every team, unit, department, division, company, municipality, agency, and so on, is built on the individual and foundational relationship that exists between the manager (boss) and the employee. Think of that relationship as the center, the hub, the nucleus, or the core. It affects all the others, like a pebble tossed in a pond. If each manager–employee relationship is healthy and functional, then each connecting level (or ring) can grow in scale, effectively, across the entire organization. (Whenever I refer to "manager," the term could also apply to a supervisor or someone who is a first-level boss.)

The best indicators of how well individual manager–employee relationships are working can be found by looking at reliable measurements of employee engagement, productivity, and customer satisfaction. Manager–employee relationships almost always lie at the core of the problem—and, paradoxically, lead to the solution!

When you start any organization, for any purpose, you are at the center of the circle. You can add a few more people, and they will likely join you in the circle. When that first circle gets too crowded and unwieldy, you probably have to add another outer circle (the next level of management).

More circles form around each of these outer rings as the organization grows more complex. These outer circles might be called divisions or departments. Within each of those outer circles, other circles may be formed into teams or units, depending on the size of the organization. As shown in *Figure 1.2*, each circle has a core, and the manager (or supervisor) and their direct report(s) are in it.

Organizational Cores

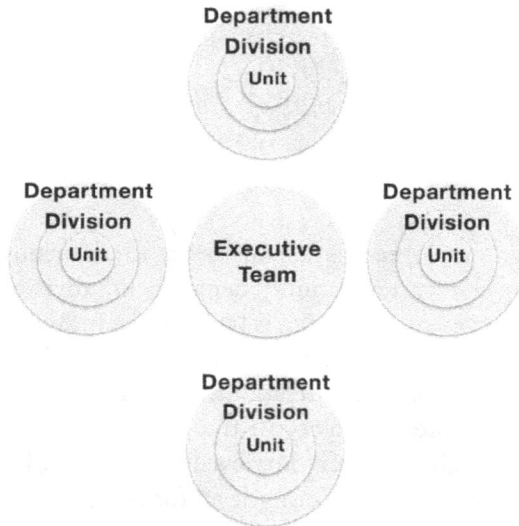

Department
Division
Unit

Department
Division
Unit

Executive
Team

Department
Division
Unit

Department
Division
Unit

Figure 1.2

In a hierarchical organization, when the leader or leaders grant the people in the next outer circle the freedom and authority to make appropriate decisions, that approach will likely ripple smoothly throughout the rest of the organization. Such an organization can function well because it has enabled a good flow of communication and decision making. But when a leader allows little autonomy for those in the next outer circle, this approach can also cause a ripple effect throughout the rest of the organization—the wrong kind, a disruptive kind. Managers in every other circle will likely behave similarly, and the result will likely be a command-and-control organization with low trust and low employee engagement.

The quality of the connections and relationships between the CEO or most senior leader and the executive team members in the core will strongly influence how the rest of the organization behaves and operates. The more contact and communication the next level of management has with the executive level, the more its members will be positively (or negatively) impacted by behavior modeling.

These modeling impacts will vary, depending on the type, quality, and intensity of power exerted from whoever stands in the center. That power might be in the form of personal power—as in the leader's charisma and influence. Or it could be in the form of expert power—the brilliance or the exceptional technical knowledge that the leader possesses. Power could also come from that position because it's the central authority for decision making that an owner, board, or other entity might give to the leader.

When people have a lousy time at work, you can be sure that something happened to change the ripples' smooth flow. It might be a wrong hire on the team. It might also be a significant personal issue affecting a key leader in one of the circles. Or the cause of the problem could be an ineffective financial system or an outdated HR process. Any one factor, or combination of factors, can have a powerful effect on the functioning of a part of the organization, or even the entire organization, over time.

As organizations grow larger and more complex, dysfunction is more likely to occur, simply because of the odds. More people = more challenges. Of course, communication is almost always one of the root causes of the problem, so we'll cover that soon.

Even if you're not a manager right now, you can still make a positive impact. So, model the type of behavior you would like to see from your own manager. However, don't tell your manager what to do (it might negatively impact you—in short, get you fired!). Instead, *show* your manager what behavior you'd like to see. Throughout this book, you'll find a range of useful ideas and actions that you can apply.

If you are a manager, always start with yourself.

Commit to forming and maintaining strong connections and relationships with each of your direct reports. Regardless of your span of control and level of power within the organization, your individual relationships with those you supervise affect the well-being and effectiveness of the whole. I believe this book can help you pay attention to the right things.

Always look to yourself first when you see a problem in your circle. Be willing to check your ego and do a gut check. Remember, you're at the core when you're the boss.

This book is about perfecting your authentic approach to interacting with people for whom you're responsible at work. Being authentic means "doing you" and always being the best version of "you" possible. The intended objective is not to *be perfect*, but rather to try hard at achieving authenticity with each of your relationships as the boss.

It's possible that you might also take away some useful lessons about people that apply outside of work, as well!

Chapter | **2**

The Number One
Characteristic
of Successful People

Think about the most successful people you know. Do you have at least one person in mind? I'll bet that, regardless of their type of work or what they've accomplished, they all share one characteristic: they are consistently *learning*.

A highly successful friend of mine, Steve, is a Boomer. Financially, he probably could have stopped working years ago (some call that retirement). He didn't. Instead, he's still very active professionally, consulting with companies and investing in others. He once gave me an important piece of advice: "You don't want to be old; you want to be experienced." Steve is the most tech-savvy person I know. He is my go-to guy for any questions I have about the latest solution to virtually any tech need I might have. The man is just up on the latest stuff in general, particularly new apps and software. When I think of "early adopter," I think of Steve.

In 2005 Steve invited me to join LinkedIn. Keep in mind that LinkedIn had not yet blown up into what it is today. For a couple of years or so, I didn't have any "links" to anyone else except him! No one I knew was using it until about 2010. I had little idea back then how useful a social network like this would be. Steve, though, must have known! I followed him onto LinkedIn because he always seems to be on the leading edge. It's because he is continually learning.

It's good to have a person like Steve in your life. It's even better if you can be a "Steve"!

How Learning Happens

Learning can often be hard, especially for adults. Real learning that sticks takes focus and discipline. Learning at its root means to "gain knowledge or skill." Not every book or article I've read, or class I've taken, always resulted in learning. Why? Because I didn't consistently apply a focused and active process to help make it happen. Sound familiar?

How easy is learning for *you*? Do you ever wonder why you're not using most of the information you "learned" in those classes you took in school and college? Would you like to be able to be a more effective learner? Here's a breakdown of how learning happens.

Learning involves a four-step process:

Step 1 - Absorbing information (content)

When you listen to, read, watch, or observe, you are absorbing content. This step can seem relatively easy because it's the most passive. Of course, the content to be learned can come in various forms: visual, written, verbal, even behavioral. When you're absorbing content, you can often kick back and be relaxed. Sometimes this can be why we don't learn what we take in: we are *too* relaxed and unfocused. Like listening, real learning requires active mental energy with minimal distractions, from the very beginning.

If you're not really focused, absorbing information will, at best, be just an experience. One that you will judge to be positive, negative, or maybe neutral. I'm sure you know what I mean. We frequently judge our experiences after an entertainment event, like a game, a show, or a movie. For example, think about a movie you recently watched. You probably have an opinion about whether you liked it or didn't like it—yes? However, you may not necessarily remember much of the content. Am I right? You may have been entertained in the moment, but you didn't necessarily absorb what you watched. The more focused and attentive you were, the more content you absorbed.

Most of us don't have exceptional memories, especially given the endless distractions around us. Taking notes on important material converts the content you target for learning to a tangible and accessible form. Notes can then help jog your memory and give you something easy to refer to when thinking about or applying the content. (This only works when you remember where your notes are!)

Successfully absorbing information—to learn—requires a different approach than when you're looking to be entertained. First, you need to make an honest choice for yourself: do you or don't you actually want to *learn* the content? If you choose "yes," then you need to be actively involved so that the information can flow to the next part of your brain for more processing.

Step 2 - Reflecting on information

If you don't invest time and mental energy to reflect on the information you just learned, what you may have absorbed will probably soon slip away and be forgotten. Just like that movie you watched last month. This second step requires critical thinking. It can also involve discussing, reviewing, or writing about the content you absorbed to help stimulate your thinking. This is why we trainers build in time for breakout sessions so that training participants can reflect on the content to help them learn.

Step 3 - Testing and discerning information

In step 3, you decide whether the information you reflected on really matters to you. *You* decide if you still want to "learn" the content, or instead prefer to move on to consider the next idea, topic, chapter, or program. You decide if you want to keep all or only a portion of the information. You make either a conscious or an unconscious choice by asking yourself:

·   "What meaning, if any, does this information have for me?"

·   "How does it change what I already know or don't know?"

·   "Do I want to change or add to what I'm already doing?"

If your answer(s) leads you to decide to keep the information, the learning process continues. You then get to the most challenging step: what to *do* with the information so that it can be useful to you.

Step 4 - Synthesizing and organizing information

This step is most crucial for learning that sticks. It involves internalizing (saving) the information so that you can access it (use it) in the future. Don't fool yourself. Unless you can access the information in some form when you need it, "real learning" didn't happen. The good news is that there is a proven method to help with this step. However, this too will take focus, time, and effort.

Practice and Repetition

What does it take for successful knowledge retention and skill-building? It takes practice and repetition. Simple, but not easy most of the time.

Here's an example of practice and repetition at an organizational level.

A senior management team of a long-standing client of mine has been relentlessly committed to having everyone follow the same approaches and apply the same standards to how work gets done in their company. They want everyone to practice consistent habits.

The challenge is that they have new, inexperienced people joining the company with little to no industry-related knowledge, along with more-experienced "free agents" who join from other companies in their industry. The newbies "don't know what they don't know," and the more-experienced types bring their own knowledge and habits that often conflict with my client's desired ways of doing things.

Getting people to learn new (or change old) habits is not easy, especially if you try to do it across an organization. Still, my client company gets mostly positive results because they do more than provide their people with just training. They reinforce the training by having each person practice what they absorbed, using the company's preferred tools and methods under active supervision. Active supervision, by the way, is *not* micromanagement.

When this company's employees practice the new habits and follow the company standards, their work and activities are actively reinforced by their supervisor. When what they do, or *don't* do, is not up to the standards, the employees get timely feedback—and sometimes more training—until the new habits are formed. Rinse and repeat. Practice and repetition until the habits stick. As new tools and methods are developed or discovered, and adopted by the company, they are integrated into the learning process. Then further training, with practice and reinforcement, begins. The learning never stops.

Consistently successful organizations and people are always learn-ing—and improving. This is true now more than ever as we all are faced with the rapid acceleration of change. No matter what you do, or how old (read "experienced"!) you may get, don't stop learning. Believe that, and it will help you to avoid the most significant risk faced by the successful. Read on.

Chapter | **3**

Avoiding Complacency

Do you remember the BlackBerry? You've probably heard about it, or maybe even had one. Before 2007, it seemed that almost everybody in business carried one. There was a time when the BlackBerry was the "it" device to have. Until it wasn't.

The company that developed it once had over 50% of the U.S. smartphone market and 20% of the global market. What do you think happened to the "CrackBerry" (as it was often called)? For a good answer, look in your pocket.

The introduction of the iPhone in 2007 began a global shift in how we connect and are connected. It was the gateway to our intimate relationship (some might call it an addiction) with personal technology. Apple's co-founder Steve Jobs called the original iPhone a "breakthrough internet communications device." It didn't take long for us users to figure out what he meant. The iPhone literally changed our individual, familial, social, professional, and commercial interactions within our world and across the world—and the BlackBerry soon lost its dominance.

Somehow the company leaders responsible for the BlackBerry failed to keep up. By 2017, BlackBerry's market share had dropped to about…0.0%. Why do you think that happened?

According to John Kotter, a former Harvard Business School professor, and a renowned thought leader, "Complacency is almost always the product of success or perceived success."

Since the Industrial Revolution and into the so-called Knowledge Age, numerous examples can be cited of companies that didn't focus enough on continual learning.

According to the American Enterprise Institute, "fewer than 12% of the Fortune 500 companies in 1955 were still on that list in 2017— 62 years later." Some 88% of those same Fortune 500 companies have since gone bankrupt, have merged with or been acquired by another firm, or even if they still exist, are no longer in the top Fortune 500 companies (ranked by total revenues).

Many of these previous Fortune 500 companies are today unrecognizable and forgotten (examples include Armstrong Rubber, Cone

Mills, Hines Lumber, Pacific Vegetable Oil, and Riegel Textile).
Some economists argue that this is the result of "market disruption"
and that the so-called churn (meaning a period when customers
stop buying your product or service) is "healthy" because it means
new industries are being created. All true!

And yet: did the entire management of these companies lose their
talent and expertise, or did they simply become complacent after
they enjoyed success? I wonder if some of the companies that got
disrupted and eventually fell out of the Fortune 500 might have
survived if only they had truly evolved and kept up with their customers' changing needs and demands.

The lesson here is to *avoid complacency* if you genuinely want to be successful managing yourself and your organization, whatever its size.
Begin by being proactive. When you are *pro*active you have more
options. When you are *re*active you have fewer options. I like options!

To be proactive, especially in a management role, be mindful of
three areas.

Innovation

"Look ahead to stay ahead" runs the old but true proverb. Today
we're not only dealing with constant change; we're having to learn
how to adapt to *accelerated* change. Everything around us is moving
faster, and changing even faster.

As a leader, always be looking ahead to stay ahead. Continually
review and update or redesign your systems, processes, services, and
products to meet both current *and* anticipated needs and expectations. Don't get too comfortable with how things are now. Whether
you are in the private, public, or nonprofit sector, you will continually be competing for talent, resources, and relevancy. Be thinking
about the *future* as well as how things need to be *now*. Allot some
time on your weekly calendar to imagine what the future may be
like for your organization, regardless of its size.

Every organization that is truly committed to being, and remaining, successful must keep up with changing demands and expectations and must acknowledge the need to be increasingly efficient

and cost-effective. Each employee, regardless of role or work type, should be *continually* asking, "Is there a better or less-costly way for us to do this?" All leaders, up and down the organizational ladder, should be encouraging these questions and—most importantly— listening to the answers. If you're the leader, be willing to quickly implement sensible solutions that emerge from good thinking.

Placing a focus on innovation could make the difference between being viable or going out of business or simply getting outsourced. In a competitive environment, continually innovating organizations have a better opportunity to positively, and proactively, influence how they are viewed (or branded) and assessed by their customers. Companies don't typically go out of business or lose market share overnight. Complacency has a corrosive impact at any level, eating away at the organization's success day by day, week by week, year by year.

During the early 2000s, Netflix and Blockbuster were both in the business of renting movies to their customers. Soon, the development of streaming technology began to advance rapidly, allowing all of us to enjoy access to a wide range of popular films whenever we wanted without ever leaving home. One of these companies adapted and became hugely successful. The other is a memory.

Everyone, everything, everywhere is moving faster with more significant consequences. Even though change has historically occurred more slowly in some sectors and fields (such as government and education), the broad social and economic challenges we face won't permit a slow pace to continue much longer for any entity. Work smarter. Pay attention. Proact. These imperatives also mean "take the lead!" If you do, you and your organization will have a better chance of keeping up with change. Otherwise, you'll likely be playing catch-up.

Collaboration

Our challenges in any business today involve how we can share and build on ideas within our company or organization and then communicate essential and significant information to each other quickly and effectively. Collaboration needs to be more than a buzzword. It must be part of how people actually work together to ensure that individual and organizational goals remain focused and aligned. As a manager, you should be collaborating directly and regularly with your employees and customers to understand what they need and expect.

Don't underestimate the power and value of face time, and I don't mean FaceTime. Even though too many of us around the globe spend an excessive amount of time coddling and staring into our smartphones, by nature, we humans are still social animals. So, find multiple opportunities, methods, and platforms to connect—in person whenever possible, and virtually when required.

The result of collaborating with your employees, and your customers, should be reflected in your organizational goals. Make sure your goals include a focus on keeping up with change and supporting changing needs by collaborating. (And maintain your attention on focusing on the right goals at the right time.)

Collaboration also involves expanding what "We" means. Support everyone involved, in any type of work, to help them focus their efforts on remaining current, relevant, and valuable in support of your business. If you allow an "Us vs. Them" mentality to overshadow "We," the value and effectiveness of collaboration will diminish.

Automation

Rapid developments in artificial intelligence by tech firms worldwide will require all workers, including managers, to become even more proactive, to avoid the perils of complacency and potential obsolescence, regardless of their industry or type of work. According to a McKinsey report, one-third of the tasks being performed by 60% of the current workforce could be automated one day by artificial intelligence! As they say, time will tell.

When you can choose, use, and manage technology, rather than have it manage *you*, you can also free up more time to invest in the areas of innovation and collaboration. Who you are and what you become are both results of the decisions you make. This is true for individuals as well as organizations. Suppose you don't make the mistake of overindulging in technology and getting consumed by it. In that case, you can focus on optimizing your devices to greatly improve communication within and outside your business to provide meaningful, usable data for faster and more effective decision making. We'll cover the importance of managing information later in chapter 10.

We're only seeing the beginning of the changing landscape of remote work worldwide. The COVID-19 experience that began in early 2020 created many opportunities for nearly all workers to benefit from the use of collaboration tools and the improvements in video conferencing platforms to virtually work with each other and interact online with customers. Easier remote working in the future will create profound changes for where we live, the design of offices, even the need for leased spaces—and much more that we have not yet considered.

To support innovation, we can also take advantage of numerous potential benefits of using the right, cost-effective automation solutions to streamline work processes. In many cases, some of that technology already exists and has been paid for by your organizations. The problem is that technology is not always being used effectively.

For example, how well do you really understand how to use all the features you already have in your current software programs? Is it possible that productivity where you work could quickly increase without your making any additional investment in more costly, time-sucking applications?

In the early dot-com era, around the late 1990s, several ambitious tech companies wanted to profit by helping to revolutionize the construction business. Because construction is an industry that has historically been slow to change, these tech companies saw the potential in that space. Their "big idea" was developing an automated system to help streamline the purchases and financial transactions between owners, contractors, and subcontractors. In their business model, they would charge a transaction fee for each purchase, and everyone would benefit. The problem was that they failed to understand the true nature of the construction business.

One of these budding tech companies met with a good friend and client of mine, who happened to run a large concrete business. This company tried to sell him on a product designed to help him buy concrete more cost-effectively by using a computer application rather than by picking up the phone or sending an email. The technology solution they promoted seemed sound and could be easily used by the construction customer. And the tech company would profit by charging a fee for each purchase.

The problem was that the tech company didn't realize that concrete is typically bought in large block purchases, maybe as few as 10 to 20 per year, from only two or three suppliers. So, unlike stocks on a commercial exchange, the small volume of these concrete purchases was made within a tight-knit circle that had no real need for streamlining. Their system was working just fine!

The tech company soon found out that there was no *way* the parties were going to let technology get in the middle of a simple transaction and pay a fee for using unneeded technology. The tech company and many others pursuing this part of the construction space all went belly up. To use a construction metaphor, when it comes to matching technology solutions with business needs, "Don't be a hammer in search of a nail."

Despite tight budgets, technology investments will still need to be continually made in many industries. Other proactive decisions will involve how you should train and use your workforce to achieve the right balance of "high-touch" and "high-tech" in service delivery.

Analyze Your Business Needs

As an effective manager and leader, stay up-to-date to know what business efficiency looks like so that you can help to determine which technologies can really help you become—and remain—successful. Most organizations consisting of three or more persons would benefit from more proactive information technology business analysis to help guide their decision making. And all IT professionals should be on the leading edge in search of new technological solutions. Today that focus is on the advantages of cloud computing, balanced with addressing privacy and security challenges. If you don't have this type of business analysis capability yourself, or in-house, consider getting some outside help. Long term, the investment will be worth it in ways that may be hard to measure.

Every organization is faced with an increasingly competitive need to respond in effective and meaningful ways to changing employee and customer expectations. So, maintain your focus on what it means to be both relevant and valuable in your line of work—now, tomorrow, and forever after.

How individuals and organizations (like you and yours) respond to change proactively or reactively will determine who thrives and survives. Or who falls by the wayside of progress or gets beaten by the competition.

The most significant risk to successful people and organizations is complacency. To avoid it, keep learning.

Chapter | 4

Two Forms of Impact

Each of us can make an impact in many different ways, regardless of our position or the roles we play in our personal or professional lives. Impact has two forms: control and influence.

Let's consider the impact you can have as a boss. See *Figure 4.1.*

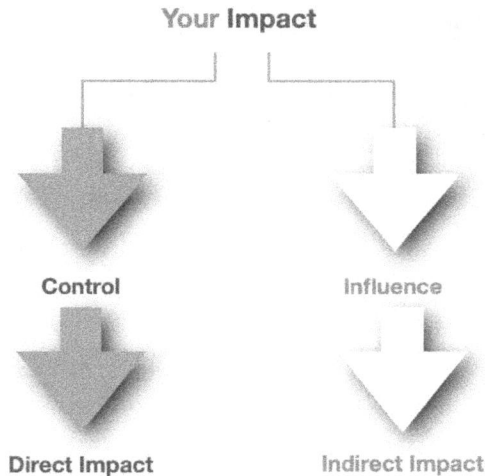

Your Impact

Control

Influence

Direct Impact

Indirect Impact

Figure 4.1

Control

One form of impact is control. When you have control, you have direct impact. Managers have many types of control that they can use: planning, organizing, hiring and firing, directing, connecting, overseeing, and so on. Control is exercised typically by a specific, or hands-on, action. If you tell a team member how you want them to process client requests, that's an example of your using control.

Control provides more immediate feedback on the results of the impact, which means that you can usually determine if it's working or not. That is, you can see relatively quickly whether or not your action or actions have been, for lack of a better word, *impactful*. Control, then, is an easily understood and visible form of impact.

Think of managers whom you know. How do they use their control? Do you think they are getting the results they want? Why or why not?

Influence

By contrast, influence is a form of indirect impact. Influence is less visible and is often underused because of our human tendency to discount or overlook its significance (and its power!). As a boss, you can use your influence and have impact in a variety of ways, including the following: how you acknowledge people when you arrive at your workplace, how you dress and keep your work area organized, how you treat people when they succeed or fail, how optimistic or pessimistic you seem, how you listen—and of course how you *lead*. When a manager openly acknowledges his or her mistakes, they are also using their influence to make it easy for others to do the same.

Unlike using control, when you use your influence you won't often get immediate feedback on the results (whether it's working not). This is why some people don't pay as much attention to using their influence. The results are not always clear or easy to see quickly.

Who are some people in your professional or personal life who have influenced you? What did they do that made an impact on you? Were you aware that you were being influenced by them at the time? Are you being influenced by someone right now? How?

When you're at the core of any-sized group or organization, you have many potential opportunities to use both forms of your impact— that is, *if* you are self-aware and attentive. Make an effort to notice how you're using your impact, either intentionally or unintentionally. Are you getting the results you want from the people within your core group and beyond? What more can you do every week to maximize, or minimize, the control and influence you have so that you can be more effective?

Chapter | **5**

Why People Are Hired

There are only two reasons why a person should be used to perform a job or a function. The first is to solve problems. The second reason is to use judgment. It's really that simple. This is true for any task at any level in the organizational hierarchy, in any industry. What should you do with a function that doesn't require a human being to solve problems or use judgment? You're probably right. Keep reading to find out.

We mainly use our analytical mind when we are solving problems. However, using judgment effectively can be hard for people to understand, and even harder to train or teach and learn.

Here's an example.

The Lesson of Rule #2

After some reflection, I realized that I learned the lessons of problem-solving and judgment early in my work experience. While in college I began waiting tables in a local bar and restaurant in Berkeley, California. When I was about to turn 21, I was eager for the owner to promote me to bartender. One day after my lunch shift, I asked him. What I heard back was, "I'll think about it...."

The next day before I started my shift, he called me into his office with some good news: "I decided to make you a bartender." I was excited and grateful. After a few seconds he asked if I knew what a Ramos Fizz was. I reluctantly told him that I didn't know. He quickly handed me a drink recipe book. "Study these drink recipes. Next week we'll start training you to make cocktails." Made sense. I took the book and started to leave his office. He then said, "Wait a minute, Jim. I have one more thing."

He then shared what I eventually understood to be one of the most important lessons about why we hire people to do work.

"I have two rules for all my bartenders," he said with a serious tone. "Rule #1 is that you never give out a free drink." He told me that I would often be tempted by my friends and other people who wanted to be my "friend." He went on, "Every shot of liquor represents revenue to this entire business. If you give away a shot of booze, or a beer, to someone, it's like taking money out of the cash register." He looked me straight in the eye and asked if I could follow rule #1. I'm an honest person, so of course I had no trouble saying, "Yes!"

He then leaned in a bit closer, locked in to be sure he had my attention, and said, "Rule #2 is that I'm paying you to know when to break rule #1." I then got a chill down my spine. In that moment, I realized the level of responsibility that he was giving me by making me a bartender. He ended the meeting and I left, beginning to feel the weight of my promotion.

Looking back on that experience, I recognized that he was willing and able to help me with the problem-solving part of the job. (That is, he gave me the recipe book and over time trained me on how to mix and prepare cocktails.) What he wasn't going to be able to help me with was the *judgment* I would need to remain employed and be effective as a bartender. The boss expected me to have the judgment to know when to give away a free drink *and* how to handle the various unknown and unexpected things that happen when you serve people alcohol in a loud and crowded bar. Knowing when to give away a free drink was one of the easier judgments I had to make!

Not long after I started behind the bar, the owner fired another bartender. She had broken one of the rules.

I've told my bartender story hundreds of times, and I'm sometimes asked about when I gave out a free drink. I always reply that I *never* gave one away for "free." Whenever I didn't charge for a drink, I had already determined that the customer had "paid" for it in some deserving way. Can you imagine a situation when I might have used my judgment and served a drink "on the house"?

It wasn't until many years after my bartending experience that I realized how universal these two rules would prove to be in any type of work or business.

———

If someone has an appropriate amount of education or knowledge to start with, they can be trained to solve most types of problems they might encounter in their work. Many people even like the act of problem-solving (say, in working on puzzles, making things, or devising better ways of achieving a goal). Although problems associated with many jobs today are indeed becoming more complex, the actions required to reach most work solutions are usually clear and often repeatable, once they're learned.

As the boss, you can help provide effective training and development methods to help sharpen your people's analytical minds and address the problem-solving requirements they have with their jobs. Their judgment can also be refined and improved with added experience and even some training.

More on Judgment

The noted authors and leadership thought-leaders Noel Tichy and Warren Bennis both described "judgment" as an ability developed by the combination of innate, personal qualities and previous knowledge and experiences. The primary application of judgment is decision making. Decision making involves making a choice when there isn't a clear or obvious option or answer. When using judgment, we usually draw more from our intuitive mind—our "gut," as we call it, which is constantly developing as we learn from and experience each event we encounter throughout our daily lives. Using judgment is especially critical to being an effective boss.

If you are curious about the function of the mind and brain and how problem solving and judgment are associated, check out Iain McGilchrist's book *The Master and His Emissary: The Divided Brain and the Making of the Western World*. In the book, McGilchrist cites various studies that indicate the existence of two hemispheres in the human brain that coexist and work together. Each hemisphere has a different focus. The right hemisphere is focused on the "big picture," and provides context about what is happening, and why. The left hemisphere is focused on the concrete, the details, the actions. According to McGilchrist's work, the right hemisphere is where judgment originates. The left hemisphere is the part of the brain we use to apply problem-solving skills.

What was your answer to my question in the first paragraph of this chapter: "What should you do with a function if you don't need a human being to solve problems or use judgment?" Here's my answer, and it shouldn't be a surprise: if you have a job to be performed that *doesn't* require a person to solve problems and use judgment, then you should probably find a way to automate that function.

Recall what I said earlier about the McKinsey report that predicts that one-third of the tasks performed by 60% percent of the current workforce could soon be automated by using artificial intelligence. The use of AI is already happening and will eventually expand into more and more industries as people working in the tech world continue to figure out how to engineer functions so that problem solving and judgment can be performed by machines.

As a boss, you can help to manage the impacts of these disruptive changes by reminding your team members of the importance of developing and using their *own* judgment, as well as their own problem-solving skills. Do what you can to help and *reasonably* support your people without doing their jobs for them. With that said, be aware when someone relies too much on the judgment of the boss, or others, to make decisions related to *how* they do their jobs. They may be sending a subliminal message that they might not be the right person in the right job.

Chapter | **6**

Role of a Manager

Since you're reading this book, you probably are already a manager or are thinking seriously about becoming one. So, before we get too much deeper into the content, I want to be clear about what the actual role of a manager is—or rather *should* be.

First of all, regardless of your role, when you're at "work," you're expected to produce a result. Producing results is simply an expectation for any person who is employed to work. For most "workers," both tangible and direct results are expected to be produced—such as a visible product or a service.

As a manager, you are also expected to produce results. These results are often less tangible and direct because they are results achieved by the efforts and work of other people: your direct reports. If *their* results are positive and effective, then *you* are also effective. That's a significant measurement for a boss.

If you're a first-level manager or supervisor, I believe you are in the most difficult management role (although not necessarily the most complex). In a first-level manager role, you're likely responsible for producing tangible and direct work yourself, *and* you're also accountable for what gets produced by your assigned worker or workers. You also have the least amount of "management power"—and impact—at this first level.

High-level competence can be useful, even critical, if you're at the first-line manager or supervisor level because you are typically very close to the production of the work itself. In this role, you may frequently have to step in to help someone directly solve a problem, or even do the job yourself.

Since the Industrial Revolution, and even before then, highly talented "doers" have been those promoted to the boss role because of their competence—meaning, the combination of their knowledge, skill, and ability. At the first level of management, technical skills can be very important and valuable. However, it's become increasingly evident that the most technically competent people don't always make the best bosses. Do you know anyone like that?

Technical skills also become much less important for managers as they advance up the organizational ladder. The higher up you go, the more your responsibilities will shift. With higher levels of management responsibility comes more oversight of people and much less direct contact with the specific work produced.

To be most effective, the competence needed for success at each rung of higher management requires a greater level of knowledge (experience), skill, and ability to solve "people problems." A good manager will delegate the technical problems to others, leaving more time to think strategically and support the people who are directly producing the work. Those most skilled at solving people problems have a high level of emotional intelligence, or EQ. High EQ is most important for effective leadership.

To be clear, the management track usually includes more tangible compensation and maybe even more status. With that said, I have seen many people pursue and accept a manager position too quickly without fully considering the pros and cons. It's easy to imagine how someone might be enticed by the boost in pay, along with the elevated title and perks associated with becoming a manager. This enticement can lead to multiple problems.

The problems I've seen are revealed when someone doesn't fully consider the actual consequences of *being* a manager—especially the personal consequences. Most seasoned managers I know and respect would agree that doing the actual work of being a good manager is not worth the extra pay and status alone.

Think about how you feel when you wake up at 2:30 or 3:00 in the morning and can't fall back asleep. When you're a manager, many different, messy, and difficult work problems will creep into your mind in those wee hours and will often keep you awake. These problems can involve other people's work issues and sometimes even personal ones. When you're responsible for people and their results, their issues can easily become *your* issues as well, at any time of day or night.

If you honestly don't really care that much about other people and only want to be a manager strictly because of the pay and benefits, you probably shouldn't waste any more time reading this book.

But if you're still considering whether or not to become a good boss, consider two questions: "What is a sleepless night worth to you?" and "Can you actually put a dollar value on your time spent staring at the ceiling?" If you want to become a manager strictly for the additional money, benefits, and increase in status, be honest with yourself about the potential cost to you as well, including the cost of many sleepless nights.

I've worked closely with many newly appointed supervisors, managers, and manager "wannabes." Here's a simple, yet thoughtful, exercise I have them do that you too should do if you are considering being a boss:

1. Make two columns on a sheet of paper.

2. In the first column, list all the reasons you think you want to be a manager or supervisor—*all* of them. Be honest with yourself.

3. In the second column, list all the reasons you think the role might be challenging or difficult for you. List as many as you can think of. Again, be honest.

Now take a long look at your second column. You'll find that a significant amount of your time and attention will eventually be focused on dealing with *this* list of challenges and difficulties. Stuff happens when you're a boss. Don't believe me? Go ask your boss.

If you're already a manager, you can still benefit from this exercise. Make your own two-column list. How much of your workday (and some nights) is already focused on the second column? See what I mean?

I don't want to prescribe what item or goal should be in your first column, reasons that you want to be a manager, even though I have my own opinions about what should be on it. I do hope that you will dig deep and find positive and authentic reasons why you want to be someone's boss.

As you proceed through this book and actually become a manager, you should do everything you possibly can to maintain a positive attitude on a regular basis.

One other exercise might help you with this. From today on, keep your first-column list (the reasons why you want to do this job) handy, and look it over often throughout your management career. Maybe even add to it. We all need positive reminders when things get tough. Go back to that list and read it over at critical times to bring you, your motivation, and your efforts back into focus.

Don't worry too much about how often to refer to the second-column list you created. The one about why things may be difficult or challenging. What's on that list will likely find *you!*

Managing people is clearly not for everyone. It can be tough to take that pivotal step from being an individual contributor to rising to manager or supervisor. I have more to say about transitioning to a manager (boss) role in chapter 14.

So how *do* effective managers get results through other people? Here's a basic list of responsibilities and activities in *Figure 6.1*:

Role of a Manager

1. Provide goals, direction, and training.

2. Monitor progress and productivity.

3. Give and receive Value-Added Feedback.

4. Provide resources, information, support, and control.

5. Help solve problems.

6. Encourage ownership and engagement.

7. Provide coaching, and set an example.

Figure 6.1

The best bosses are leaders as well as managers. Exercising effective leadership is how the most favorable results involving other people will be produced. Each of the responsibilities and activities above will be covered in this book to some degree. Your objective as a boss should be to find a rhythm in your work that allows you to consistently focus on these activities naturally.

What you do at work, and how you feel during and after work, significantly affects your quality of life. I'll reiterate why I've written this book. I want people like you to make the right choice about whether or not to be a manager—for yourself and for others. Why should I care? Because I want the right people to be bosses *for the right reasons.* There are far too many "nightmare" bosses at large today. My intention is simple: I don't want people to have a lousy time at work—and that includes you! I hope you share my intention. The world of work definitely has an ongoing need for good bosses. I'll do my best to help you become one as you read on.

21st Century Approach

When you're the boss, be demanding without being an a-hole. The 21st century approach requires a blend of both management skills and leadership skills to be most effective in producing positive results in any organization.

If you expect less, you'll get less. Have a "championship" mind-set, which means focus on helping people be the best they can be in their individual roles and as team members. As your team understands and learns how to become their best, you will eventually attract and retain others who also want to be their best.

Whether in sports or in business, this is how a successful organization begins and continues. Being the best is rooted in the culture. A good boss sows the right seeds and provides each individual and team the care and feeding needed to develop.

In my experience, the best 21st century bosses, regardless of industry, share the following characteristics.

They Like People

Here's an obvious fact. People are unpredictable. Effectively dealing with their emotions, whims, and personalities can often be messy. If you don't like "people," it can be really difficult and draining—*and* hard—to be a good boss.

We all have our "crew" that we like to be with. Most everyone likes *some* people, whether they are close family members or a few choice friends or whatever. Effective bosses just *like* People (with a capital "P") overall. They accept their differences, their quirks, their moods and feelings, and even their failures and imperfections—all the qualities that make us human.

Good bosses accept all the messiness that comes with each and every individual person. They're able to reframe the frustration created by some people into a welcome challenge—because they really like People.

It's clear that many of us spend more time actually interacting with our smartphone or tablet or laptop than we do with human beings in-person. We now have personal, professional, *and* digital relationships. Talk about a complicated triangle!

Whether we're conscious of it or not, we are being trained and conditioned by the speed and capabilities of the technology around us, and even *on* us (like a smartwatch that tells us to walk more or do less). Some of this technology we control, while some of it, maybe even most of it, controls *us*. An unintended consequence of our increasing reliance on our electronic devices is that our expectations about how people should "operate" can be affected. If you've been paying attention, you'll know that our 21st century technology has changed how we interact with each other. And we don't really know what changes are still ahead.

With a few exceptions, technology mostly works as advertised. When it doesn't, it might require an upgrade or replacement. We learn, often through trial and error, which keys and buttons to press and which commands to give to get the results we want. Each time I sit in front of my laptop and click the word processing icon, it loads, and I can create a document the same reliable way I did yesterday or last week. How often do interpersonal problems occur because you unconsciously expect your coworker, your boss, a friend, or even a family member to respond as consistently as the technology you use?

Managers too often expect workers to be constantly available, just like the smartphone that they never turn off. As our world, and especially our workplaces, become increasingly automated, remember that people don't operate as effectively 24/7 every day of the year, like the bits and bytes in your laptop do.

People can sometimes behave like "buggy" software! Dealing with them is often unpredictable and even messy. One day they are in a positive mood, another day, they are cranky. One hour they are incredibly productive, and the next, they are staring at their phone scrolling through the latest nonsense they discovered and wasting company time. As skilled as some of us may be in operating and even programming our computers and cell phones, as humans we are still buggy! We have moods, with different abilities to communicate that other people have to respond to and adapt to. Doesn't most all of the above apply to you too?

Certain challenging and sticky truths can affect specific people at work, as well as outside it. Some of us have personality disorders, or even more serious psychological problems, that are brought to the job.

Other complications can affect people in your workplace: like alcohol and substance abuse. People will exhibit the effects of their disorders or addictions, to varying degrees, while at work. Some of these effects may not be so obvious as to require corrective action or even termination. Yet, they *will* directly or indirectly affect how these people do their work and how you will need to manage them and others around them.

By now, you must know that managing people is not the same as managing a calendar application on your phone or laptop. A great deal more patience and flexibility is required to prevent the frustration that can spill over to those around you. If your frustration gets out of control, it can contribute to dysfunction in the workplace. When this happens too often, it might be a sign that you have difficulty managing *yourself* and perhaps shouldn't be in a management role to begin with. Have the courage to face this question.

When you're the boss, focus on maximizing *all* your resources, especially your people. And accept their limitations while remembering that people are not machines that produce consistently reliable results *on demand*. Even though people are imperfect, they have a big advantage over technology: that is their problem-solving ability, judgment, and creativity.

The most effective 21st century leaders always stay connected to others and to their "issues," particularly when they are difficult. When people feel liked and valued by their bosses, they bring their focus, energy, talents, and effort to their work. They then successfully deal with ambiguity and uncertainty, particularly during challenging and changing times like these. Computers can't do that quite as well—at least not yet.

They Are Trustworthy

When a leader isn't trustworthy, they had better produce near-perfect results if they expect anybody to follow them. Even *then* they may not gain any followers. Trustworthiness is the degree to which someone deserves to be trusted. A good boss takes the first step by starting the cycle of trust. They show that they can be trusted before expecting that others show that they themselves are trustworthy. And even then, a trustworthy leader may not get others to follow them consistently. It can be really complicated (see the previous section!).

Trust is the foundation for every successful relationship—personal, social, professional, and even digital. There isn't a worthwhile management or leadership book that doesn't include trust as a topic. It's that important! We'll examine what trust is in more detail in a later chapter.

They Like Problem-Solving

If you like to problem-solve, that doesn't necessarily mean that you *like* problems. To be a good boss, you'd *better* like problem-solving because most of the sticky and complex problems get passed on to you when you're a manager. Often you are expected to be the all-star problem-solver.

Remember why people are hired to do a job? The answer is to solve a problem, or a set of problems, within the scope and level of their responsibility and work assignment. As a manager, you are always expected to bring a high level of skill to problem-solving in your job as a boss.

The problems associated with managing work and leading people are endless. Good bosses don't try to avoid problems, especially the tough ones that tend to be the people-oriented ones. The most successful bosses don't cringe and get annoyed when a problem presents itself. The better ones get over the frustration and soon pivot to problem-solving mode in search of a solution. They adopt a positive attitude when there are breakdowns, and they even learn to *like* problem-solving. If you can do that effectively, you will likely distinguish yourself from the herd and will be a better boss.

They Have Courage

If you're a first-level manager, there are more management levels above you and none below you, which means you've entered what Barry Oshry, a highly regarded sage in the field of human systems thinking and organizational development, refers to as the "torn middle."

In this torn middle, the managers above you in the hierarchy push *down* to you to get you to meet their needs and expectations. At the same time, as a boss, the staff below you reach *up* to you to get *their* particular needs and expectations met. This can be an uncomfortable spot to be in that requires courage to push back when necessary. You will sometimes find yourself faced with difficult choices that will require you to assert your beliefs in defense of a person or a value you may hold.

They Are Humble and Empathetic

Humble bosses don't place themselves or their needs above others. They have the confidence of knowing and accepting who they are and don't need to be showing off their power. One thing you may be surprised to discover as you move into higher levels of responsibility with more power (if you haven't learned it already) is that people at their core don't change that much. No matter the role, job title, or span of control, you and they are the "same" people. So, stay humble (and don't allow yourself to be intimidated by others).

Good bosses use their humility to be empathetic—that is, they make a sincere effort to notice and understand what someone is experiencing and feeling. When you are empathetic, you begin to comprehend the thoughts and beliefs that are behind others' words and actions. Striving always to be empathetic allows you to make personal connections and build trust that will encourage others to follow you.

They Fit In with the Culture

Culture is determined by the shared assumptions, values, beliefs, and mind-set of those within a group or any organization. "Culture" is the *way* things are done. You can sense it. For example, is the look, feel, and language used at your worksite formal or informal, casual or stuffy? An organization's culture broadly determines how people within it behave. Its culture also determines what's required for success, both individually and collectively.

Over the last 20 years or more, I've seen quite a few people move from company to company within the same industry. A few years ago, I worked with a midlevel manager at a client company who was very bright and successful technically. He also had a 21st century approach, yet his style and personality just didn't fit in with that company's culture—with how they did things there. Consequently, he was not promoted into another leadership position.

I recently watched that same manager leave that company and go to a competitor where his style and approach were a better fit. He found greater success as a leader in his new position because he was simply a better fit for how things were done at that company. He fit in with *its* culture.

If you are an aspiring leader and don't feel that your skills are appreciated or valued where you are, you may need to make a change if you want to advance up the leadership ladder. But don't quit too soon before making a real effort! Just realize when your success in your current role might not be about what you can do, it might be about how you *fit*.

Being a good boss does not mean that you are better than others. It's about *helping others to be better*. Often it requires being an effective advocate.

What Being an Advocate Means

The word "advocate" is both a noun and a verb. It's a role as well as an act. To be an advocate means to push for an idea or a position, or to defend. It means you are willing to take a stand *about* something or *for* something—for either others or yourself. A good advocate is ready to be uncomfortable. A good advocate is humble, empathetic, and courageous. Sound familiar? (If not, reread the section above!)

Effective bosses can only navigate the tricky and touchy topics and needs that arise when they are in the "torn middle" *if* they are an effective advocate. This involves being an advocate for the organization, for their employees—and even for themselves. Let's consider what it means to advocate for each.

Advocating for the Organization

A manager is often the first to tell their employees about a new direction, new policies or programs, changes, and the like, that are typically determined by someone above them. When you agree with the decisions made from above, it's much easier to advocate for the organization *and* for your boss as well. It gets more challenging when you don't agree with decisions or directions handed down from above. It can even take a good deal of courage to be an advocate in these situations, especially when you need to get your employees to follow and implement those decisions made from above you.

In these situations, be careful not to fall into the trap of wanting to play the "good guy" or "good gal" role with your team. This tendency can pop up as soon as you tell them that it wasn't *your* decision and that *you* don't agree with it. In the short term, you can probably avoid conflict, stress, and discomfort with your team members. Your team may like you more and consider you "one of them" and not associate you with the other "them" (read "senior management").

A good boss communicates the senior leaders' higher-level decisions by using terms like "we" and "us," regardless of their personal views. If you frame your senior management's decisions in any terms that sound like "*they* want us to do this" or "it's because of *them*...," be clear that you are *not* advocating for the organization. Even if done subtly, in the medium- to long-term, your boss will probably figure out that you didn't support him or her and the decision they made. This lack of support will erode your boss's trust and respect for you and will probably limit your advancement opportunities.

When you're a manager (including a first-level supervisor), you're also on the management team. *You* are management too. So act accordingly.

You won't always agree with your boss. Nonetheless, when you make it known to your team that you don't support your boss's decision, you're also signaling to them that you have zero management power. If you separate yourself from your boss's decision, you may be unintentionally communicating that you're really just a mouthpiece for senior leadership. Then when your direct reports need some significant action from you, some will likely go around you—directly to your boss. Why? Because you've made it clear to your team that you are not on the *management* team, you're only on *theirs*. Consequently, they may like you more *and yet* have less respect for you and your position.

A young manager named Nick, whom I often work with, shared a recent experience. His director (Sandy) made a decision he disagreed with that involved giving the client a rebate of 50% off the amount the client was contractually obligated to pay for a change in scope to their project. Nick and his team had worked for *weeks* to get the client to pay the full amount—until Sandy overruled their effort.

When Nick reported back to his team, he framed Sandy's direction as "Here's what *we* are going to do for the client." When pressed by one of his team members about whether or not he agreed with the decision, Nick responded by saying, "Whether I agree is not important now. We need to work with this client moving forward, and we'll figure out how to follow through with Sandy's decision."

Nick avoided the easy trap of pointing responsibility for the decision away from him to his boss. He redirected the focus back to him and his team to get the job done.

Whenever you disagree with your boss's decision or decisions, have the courage to state your position with her or him privately or with your peers, and ask for more information if needed without being obstinate. Unless you are asked to do something illegal, immoral, or unethical, move ahead and confidently represent "management's" decisions to your team—or move on and join another organization. Regardless of how you may feel about your boss or the decisions they make, never disparage them to others. It will eventually reflect poorly on you and your character. And it almost always creates or perpetuates a toxic environment for all. If you really don't respect your boss, and can't be an advocate for the organization when needed, you should find another gig.

Advocating for Your Employees

A good boss doesn't merely take a stand to support the organization's management. A good boss also shows the courage to advocate for their employees' needs up the chain of command to senior management. These needs could involve asking for more time or other resources to complete a project or assignment, communicating employees' sensitive or challenging concerns to senior leaders, or advocating for more compensation or more flexible work arrangements.

Advocating for your employees can sometimes be uncomfortable, especially if you have an "unreceptive" boss. Be aware that if you lack the courage to face your boss on behalf of a team member or members when needed, you may avoid short-term conflict, but you'll also generate longer-term disrespect. It won't be a secret for long to your employees that you didn't support them by taking a stand when they needed you to.

Remember the consequences of not advocating for the organization? Similarly, if you fail to advocate for your employees at critical times, their trust and respect for you may also erode. If you rarely or never go to your boss on behalf of your team members, your boss, too, may lose respect for you and your effectiveness.

Advocating for Yourself

It often takes courage to be an advocate. To constructively advocate for the organization, as well as for your team, at times you'll have to step up, hold firm, or push back—for yourself. When—not if!—you disagree with your boss, be willing to ask for clarification to better understand the "why" behind decisions that are made. That information will help you to lead. But don't do this in front of your team members!

You'll also have to ask for what *you* need to be successful in your management role. Typically, that "ask" will be directed to your boss, who may not want to be asked for anything. Doing this can make you feel uncomfortable, especially if you're conflict-averse. Being uncomfortable is part of the job, so accept it and don't retreat.

If you can maximize your impact as an advocate for yourself, you will increase your effectiveness as an advocate for others—and be a better boss.

Be Authentic

To be an effective advocate for the organization, your employees, or yourself, make every effort to be tactful, confident, and authentic. You'll likely get better results. Being authentic means "doing you." Communicate naturally, using your words, in your voice, in your style. Don't try to sound or act like your boss or your favorite consultant or coach. Just be yourself, because most people will know when you're not. Sometimes it takes courage to be yourself!

Be Comfortable Being Uncomfortable

When I began my formal training in organizational development, I was fortunate to attend several workshops led by Peter Block, the author of *Flawless Consulting*, who also wrote many other best-selling books related to leadership and management. Block's ideas and approach to working with people as well as organizations continue to influence me significantly. At one of his sessions, I recall Peter discussing a thought-provoking mental approach for dealing with significant problems. He said when you're struggling with a problem, dive deeper to find the answer.

Peter may or may not have shared this "deep" analogy. But this is the way I remember it: When you're underwater, in the middle of a pool, you may find that the best way out is to dive deeper. Now, I know that it's counterintuitive to think that way. Naturally, it's because we have been conditioned to swim "up" to get out. However, suppose somebody covered the very top of the pool after you dove in. Imagine that the only way out is through an opening at the bottom of the pool (think James Bond in *Thunderball*). The message is: don't always look for the easy way out (the most comfortable and familiar answer to the problem) because it may not be the *best* way out.

Peter McWilliams, a self-help author, is credited with this quote: "Be comfortable being uncomfortable." This is the fundamental mind-set that effective managers adopt, whether consciously or unconsciously. If you want to be mostly comfortable in your job, you probably shouldn't be a boss. Effective bosses are rarely comfortable. They get used to the feeling and adjust to it.

A *Harvard Business Review* article described a study that revealed that 69% of managers say they're uncomfortable when communicating with employees. That's a lot of discomfort! Being an effective boss requires more than the learning and practice of a set of skills and methods. Being a better boss sometimes involves developing a mind-set that may run counter to your natural style and personality preferences.

An excellent place to start is to become comfortable with learning. Learning can make you uncomfortable, especially if it involves reflecting on a negative experience. Have you ever felt regret when you learned new information about a previous situation? Did you ever wish that you could get a do-over, knowing what you know now? Sometimes avoidance of regret can become an obstacle to learning.

It helps to have a long memory for successes and a short memory for failures. Failures can be useful experiences when you incorporate the learning quickly. The best approach to deal with them is to move on, and through the problems you encounter, without slowing down to dwell on the past's negative experiences that you can't learn from.

Imagine your past as an attic. It's okay to spend occasional time up there—sifting through memorabilia and reliving memories. You can even collect some of what you find there to put to use down-stairs—in the rooms where you live. But most things in the attic are better left there; they are of the past. Spend more time in the rooms where you can be present and focused on your future.

That said, your previous successes can be useful to revisit. Calling upon them can help boost your confidence. Although there is learn-ing from failure, recalling a related success can often help you to positively focus on your current problem, especially during peak discomfort (when times really suck). Like when you must deal with an unexpected budget shortfall involving one of your best perform-ers or need to handle a harassment claim.

The temperament of your personality, as well as your cognitive understanding of what's going on, will significantly influence how easily you can learn to be more (or less) comfortable with being uncomfortable. For instance, if you have a conflict-avoidant per-sonality, adopting this mind-set will take time, a strong desire, and practice through exposure. The good news is that it can be learned.

When you see and experience that working *through* problems—and not around them—eventually leads to more effective solutions, you'll likely be more willing to be uncomfortable more often.

The more experience you have, the more comfortable you will be. Be patient and gain experience *wherever* you can find it. It all helps your learning. The eventual (and maybe unexpected) result will be more overall success and enhanced job satisfaction in your role as a boss or an individual contributor. It will also help *you* to not have a lousy time at work!

You're Always On

Never forget this maxim: when you become the boss, "you're always on." It's as simple as that! Being "on" begins as soon as you are visi-ble to others—in the parking lot, in the building, or on the job site. It's also true when you dial-in to a telephone or video conference.

As a manager or potential manager, recognize that "being on" hap-pens as soon as you're "the boss." It's not a choice; it's a *condition*. Within the context of your boss role, everyone connected to you in the organization will pay attention to almost everything you do or don't do, what you say and what you don't say, your mood, your attitude. Kenneth Nolan, an American painter, once remarked, "For me, context is the key—from that comes the understanding of everything."

People scrutinize how you behave when you're the boss and even make assumptions about what they *believe* you are thinking. People pick up on your "bossness." It tends to come out of your pores just by your occupying the manager role.

You influence others when you're the boss. When you show up, in person or virtually, you affect how people think and feel about you, and even themselves, at a given moment. And maybe for the remainder of the day—or longer.

This can have a positive effect, of course, when the boss is thinking and acting positively. Unfortunately, there can be a negative effect as well, even unintentionally. When the boss is around, any perceived slight or perceived negativity coming from him or her can trigger internal questions in their direct reports like "What did I do or *not* do?" and "Did I do anything wrong?"

Effective bosses are more self-aware. They even have a second level of awareness. At the first level of awareness, you're more spontaneous and not particularly self-conscious. For example, you say something, the other person responds, and then you respond, and so forth. You mostly get a quick read on the other person at this first level and then react and respond quickly, without much thought or filtering.

At the second level of awareness, you use an additional filter. You're more self-conscious and attentive to your actions and their impacts. You quickly look inward *before* responding or behaving and so determining how others may perceive your actions and reactions. These actions include your verbal as well as your physical body language.

Most of us already have this second level of awareness with certain people in our lives. They could be *our* bosses, maybe our young children or older parents, and other people whom we respect and care about how they perceive us. Unfortunately, many of us don't always use this filter with the people we *should* care about the most, like our significant others or those team members who report to us. We may take these relationships for granted, and in so doing, we become less effective and successful.

Unfortunately, many managers tend to forget this fact or condition of "always being on." I've found this to be particularly true at the most-senior levels of management. Many well-intentioned CEOs and director types believe that no one notices them when they walk through the office or on the job site. Or, worst case, some just don't care about how they are perceived because they are too self-important. The reality is that others know they're coming for a visit, often before they even show up!

Be aware that virtually every situation you are in is an opportunity to teach—directly or through your influence—how you:

- Adapt to change
- Admit to and address mistakes
- Allocate resources
- Consider the perspectives of others
- Deal with feedback
- Deal with frustration and disappointment
- Follow and enforce established or new procedures
- Follow through on commitments
- Give credit
- Make decisions
- React under pressure
- Run to and participate in meetings
- Share information
- Spend your time
- Talk with and treat others

Because we all tend to be somewhat self-conscious at work when the boss is around, we can make projections about what we believe they may be thinking about *us*. It could happen with something simple. Like if your boss typically says hello to you in the morning and on one particular Monday, they don't. If you're sensitive or insecure in your job for some reason, you might assume that something's up. You may begin thinking about what *you* might have done or not done. Maybe you screwed up—but what was it? You might also be thinking about how lousy your boss is because they didn't say hello. Before you know it, a lot of your time is spent consumed by that distraction. Only you find out later that everything was fine with your boss. Has that ever happened to you? It's a type of work "paranoia" that almost everyone with a boss experiences sometimes.

To be a better boss, do everything you can to maintain the second level of awareness. Be more mindful of the impact of what you do, say, don't say, and so on. I'm not suggesting that you adopt your own kind of paranoia. Instead, as a manager be continually aware of both the direct and the indirect influence you have. Add that second-level filter. You can then avoid many of the unintended negative consequences that often result from being less aware. By being *more* self-aware, you can leverage your positive influence as the boss.

If you prefer not to be always on and want to avoid additional scrutiny, remain an individual contributor. It's okay! Choose what you do with your work life wisely—for your sake and for others'.

In one way or another, when "you're on," you are always setting and signaling the tone.

Setting and Signaling the Tone

Your early experiences with parents, caregivers, teachers, or coaches offer a rich set of examples of what it means to "set the tone." These influential people in your life affected how you behaved when you were younger. You learned then how things worked and how you fit or didn't fit, simply by the tone those important people set—at home, in the classroom, or on the playing field. Similarly, as a manager, *you* hold power to set the tone—either a positive or a negative one. You create the atmosphere within which your team members interact with you, with each other, and with those beyond your team.

Setting the Tone

Tone is often described as a sound, one with a particular quality and strength. When a tone is set in a group, team, or company, you get a feeling or an impression, or you adopt a way of thinking when you are part of the group. As with a sound, a feeling can also have a certain tonal quality and type of strength.

The tone of the workplace can be loud or soft. It can be transparent or opaque. It can be open or closed. And it can resonate at multiple levels in between. I've been in and observed hundreds of workplaces. Every one has a tone to it. You might even call it a vibe.

Managers have a significant impact on the tone within their "core." It happens in the way they use control and influence. You can set the tone in person, nonverbally, virtually, and even by email or text message.

As the boss, how you manage yourself and your moods, along with your day-to-day approach to your job, will create an atmosphere— that is, a tone—that will affect how others behave. Your tone impacts the culture in the short term and long term. Remember, *you are always on.*

Certain team members will be more, or less, influenced by you as the boss. Some might even begin to adopt and model your behavior. If you're often quiet or get angry and frustrated quickly when things don't go well, you'll be setting the tone through your example, so don't be surprised when you see others model it.

To be clear, you may not be the only one who determines the tone for your group. Depending on personality types and group chemistry, others can also shape it. However, in your role as the boss, you should have a more significant and consistent impact on setting the tone by how you act and react to what goes on around you.

I have a coaching client whom I have observed over a few years. He's responsible for leading a team in a health services business. Each time he walks into the team office, you can feel the energy shift—always positively. He is quick with a smile and tries to find humor no matter what the situation. The team responds to his positive tone because the mood and chatter there is always light, regardless of the stress level. It's not by accident that the team feels safe speaking up, especially when mistakes are made.

The tone you set can attract or repel others. It will depend on several factors, including your personal style and intentions, the personalities and experiences of the people around you, and also the circumstances at the time. Whether or not the team is enjoying a lot of success, or dealing with failures, will likely affect how your tone is perceived at any given time.

Signaling the Tone

In addition to setting the tone, as the boss you also have the power to reinforce it by "signaling the tone." This is related to setting the tone, yet it's a bit different. Signaling the tone is much more immediate and proactive. It happens *after* you've set the tone. Setting the tone can be done passively, by "how" you speak. Signaling the tone is more active, and yet can also be subtle. You can signal it by "what" you say. You signal the tone by purposefully sending information to reinforce your intent. That information could be instructions or encouragement to your team or others, whether using verbal, non-verbal, or written means.

Here's an example: a client of mine is a senior project manager. She meets with her team every morning in a daily huddle. She has set a tone for her team that makes them feel as if they can always rely on her support and be open about what they need. She wants each person to know that it's okay to ask for help from her or any other coworker. She signals the tone by quickly checking in with each individual to do the following: review the goals for the day; assign specific responsibilities; identify resources required; address relevant concerns; and acknowledge what worked and which improvements need to be made from the previous day's work.

Her team *knows* that she is connected to them and is concerned about their needs because she is active and intentional. As a result, her team members also communicate openly with each other throughout the day and look for ways to pitch in when someone else is struggling. She is an effective boss.

Most reasonable and attentive employees align how they behave at work to fit with their manager's expectations. These expectations include what's acceptable to say and do. You, as a boss, consciously (or unconsciously) align your expectations with your direct reports by what you prioritize, what you get excited about, and what you praise, as well as by what you discourage. By doing these things, you signal the tone for the workplace—and nourish and protect the culture.

Management by Walking Around

MBWA, meaning "management by wandering (or walking) around," was popularized in the 1980s by the management consultants Tom Peters and Robert H. Waterman in their seminal book, *In Search of Excellence: Lessons from America's Best-Run Companies.*

To be clear, MBWA is not a "gotcha" type of management surveillance. Rather, it's about *connecting.* That means finding connections, making them, fixing them when necessary, and maintaining them with the people in your core.

Effective MBWA is done informally and randomly. Most important, it should be done authentically, with positive intent. If you simply show up at someone's desk or field site and don't really listen, don't ask follow-up questions, and aren't "real," they will sniff you out as a phony. And if your employees feel as if you are spying on them to find out if they are screwing up, they'll treat you with suspicion each time you appear.

As we discussed in a previous section, if you truly *like* people, find something that will connect you to each person in a sincere way so that you can help build your relationships, one by one. MBWA is still today highly effective approach to maintaining and building connections, despite ongoing changes in the nature of the current workplace (i.e., remote work).

———

As a manager, you both set the tone and signal the tone—consciously or unconsciously, directly or indirectly. You bear a crucial responsibility for the look, feel, and operational efficiency of your team.

To become most successful as a boss, be positive, optimistic, open, and available. Sincerely interact with people, rather than just showing up and then blindly walking through the office or job site. Invest in face-to-face time with each of the individuals who matter to you at work, before leaning on your technology and other media forms to communicate. Even if you're an introvert, or are trying to relate to one, find a way to connect that's effective for both you and them.

Fear Interferes

Charles Duhigg, the noted journalist and author, described the findings of a study by Google that focused on identifying the qualities of the "best" teams. The Google effort was called "Project Aristotle." One of the key discoveries was that high-performing teams shared a similar characteristic: they all felt "psychological safety." They were not afraid to take risks, speak their mind, or be themselves.

I learned early in my career that fear often interferes with the most successful performance.

A few years ago, a good friend and I decided to start competitive sailing. Before then, he and I would sail cruising boats out on San Francisco Bay. Occasionally our skills and nerves got tested when we found ourselves in some dicey weather conditions, but typically the sailing was not overly challenging. We figured that learning to race would provide us with an incentive to take our learning up a notch or two.

We soon became members of a newly established team on a large race boat. Our crew were all inexperienced racers like us, including the boat owner. But we were 12 strong sailors ready for a challenge and ready to learn the ins and outs of racing. After our second or third practice race, a more experienced local sailor volunteered to coach our race crew and help us become more competitive sailors. We agreed to bring him onboard to lead us. It wasn't long after we left the dock that I was reminded of the power that leaders have and how they can also *negatively* affect performance.

Here's how it went.

Once we were out on the water, it was clear that our coach's style was to yell and frequently demean the crew—us. We were all big boys and girls, and for most of us, it was humorous at first. I hadn't really been yelled at since I played high school football. At first, I assumed the screaming was a "performance" for dramatic effect to get our attention. But it never ended. Our sailing coach would bark orders and run around the boat as if his hair was on fire. Do you know the type? Even though we believed he was there to help us, the result wasn't better performance or learning. It was fear.

It wasn't long before each of us was afraid of screwing up and getting yelled at in front of our other crew mates. That fear then created hesitation, often at the wrong times. When he yelled "Turn to starboard—STARBOARD!" or "Bring that line in NOW—DAMMIT!," it was surprisingly easy to lose focus and do the opposite—or just freeze. Instead of avoiding mistakes, we were committing *more* of them. Instead of improving, we got worse. And of course, we weren't having much fun. The last straw was when my friend got so frustrated with the "coach" that he jumped onto the rail of the boat, hung on to the lifeline, and yelled back, "I'm going to let go if you don't shut the F*** up!"

On a large, powerful sailboat, there are many moving parts that can hurt you, like winches and a big, heavy boom that can cause severe injury or even death if it hits you in the head. Being a *little* bit afraid of what can happen on such a boat is smart and appropriate. Even in business, when you're the boss, it can sometimes be constructive to instill a measure of apprehension or even fear *if* it keeps people focused so that they don't make dumb, costly, or dangerous mistakes. However, at some point, too *much* fear can result in paralysis of thought and diminishment of good judgment, which can also produce tragic errors.

Think of it this way: fear is to people like heat is to food. Managing people and cooking food require some understanding of chemistry. When cooking, you have to apply the right amount of heat, to the right food, for the right amount of time, to get the right results. If you apply too much heat, the food gets burned. Too little heat and the food won't cook. Same with managing people. Know who you are dealing with, and understand what needs to be done and why. You need to find the right balance of "heat."

Remember that every team and organization has its own culture. Here again, the manager influences that culture by consistently setting and signaling the tone. For instance, if the culture is competitive, hard-charging, and testosterone-driven, some level of fear might be appropriate to get people to produce results. By contrast, overthinking, worrying about making a mistake, and not feeling psychologically safe can distract and interfere with helping a customer, client, boss, or coworker.

Don't be the type of manager who creates too much fear if you want to be effective in the long run. It's true that if you expect less, you'll get less. Yet, you can still be demanding without being an a-hole.

By the way, we "fired" our sailing coach after two races and finished the season performing a lot better—without his help.

Chapter | 7

Management
and Leadership

To be an effective boss, you need to be skillful at both management *and* leadership. Although the verb or noun phrases *managing and leading*, or *management and leadership*, or *manage and lead* are often used interchangeably, the meaning and concepts are distinctly *not* the same. Yes, management and leadership are related, but the skills, abilities, and approaches for each are different.

The 21st century approach to being a better boss requires both cognitive agility (IQ) as well as emotional intelligence (EQ). You need to toggle back and forth between managing and leading so that you can produce the best results.

The choice between managing *or* leading should depend on the results you want or need to achieve at the moment. Keep in mind that those results will not be determined by you alone. What you *can* reasonably achieve will also be affected by other variables—such as the person, team, and situation you are dealing with. Successfully navigating among those often-unpredictable variables is what good bosses consistently do.

As in all successful learning, you'll need real desire and a commitment to practice if you're serious about being the best boss you can be. The good news is that the knowledge, skills, and abilities for both managing and leading can be learned. Although some are born with these skills and may have an easier time applying them, all of us have to put in some work if we want to continually improve and be the best version of ourselves when we are the boss.

Peter Drucker, one of the most influential and prescient business thinkers of the last century, wrote: "So much of what we call management consists of making it difficult for people to work." As a management consultant, educator, and author, his books, articles, and teachings still provide the conceptual foundation for most current management and leadership theories and practices. I highly recommend looking him up.

What Is Management?

When you're managing, you're focused on the "what" and "how" related to the desired and expected results of a job or function. When you say to someone in your department or company, "Here's what I want you to do this week, and so on…" or say, "This is how I want you to handle this…," you are managing. For the most part, management is technical and is primarily focused on process and tactics. An organization can give you, or anyone, the title of "manager." And with that title, position power, and authority can also be given.

When you're managing, you have the power to ask (and, with luck, also to answer!) questions like these:

· Is the work organized so that people can work smart?

· Do our policies and procedures make sense?

· What changes should we consider to help achieve more consistent outcomes or results?

· Are all the tasks necessary?

When managing, you may even be inclined to ask a classic question posed by one of "the Bobs" in the cult film *Office Space*. "What would you say . . . you do here?"

———

Management also involves ensuring that employees "can do" their jobs at the level required. When managing effectively, you should also be asking questions like these:

· Does each person have the skills or competence necessary so that they can do their job?

· Are the expectations clear and understood?

· Would they benefit from additional training, direction, or other support or assistance?

To be sure, management activities are critical to getting work done. Most reasonable people need and want to know *what* they're expected to do and *how* they are expected to do it, whatever their job is. Unfortunately, too many bosses think that "management" is their sole significant responsibility. They are what I might term "manager managers" who almost entirely rely on using management practices to get results and who rarely incorporate leadership practices in their approach.

These "manager managers" often get frustrated when people reporting to them don't consistently (or ever) perform to the level they are expected to. These bosses then push a "management" approach even harder. Despite their elevated focus and pressure on managing, they usually *don't* get consistent results from people in return. What's been your experience with "manager managers"?

When you transition from individual contributor to manager, you might struggle for a while as you settle into an effective approach. It often happens to new managers. It's easy to get fixed on being a "manager manager" and continue with an individual contributor mind-set. The action-oriented, reactive, and tactical focus of management activities can often pull you in that direction. I have more to say about this transition in chapter 14.

In management mode, one of the advantages is that you can often see more immediate results. Because the details about "what to do" and "how to do it" are probably already familiar to you from your experience as an individual contributor, both can also lead to your getting stuck in that management mind-set. Unfortunately, *your* manager may even be subtly encouraging you to stay stuck in this management-only realm. It's understandable why you may be inclined to do it, but it's not advisable.

Historically, more emphasis has been placed on management skills within organizations because management is thought of as more of a science. Management is process-oriented, and management results can be largely tracked and measured because they are often more tangible. Until recently, many more colleges and universities have offered management programs than have offered leadership programs. Fortunately, that's beginning to change.

Significant shifts in understanding what it means to be an effective boss have been gradual and are now accelerating in response to the changes in the current workforce's expectations. Many of these overdue changes have been driven by the needs and expectations of millennials, and now by members of Gen Z. People working today generally expect more from their bosses, in-person and (lately) virtually, and if they don't get what they're looking for they might not stick around for long. What they're looking for is genuine leadership.

If you want to keep pace with the current and future needs of your workforce, be sure that you understand the importance of leadership as well as management. Then be willing to invest the time necessary to learn and apply leadership best-practices. I believe your future success as a boss in almost any organization will depend on how well you can lead as well as manage. See *Figure 7.1*.

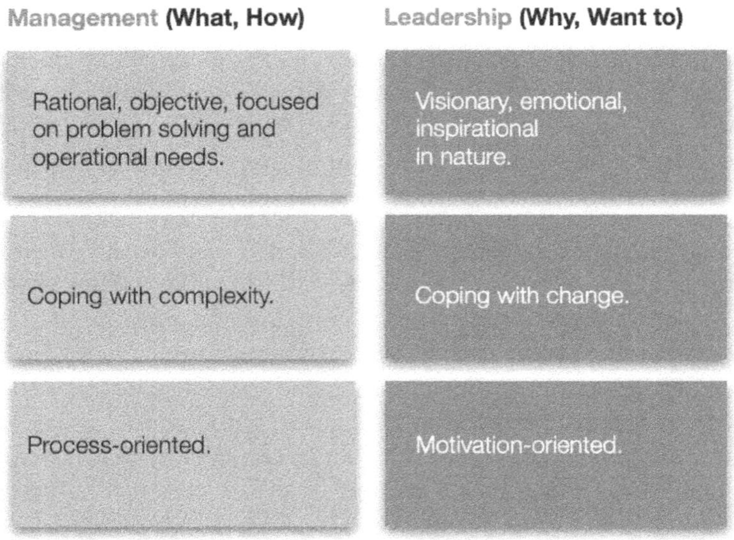

Management **(What, How)**	Leadership **(Why, Want to)**
Rational, objective, focused on problem solving and operational needs.	Visionary, emotional, inspirational in nature.
Coping with complexity.	Coping with change.
Process-oriented.	Motivation-oriented.

Figure 7.1

What Is Leadership?

Warren Bennis, a renowned American leadership authority, concluded that there is not enough of true "leadership" in the world today. Leadership is more of an art. Unlike management, it can be difficult to measure. Leadership is focused on communicating *why* something is to be done, to get those involved to *want* to do it. Effective leaders are proactive.

Leadership involves:

- Thinking ahead and anticipating—not reacting.

- Seeing at a higher level and interpreting the "big picture."

- Developing strategic objectives that will influence your lower-level, day-to-day, tactical actions that you will take when you are managing.

- Focusing on your people as well as both your goals *and* the results you are responsible for achieving.

You can be doing all these leadership activities and still you will only become a real leader when someone decides to follow you! Anybody, at any level, can become a "leader" by having at least one follower.

Some people are born leaders. They possess many natural and relevant skills for leadership. Like management, leadership skills can also be taught. Unfortunately, too many good managers aren't willing to put enough effort into doing the hard work often required to develop into true leaders. That hard work usually involves "the people."

Leadership—or the lack of it—impacts people personally. Leaders reach people emotionally, not just logically. I trust that most of us have figured out by now that people may be similar, but they're not all the same. Unlike management, leadership often requires a great deal more time, energy, focus, and especially patience. This last requirement—patience—can be the most challenging.

Effective leadership involves tuning in to each person you are trying to lead, individually, until you make a connection. With that connection you can then begin to understand what *they* need for them to follow you. I'll describe what employees need in chapter 8 so that you'll always be clear.

Learning how to apply leadership skills can be difficult because it requires understanding the "drama" and many variations related to individual people and their emotions. This is why I emphasized the importance of liking people early on in this book. People are unpredictable. Our moods change due to what is happening around us and *to* us—not just when we're at work, but also in our home lives.

As a result, what motivates someone on the job one day may not apply the next day. Effective leaders can guide people to the point where most days they "want to do" what is being asked of them without that leader always looking over their shoulder to ensure it's getting done.

The key questions leaders continually ask themselves include the following:

· Does each worker have the necessary motivation and attitude to do their job well and be a positive contributor? If not, why not?

· Are there obstacles in their way that are preventing them from being fully committed while they are at work? (These may include personal issues, problems with coworkers, fear of change, coping with shrinking resources, frustration with the current work process, or other difficulties.) What can be done to help remove these?

· Do they have any other unmet needs that can be provided?

If you don't invest much time and energy to lead, you're probably more of a "manager manager." And if you find yourself mostly frustrated with your team and thinking more about the question, "Why can't they just do their jobs?!" you probably aren't leading that much at all.

At any point in time, each of us lies somewhere on the Compliance-Commitment Continuum (*see Figure 7.2*). Whether you're managing or leading, the impact you have will affect which end of the continuum your direct reports generally are on, and for how long.

Compliance-Commitment Continuum

Motivation is the internal fuel that drives our behavior. The Compliance-Commitment Continuum is a simple calibrator to identify a person's type and degree of motivation at any point in time. The continuum ranges between *having* to do something and *wanting* to do something. This "reading" applies to all of us, including at this very moment. Stop and think: How motivated do you feel to be reading this book right now? Do you believe you really *have to* or kind of *want to*?

Compliance-Commitment Continuum

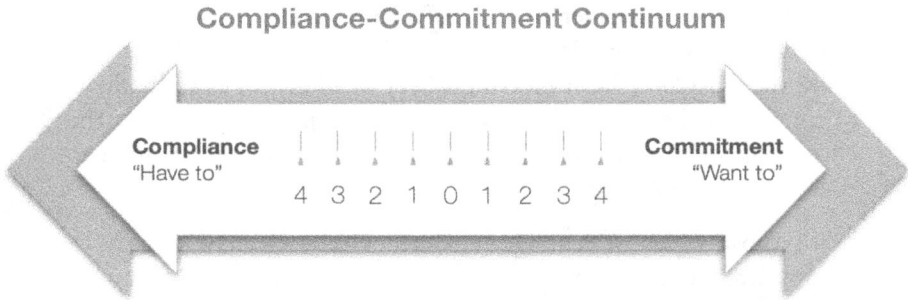

Figure 7.2

Compliance

When our motivation is on the compliance end of the spectrum, we do what we do because we believe we "have to." Unless you're a hermit living on a mountain top, a civilized life often involves being motivated by compliance at various times. What's also true is that the consequences of noncompliance are usually clear and direct in the most common situations we encounter.

For instance, we collectively agree (most of the time) to comply with traffic rules, even if we sometimes disagree with the need for them. We may not want to follow speed limits or abide by "No U-turn" signs, yet we do because we believe the result will be personal safety and more-efficient traffic flow. There is also a clear consequence if we don't follow the traffic rules. For example, if we run a stop sign, we risk being given a ticket or getting T-boned by another car.

Most aspects of modern life involve having to comply with some rules and norms. Every job imaginable has at least one policy or procedure that *must* be followed if you're going to keep it. Each work team usually adopts its own explicit or implicit standards, rules of conduct, and the like, that must be followed. Organizations are also affected by a broader range of compliance requirements or mandates. Federal, state, and local laws like ADA, EEOC, sexual harassment laws, and a great many others, affect all organizations and must be complied with. At some point, all of us must comply with something if we are to get along.

Unfortunately, "manager managers" typically focus most of their attention on getting team members to comply with their jobs. They then neglect the leadership effort needed to get individuals to commit to their jobs. "Manager managers" usually just stress the consequences of noncompliance—if, that is, they are attentive to their people at all!

With those types of managers, some employees may comply or follow directions primarily out of fear. This management-centric approach may yield faster, short-term results. But in the long term it likely won't support attracting and retaining high-performing team members who have the most skills and talent, not to mention options for other places to work.

I can remember hearing more than one of my bosses say, "You're lucky to have a *job*!" That's classic "old-school management think-ing" that unfortunately may still be prevalent in some workplaces. Too often, I see bosses who are highly compliance-focused, with a "do it my way, or go work someplace else" tone. Boomers are famil-iar with this attitude, and many have grown to accept it from their managers. Managers who strictly rely on this type of motivation, and have a transactional attitude toward their team members, usu-ally have to provide more attention and oversight to get people to perform. This one-sided, compliance-oriented approach is also not flexible or adaptable enough to meet today's workforce's current needs, desires, and challenges—not to mention tomorrow's.

Commitment

The other end of this continuum is commitment. When we feel committed, we "want to" do something, follow a plan, and the like, because we have either "bought-in" to it or have convinced our-selves of good reasons "why." Result: we feel "ownership" for what we are doing.

Here's an example of a committed team.

Imagine a group of employees involved in examining work flow design. They are making changes to their work process so they can improve how things are done in their department or area of the business. Because they are directly involved in the process and the approach, they can directly explore the reasons "why" and "how" work flow improvements can benefit them as well as the company. This direct involvement will most often result in helping them make better use of their strengths and abilities, not to mention better suiting their own interests, as they consider the work process they're following.

———

The current multigenerational workforce comprises people who have various expectations for what they want to get out of their work experience. The best and the brightest—your "A" players!—have the most options for alternative places to work. If you don't create a workplace where they can truly feel committed to their jobs, they will likely find another place to apply their skills and talents. This is true for most high-performers, regardless of one's generation.

When you make sincere efforts to consistently involve your team, that will help to support their increased motivation and commitment to the work itself, as well as to customers, coworkers, and the larger organization.

I hope you can see that "compliance," then, is more of a management focus, while "commitment" is more of a leadership focus. As the boss, you'll discover that some individuals will require more leadership attention and effort than others. This is where your patience may be tested. If you give up too soon on individuals and slip back into relying on compliance, remember that you may ultimately be creating more work for yourself. Many employees who barely do their jobs in order to comply may require more time, attention, and supervision to produce consistent results. In other words, when you are not around, their productivity may drop off.

Skilled managers can find the right balance between directing people to do what they *have* to do (compliance) and inspiring people to do it because they *want* to (commitment).

Eva, a manager at a biomedical company, is skilled at achieving this balance. Numerous laws and guidelines regulate her industry very tightly. The products her company produces must consistently meet high standards. Otherwise, it will be subject to hefty fines that could potentially cripple it financially or even cause it to go out of business.

Eva regularly communicates to her staff what the standards are and the importance of complying with them so that they understand "why." She makes it clear that although the compliance standards are indeed strict, they exist to protect their customers. These customers are medical patients who rely on the high quality and safety of the company's products.

Eva's team sees the whole picture and also sees how what they do fits within it. They understand what they *have* to do and *why*. Because of Eva's leadership approach, they feel motivated to *want* to follow the standards as they perform their work. They're committed.

Like Eva, when you keep your team members in mind *and* focus on the results you and they are expected to produce, you should be more aware of how to strike a balance that will be most effective. And that balance should lean more toward getting people to be committed to their work, if you also want to be a leader and follow a 21st century approach to being a boss.

Hub and Spoke vs. Roundabout Leader

The last time I researched the topic of leadership styles, I found at least 10 common descriptions—all of which make good sense. Since I'm a practitioner and like to keep things simple, I've identified two distinct leadership styles and created models that I believe come closer to describing how bosses actually lead. They are leadership styles that I call "Hub and Spoke" and "Roundabout" (see *Figures 7.3* and *7.4*), each of which can be appropriate and effective in different situations. Good bosses can switch between both as needed. Which one you choose to use should be based on your individual team members' needs as well as the needs of your team or organization.

Hub and Spoke Style

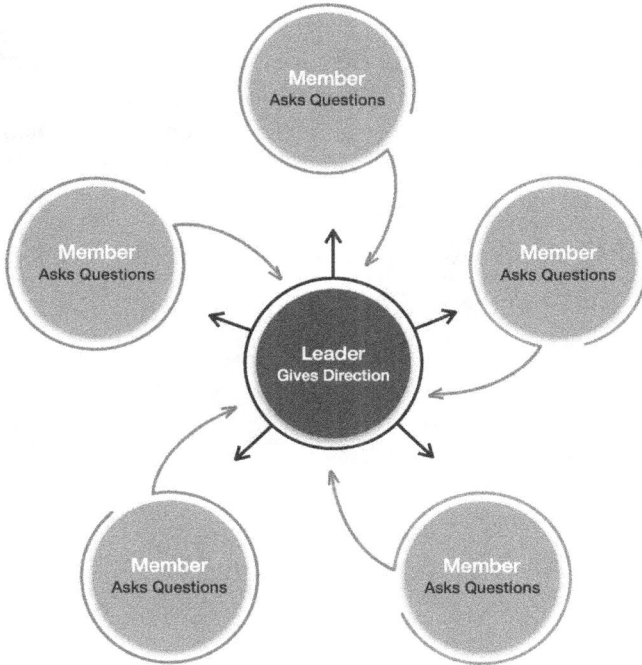

Figure 7.3

If individual team members' standard work can be performed independently and doesn't require much collaboration with the other members, this leadership style might work best. It can also produce effective results in certain other situations—as, for instance, in a crisis or when a problem must be solved with little or no time for debate between team members.

How about when a new team member joins the team and is in the process of onboarding? Do you think that might be an appropriate time to use a Hub and Spoke leadership style? It's likely that this more-direct, one-on-one connection with the leader from the start might support a more successful integration for a new member into a team. A Hub and Spoke style might also be optimal if one of the team members develops performance or conduct issues and requires more-direct attention from the boss.

The Hub and Spoke leader is typically in the center of the action. Hub and Spoke leaders provide direction to each team member and are generally available to answer questions. The members who follow a Hub and Spoke leader often operate in silos and have little to no contact with each other. They rely on the leader for more direction and can sometimes be overly dependent on them. When overdone, this leadership style can also be a form of micromanagement and reflect an "old-school" approach.

Be mindful of the pros and cons of this style, and choose your approach wisely.

Hub and Spoke Leader

Pros	Cons
Can be effective when a team member is brand new, typically during onboarding	Limits the growth and development of the team members
May be appropriate when time is limited to decide or perform	Fosters dependency on the leader
May be approriate when the members do not have the skills or experience needed	Requires more time and attention from the leader, limiting their growth
May be appropriate for some high-risk decisions or tasks	May lead to disengagement and eventual loss of talent

Roundabout Style

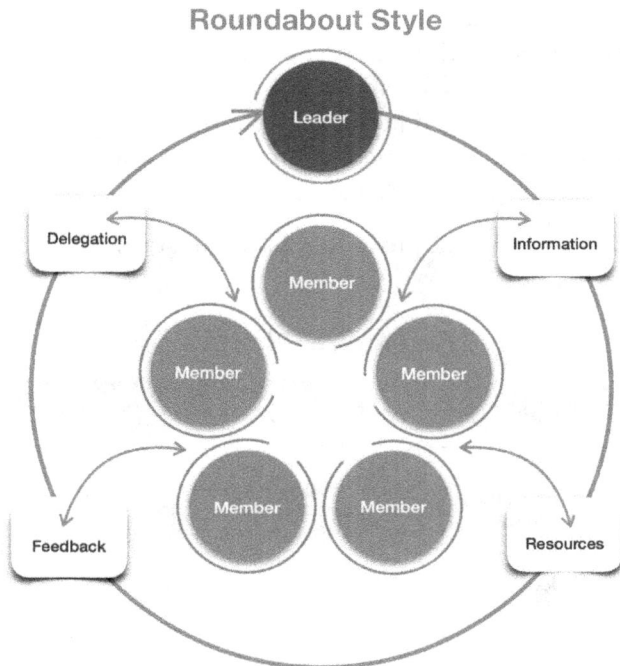

Figure 7.4

The Roundabout style of leadership puts the team members in the middle, figuratively and maybe even literally, depending on the nature of the work. The Roundabout leader is connected to the team but differs in approach from the Hub and Spoke leader. When you're a Roundabout leader, you interact with the team members by focusing on what you can do to meet their needs, mainly those involving information and resources. This leadership style is less direct and less directive.

A respected client of mine is a classic Roundabout leader. His accounting team works closely together, even when they are working remotely. He regularly checks in with each team member and is available when they need him. Otherwise, he stays out of their way and expects the team to determine how they will coordinate their work as they process numerous, complicated financial reports for the company. When they get stuck, they go to him, and he steps in to help.

If you act as a Roundabout leader, the relationship between you and the team members will be mostly collaborative. Your team members should feel safe and sufficiently comfortable to share information, resources, and candid feedback with you—as well as with each other. They also can delegate certain tasks back to you when they believe you can help them achieve the most effective result.

Here again, consider the pros and cons of this style, and choose your approach wisely.

Roundabout Leader

Pros	Cons
Promotes interdependence between team members	May be ineffective when a team member is not clear about their specific role and responsibilities, particularly when they're new
Allows for individual leadership qualities to develop, and builds capacity for succession	Poor individual performers may harm the team if the other team members are not able to adequately handle the situation at a peer level
Permits the leader to focus on more strategic thinking because they can spend less time having to direct day-to-day activities	When a decision or task is time-sensitive, the collaborative approach might take too long

As the boss, always strive to be aware of the overall situation you are facing. Then you can factor in each individual's circumstances to determine which leadership style is most appropriate. Leadership styles fall within the two extremes of Hub and Spoke or Roundabout, and can sometimes even be practiced at the same time with different individuals within a team.

Humility

A leader should be humble and someone whom followers can relate to: a person who makes their followers' needs a priority. Robert Greenleaf, the founder of the "Servant Leader" movement, wrote as long ago as 1970 that *leaders should serve the people they are leading.* Since then, many other leadership thinkers and writers continue to echo this intent. Yet, this mind-set can still be challenging for managers to adopt, especially when they are beginning as new bosses.

A good boss leads by leveraging the strength of their humility. One of the most significant challenges new managers face is controlling their ego needs. Controlling your ego means caring about others and focusing on them without feeling personally diminished.

Successfully transitioning from an individual contributor to an elite-level manager requires the ability to redefine what a "win" means for you. Once you're clear about that redefined win, the challenge can be getting satisfaction from it. Here's why.

When you accomplish something as an individual contributor, the result you produce is mostly *your* win. Even as a team member, you can look back on your day and often see a tangible impact in whatever sort of work product or service you provide. When you take time to notice what you've done, you can derive personal satisfaction from your direct efforts. Sometimes others (maybe even your boss!) recognize and acknowledge what you've produced. Simply put, it's clear to you what your "win" is.

When you're a good boss, however, your win will be different and often indirect. You win when you give your team members what they need to learn, grow, improve, and produce results independently. When *they* win, *you* win, too.

Steve Kerr, the head coach of the NBA World Champion Golden State Warriors, is an excellent example of a manager who has successfully redefined what a win means for himself. Kerr was a championship-caliber basketball player with a great three-point shot. When he stopped playing, he eventually became a winning head coach. As a long-standing Warriors fan, I've watched Kerr from the start. When you watch and listen to him, it's clear that he is always focused on his core (the players) and is also driven by a set of underlying values that he developed throughout his life and all during his championship-level playing career. Kerr doesn't derive satisfaction from clutch three-point shots now, because he is no longer a player on the court. Now as a coach, his "win" is what his team can achieve when *they* are on the court.

One of Kerr's responsibilities is to call situational plays and "manage" the game when necessary. He consistently sets a positive tone, regardless of the circumstances, and encourages all his players to have fun and not be afraid to take an open shot. It's evident that he connects with each individual player and tunes in to supplying whatever he thinks they need to always perform at their best.

Coach Kerr is a highly effective leader. He gets buy-in to his vision and direction, and consistently earns his players' trust. Even when he doesn't have an all-star bench, he still supports his team members so they can learn and develop to be the best they can be.

Kerr doesn't make the team or even any part of a specific game be centered on him. Despite his personal accolades and exceptional professional experience as an NBA champion, he never has to remind people how much he knows. His players respond to his coaching because he leverages his *humility* by sharing his knowledge and experiences with them. He does this by always focusing on them and their needs.

When you watch his players' body language on the court or on the bench, it's clear that they *want* to follow him. I believe Coach Kerr gets some of the most talented athletes in the world to work together and achieve high-performing results by his *humility*, not by his swagger.

Managers don't usually get positive strokes for work they directly do themselves. The kudos that elite managers receive (if any) are an acknowledgment for supporting the successful performance of their team members.

If supporting others' success doesn't provide you with the type of ego gratification *you* need, then you should probably remain an individual contributor—for everyone's sake! You can choose to stay on the "court" and get your individual wins there. But if you genuinely want to be an effective boss, be humble and willing to stay on the sidelines until you're needed. Find ego gratification and your personal "wins" by doing everything you can to support your team members to get *their* wins.

———

Develop your ability to naturally flex between management and leadership and between the Hub and Spoke and Roundabout styles when required without being stuck in a habitual, one-size-fits-all approach. Be forewarned that if you can't be flexible these days, you may find that your potential for career growth and advancement can be limited. Skilled leaders need to be attentive and agile so that they can change strategies, approaches, and methods as required. This is how better bosses thrive when faced with continual change.

Chapter | **8**

The Boss Triad

I firmly believe that everything that has ever been said, or written in any form, relating to both management and leadership involves three indicators. If you want to be a better boss, you need to continually keep track of these. When these areas receive the right amount of attention, individually and collectively, they represent good management and leadership. When you regularly focus on these three, you'll build and maintain the foundation for safe, healthy, satisfying, and productive workplaces, no matter the job or industry. Each of these indicators can overlap and impact the others. By neglecting any aspect of one, dysfunction will eventually occur. You can bet on it.

Together these indicators comprise The Boss Triad (see *Figure 8.1*). They are:

1. Trust
2. Needs
3. Morale

The Boss Triad

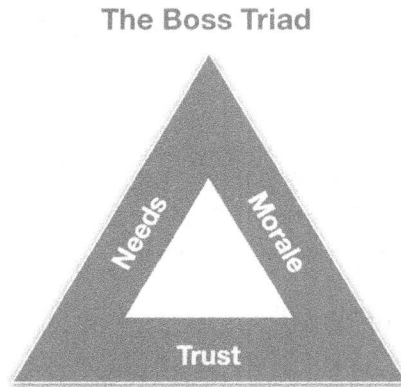

Figure 8.1

The words "trust," "needs," and "morale" on their own can be abstract concepts with different meanings and connotations for each of us. Since you're reading this book, you have likely worked at some type of job long enough to know how these words are associated with work. In fact, you may have had a lousy time at work because one of your managers ignored one or more of these indicators.

In the following sections, I'll describe a framework for how each of these three indicators is complementary and applies to every one of your team members (and also to you!). This is true whether or not you notice or deliberately measure them.

If you want to fully notice the impact of the Boss Triad on your team, you have to see each of the indicators clearly, so you can act and react accordingly as an effective boss. When you consistently keep these three indicators on your boss dashboard, they can be highly reliable measurements, but not for strictly financial or operational results. Rather, they indicate the well-being of the people in your organization—those who ultimately produce the results.

The many different managers I've worked with have had various levels of understanding about the importance of each of these in creating a satisfying, effective workplace. For some, Trust, Needs, and Morale are words that are devoid of any practical significance, especially for "manager managers." Just look at employee survey results worldwide for evidence. When you pay sufficient attention and use these indicators as diagnostic tools for an individual or a team, you'll understand the reasons why far too many people have a lousy time at work.

My objective is for you to recognize how important it is to invest time and attention into this Boss Triad. If you do that, I'm convinced that you will build a solid, stable framework for a high-performing team or organization of any size.

Four Elements of Trust

Trust forms the foundation for all relationships, whether personal or professional. The existence, as well as the strength, of trust also determines the quality of any relationship. It even determines the relationship's potential—whether it will move forward or backward or will stagnate or disintegrate. Trust between people is never static. It's either increasing or decreasing, often imperceptibly due to each interaction, or lack of one.

Trust is similar to money, and even to forms of power, in that it's entirely dependent on belief or perception for its existence. The quality of trust can sometimes feel like the quality of air. You believe that air is around you, don't you? You know when the air feels or smells clean or is just plain bad. Yet air is not something you can always see clearly unless it is really substandard, like when you're near a fire and visible dark smoke particles are floating around.

We typically treat trust like we do air in that both are somewhat abstract. Most of the time, we take air for granted, even though it is critical to our physical survival. Trust is essential to the survival of all our relationships, and unfortunately we may take it for granted as well.

The existence and quality of trust is not necessarily determined by fact or reality, or even by the actual intention or motivation of the other person or persons involved in the relationship. Because we're imperfect humans, our intent may drive our behavior, but our behavior doesn't necessarily, or always accurately, reflect our actual intent.

Imagine two coworkers, Casey and Stefan. One day Casey sits next to Stefan at a meeting, in a row of their own, and at the end of the session, Stefan walks out and suddenly realizes his wallet is missing. The truth is that Stefan's wallet fell out of his pocket on his way to the meeting. Here is the perception part: Because Casey was the only one who sat next to him, Stefan somehow believes that Casey took his wallet. Stefan thus questions Casey's integrity, even though Casey was not responsible for taking the wallet. And now Stefan's trust in Casey will likely be damaged or lost altogether.

Stefan might choose to confront Casey about the wallet. Let's say that Casey convinces Stefan that he didn't take it. They both might move on, with trust a little shaken but eventually regained. However, if Stefan never finds his wallet and doesn't believe Casey's denial about taking it, Stefan's loss of trust in Casey may never return. This could easily happen simply because of what Stefan *perceives* to be true, not what is *actually* true. (The fact in this example is that Stefan's wallet is still lying in a bush next to a walkway he uses to get to the office.)

Here's another example. There's a team leader, Jordan, with her team expecting information they need from her about a project they are working on. Jordan gets caught up working on another critical assignment for their boss and doesn't follow up with the team, so they're all left waiting for what they need. This isn't the first time Jordan is late getting the team information. The team's belief in her reliability will likely decrease.

Without trust, you won't get people to follow you very far, or for long. Without trust, you might get people to comply, but they won't commit.

A lot has already been written and said about the topic of trust—and with good reason. As I began my organizational development career, I was highly influenced by Stephen R. Covey's book *The 7 Habits of Highly Effective People.* Covey described trustworthiness as having the courage to act, combined with consideration for others. Covey's son Stephen M. R. Covey further expanded on the topic of trust in *his* book, *The Speed of Trust,* in which he described 13 behaviors that can be extremely useful for leaders to build and maintain trustworthiness.

I learned early on from the work of Covey the father that it's essential to "diagnose before you prescribe." With all due respect to the Coveys, as a practitioner, I wanted to find a simpler construct with familiar terminology so I could more precisely diagnose and "see" the trust issues between the people and teams I consulted with and tried to help.

After some more research and thoughtful consideration, I landed on the following four elements (*Figure 8.2*) that can help determine whether trust does or doesn't exist between people—and why.

Four Elements of Trust

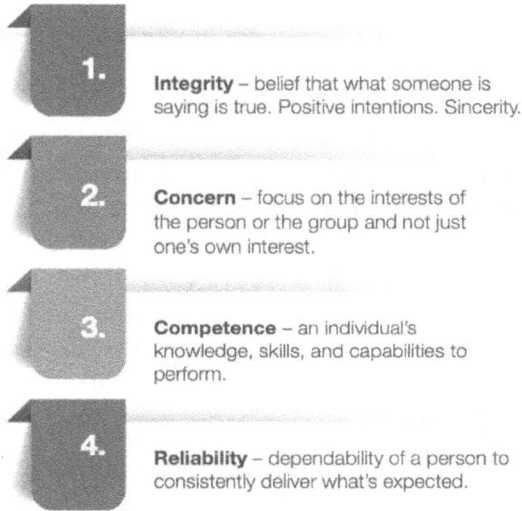

1.
Integrity – belief that what someone is saying is true. Positive intentions. Sincerity.

2.
Concern – focus on the interests of the person or the group and not just one's own interest.

3.
Competence – an individual's knowledge, skills, and capabilities to perform.

4.
Reliability – dependability of a person to consistently deliver what's expected.

Figure 8.2

All it takes for trust to be lacking or eroded is a perception that any one of these four trust elements is low or nonexistent. Two people may not trust each other for various reasons. One person might question a coworker's concern because they failed to offer help when needed. This coworker might have an issue with the other's competence because they have made multiple mistakes, despite being given adequate training and direction. Consequently, the result between these two would be low trust.

The primary reasons why trust exists, or doesn't, can be more easily understood by considering each of the four trust elements individually.

I frequently use these four elements to diagnose trust issues between individuals and even between teams. You can focus on each specific element as if it were a lens to help you see and understand how trust is built or eroded. When I don't trust one of my neighbors, or even my dry cleaner, I can see and understand the reason why by using these four lenses.

Remember that trust involves perception and belief, not necessarily reality. When all four elements are perceived to be high, solid trust exists.

Integrity

Integrity is a measurement of whether we believe that the other person is honest or behaves with positive intent. Integrity is the primary element that most of us typically attribute to trust. Although each of the four elements are necessary for a high level of trust to exist, if your Integrity is questioned, so too will the other trust elements be. If you deceive, lie, cheat, or steal, any trust you may have had with the other person will likely disintegrate, as will the quality of the relationship. And if trust wasn't there at all, you'll have a difficult time building it.

A senior manager I know, named Ari, continually told his team for months that the company was doing fine financially, even though it wasn't. His team believed him until they eventually found out the truth. Ari knew about the revenue troubles all along and failed to tell them when he should have. Ari's integrity was questioned, and his team struggled to follow his leadership. Not long after the truth came out, a few team members left the company, but not because of the financial problems. They left because they had issues with Ari's integrity.

Some people wait for other people to prove or demonstrate their integrity before "trusting" them. Others—like me—believe that people behave with integrity until they prove that they don't have it. What assumptions do you make about a person's integrity?

Concern

As a trust element, Concern is the belief that another person cares about you and your interests as well. If you think that someone's actions and behavior are motivated by selfishness, or if you perceive them to be self-serving in any way, it will negatively affect your assessment of their level of concern for you and *your* interests. This is true, regardless of what someone may mean or intend to do.

Concern is the trust element that you have to "show" more than just "tell." As a new manager, it would be appropriate to tell your team early on that you are there to support them and give them the direction they need to be successful. You should also tell them about your goals, plans, and expectations for them, as well as for yourself. However, what they likely will be thinking is, "We'll see."

To positively affect if or how someone perceives your concern, words alone will not build trust. When you're a manager, team members and others who may be new to working with you will likely take a wait-and-see approach before deciding if they really believe that you are concerned about them and their interests. Your relationships are influenced by the quality and frequency of the connections you make. Making a personal connection with those in your core circle begins to show that you are concerned. You can build trust from there.

Competence

The trust element that each of us has the least control over (because it doesn't change very quickly) is Competence. It involves the belief or perception that a person has the knowledge, skills, or ability to do whatever is wanted, needed, or expected of them in their role. That role could be friend, spouse, mother, food preparer, coworker, plumber, or boss. When it comes to knowledge, skill, and ability, we are only as competent as we are at this moment. We should hope to be a little more competent at the end of each day, *if* we are committed to learning.

Imagine that you have a coworker who is a project manager, someone well-qualified and reliable—someone you can trust in her role. You trust her also because she has a high level of concern for you and acts with integrity. Despite this high level of trust, she would not be the person you would call if you needed surgery next month because she lacks the competence necessary to do what you need done: surgery. If you insisted that this trusted coworker be your surgeon, she would fail, and you and your family would be seriously disappointed!

To be an effective boss, it's imperative that you assign people to the right jobs and roles matching their competence. The phrase "setting people up for success" refers to putting people in positions where they possess enough competence to succeed. This is critically important for a people manager. Trust can continue to be built, *if* the competence is there.

Reliability

The most actionable of all the trust elements is Reliability. This relates to the perception or belief that one will *consistently* follow up or follow through with whatever you need them to do in their role. This is true for your boss, a coworker, a friend, a family member, or even your barista.

To help build trust, you can demonstrate your reliability every day. Respond to an email soon after it was received. Return a phone call promptly. Complete an assignment on time. Provide all the information that someone requests. Meet a project deadline that was agreed to. You get the idea.

Despite our best intentions to follow up or follow through, we are all still human. There will be times when we don't do what others expect from us, for a variety of reasons. Regardless of whether or not you're the boss, accept your responsibility for missing a deadline or expectation. Make clear the reason "why." However, never use "why" to try to give yourself a pass or an excuse. When you provide the reason for missing a commitment, the other person can better understand your side of the story, before making assumptions and possibly forming mistaken beliefs about your intentions. However, if your integrity is questioned, your "why" will likely not be believed.

Consistently follow up or follow through with what is expected from you in your relationships. Then when you provide a reasonable explanation for an occasionally missed deadline, the other person's perception of your reliability probably won't be affected negatively. It may only be a problem when a person believes that dropping the ball is typical of your behavior. If that happens, it will be more difficult for you to build trust.

Building Trust Using the Four Elements

When a given relationship matters, first focus on reliability if you want to build trust. If you are consistently reliable, eventually the other person will believe that you are concerned about them and their interests, too. As I indicated earlier, you can say that you are concerned about someone; however, this trust element is most affected by your *actions*.

When you consistently follow up or follow through with what someone expects from you, it's a significant way to show them that you are also concerned about them. By focusing on being reliable, you begin to positively address two trust elements—Concern and Reliability.

Since we have little control over Competence in the short term, just do your best at whatever you are doing—period. If you are in the right role and the other trust elements are in place, most reasonable people can accept that you are less than perfect. That leaves Integrity.

All I can say about your integrity is, "Don't screw it up!" When your integrity is questioned, it is tough to change other people's perception or belief about you. So do everything you can to act with integrity, no matter what your role is. Just be honest and behave with positive intent toward others. It's that simple.

Trust is *not* a static state. Keep in mind that we're always assessing each other against these four elements, consciously or unconsciously. Whenever you have direct or indirect contact or connection with another person, your trust in that person will either increase or decrease. Your trust in them will be influenced by your perceptions of how they behave with you, or around you, at that time. And vice versa.

In a mutual relationship, trust is what links us and shapes the quality of our relationship. For a person to be considered trustworthy, all four elements need to be in place.

Use the "Employee Trust Worksheet" (*Figure 8.3*) to consider what trust elements may be currently affected within your team.

Employee Trust Worksheet

Employee Name	Integrity	Concern	Competence	Reliability	Follow-up Actions

Figure 8.3

Four Employee Needs

Want to know what life's about? It's simple. Life is all about getting our needs met. This is true for a newborn infant at the beginning of life as well as for an older person approaching the end of life. In between birth and death, the rest of life still involves meeting our individual needs. When we know what we need and have those needs satisfied, we can be productive and hopefully even happy! This is a simple truth, but one not always easy to achieve.

At work, every person, regardless of their role, has needs in each of four categories. When those needs are met, the person can be effective at solving problems and using judgment in their jobs. This is true for the CEO, the office intern, or the apprentice carpenter. What differs between them is the scope and specific type of need.

The four primary employee needs that I've identified are Resources, Information, Support, and Control. (See *Figure 8.4.*) The acronym is R-I-S-C.

Four Employee Needs

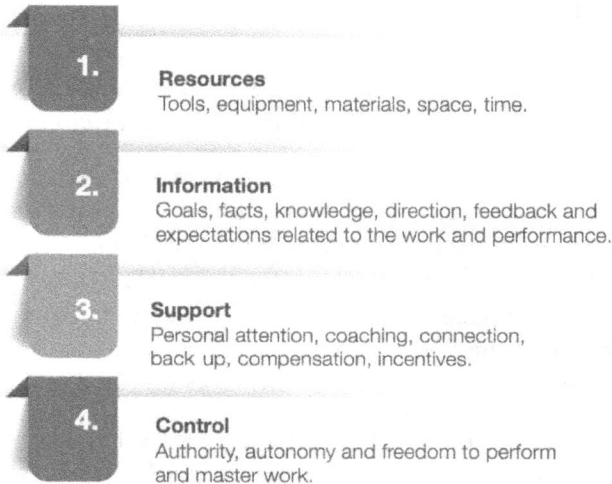

1. **Resources**
Tools, equipment, materials, space, time.

2. **Information**
Goals, facts, knowledge, direction, feedback and
expectations related to the work and performance.

3. **Support**
Personal attention, coaching, connection,
back up, compensation, incentives.

4. **Control**
Authority, autonomy and freedom to perform
and master work.

Figure 8.4

Resources

Tangible and intangible needs are met with Resources. For instance, tools, equipment, materials, supplies, and space are tangible. Time is intangible. As with all needs, the resources required will vary, depending on the role and scope of responsibility. When you are in a management role, responsible for a unit or large organization, financial (budget) and human resources (staff) are needs that would also be categorized under Resources.

I once worked with a group of maintenance engineers who realized that they could be more efficient when lifting heavy metal plates from the work floor. The task had always been a two-person job. One of the team members, Jorge, did some research and found a specific winch-like device that was available from a local supplier. The group approached their supervisor, Larry, with a request for the winch. Because they had less staffing due to cost reductions, they now "needed" another resource (equipment) to remain efficient. Larry listened and then successfully advocated for the employees to his manager. The unit purchased its latest piece of equipment and filled a resource need.

Information

The umbrella category of Information can include anything related to the facts, figures, details, or knowledge required for someone to do their job successfully. As with all work-related needs, information needs also depend on the individual's specific circumstances.

For example, technicians in a laboratory would need information about scientific means and methods, along with processes and procedures to be followed to produce results. Goals and action plans for a project engineer would involve information about what she should focus on to complete her project on time and on budget. Direction to a laborer in the field about how to set up concrete formwork is information he needs to complete his tasks for the day.

I coached an experienced data manager named Jen who was highly competent yet was struggling to keep up with the expectations set by her IT director. The director, Sarita, recognized that Jen lacked the ability to use the latest analytical tools she had available. So Sarita reallocated Jen's workload and priorities and arranged for her to attend offsite training to get the information she needed to maintain her skillset.

Feedback, both positive and negative, can also be a critical information need for anyone, including a new supervisor. Anything related to learning about what's working and what isn't would be needed information to avoid or minimize mistakes. A list of performance expectations is also an example of information that every worker needs to know to consistently produce desired results.

Keep in mind that Information (data) should be accessible, sensible, and actionable. More on this later.

Support

Each employee may have different Support needs, so support can be provided in various forms. One person might need coaching, while another might need backup from a manager or the organization. Leadership is a form of support. Most of us also require some degree of social interaction at work, whether we're extroverts or introverts. This interaction can fill a need we have for support from others.

Support also includes pay and other forms of compensation, benefits, perquisites, and incentives. It includes formal and informal recognition for achievements—the "atta boy!" and "atta girl!" remarks from a boss.

A respected director, Miriam, at a company I consult with recognized that her senior project manager, Jose, was becoming impatient with the pace of his career advancement within the company. Although he was producing quality work, he was having difficulties delivering "bad news" to clients. Miriam determined that Jose needed coaching. She decided to spend time with him at their one-on-one meetings to work through the communication challenges he was having. Miriam provided support to Jose by giving him helpful tips and allowing him to practice some new communication approaches with her before taking them to actual clients.

Although everyone needs some amount of support, it's worth noting that workplace surveys show that Gen Z and millennials generally have a greater need and expectation for support than their predecessors. This is particularly true as it relates to coaching and mentoring.

I have also found that solid and high-performing employees don't merely want to be directed by their manager. Most want to be coached on how to do their best work and how to continue to learn, grow, and advance. Coaching will be covered in more detail later.

Control

The Control need is defined by the freedom, authority, and autonomy someone has to make decisions and use judgment regarding how they perform their work. Everyone needs a certain degree of control, whether the job is digging a ditch or making strategic decisions for a global business conglomerate.

If a boss allows little to no control over *how* work gets done, they are probably a micromanager. This can result in overdependence by employees on their manager. This is a primary reason why employees become disengaged and can stop using their brains and creativity. They stop learning. This can eventually lead to stagnation and obsolescence, for the person as well as the company.

Do everything you can to provide each of your employees with as much control over their work as you think they can handle, based on their competence. Provide continual training and experiences to them to help increase their knowledge and skills. More than likely you'll see an increase in the quality of their judgment and ability to handle more control.

Keep Their Needs in Mind

Continually pay close attention to the needs of *each* of your direct reports. Don't wait for them to ask you, because they might not know what they need! So be proactive and find out about their needs. Your one-on-one meeting is an ideal time for this type of exploration. See chapter 11 for tips on one-on-one meetings.

When you identify a team member's needs, do everything you can to provide them. Be as open and transparent as possible if and when reality prevents you from giving your employees all they need. Let them know "why." If you are not upfront with them, they will make their own assumptions and projections, which may be incorrect or inaccurate. Treat employees as adults and trust them with the truth—until you can't.

The Four Employee Needs (R-I-S-C) should always be on a boss's "radar screen." Your attention to these needs matters greatly, because how well your team members believe you and the organization deal with them will also affect their morale.

Use the "Employee Needs Worksheet" (*Figure 8.5*) to analyze what your employees need to continue or increase their performance.

Employee Needs Worksheet

Employee Name	Resources	Information	Support	Control	Follow-up Actions

Figure 8.5

Four Factors of Morale

Morale is generally understood to be a barometer of how people feel, typically when they're at work. The collective morale of a group usually gets more attention than an individual's morale. However, any group's morale is actually determined by the sum of each individual member's morale.

The collective morale may be low or high, for a variety of reasons. To positively impact the group's morale, you need to see and understand how each individual's morale is being affected. For every person on your team as well as across your organization, morale is significantly influenced by how well and how much they are getting their four needs met—Resources, Information, Support, and Control. Beyond having needs met, a person's morale can also be affected by broader circumstances that may or may not be in a boss's control.

I coached two program directors at a nonprofit agency. Both had low morale, but for different reasons. One director, named Lane, felt that her executive director played favorites and held her coworkers to inconsistent performance standards. She also felt burned out due to the long hours she had been putting in over the last year.

Another director in the unit, Alex, had frequently approached the executive director with suggestions and ideas for improving services—yet was repeatedly turned away or ignored. Alex felt that he might be targeted for layoff because he thought his input might have been viewed as being a "problem" for his boss.

Even if what Lane and Alex separately believed wasn't actually true, what's relevant is what they *perceived* to be true. Their perceptions defined their reality and caused them to have low morale, though for different reasons. All it takes for someone's morale to be negatively impacted is their perception or belief that one of four morale factors is low. Morale is similar to trust in that it is also based on perception or belief, not necessarily on fact.

(After you read more about the four morale factors, see if you can tell why Lane and Alex had low morale.)

When people have "a lousy time at work," you can bet that one or more factors of their morale are low. Effective managers diagnose *before* they prescribe how to address critical morale issues. Too often, when a boss senses low morale in the team, they prescribe a version of the quick fix. Of course, you know what that might be: "Have a party!" or maybe "Let's throw a potluck" or "Happy hour!" or perhaps even "Let's schedule a team-building session" with someone like me! Despite good intentions, this is a common misstep that I've seen taken by too many bosses.

How many at-the-office potlucks have you attended where you and many of your team members pick up a plate, grab your food, and go back to your workspace without hanging out together? To be clear, I don't think there's anything necessarily wrong with making time for people to share a pizza and socialize. However, when people are having a lousy time at work, that might not be the best prescription or approach for improving their morale. In fact, it could make it worse if you don't understand what's going on.

If you want to positively address morale issues, make a real effort to accurately diagnose *what* is affected, *who* is affected, and *how* they are affected before you take action. Diagnosing a problem or issue is an instance when it's best to "go slow to go fast."

Each of your team members' morale is determined by their perception of each of four factors (see *Figure 8.6*).

Four Factors of Morale

1.
Security
Physical, emotional, psychological, economic.

2.
Justice/Fairness
Treatment by a manager, coworker, or the organization.

3.
Meaning/Achievement
Meaning and sense of accomplishment for the work being performed. Quality of personal-professional life.

4.
Participation
Level and type of involvement and connection to peers and others. Receptivity to providing ideas and input.

Figure 8.6

Security

When someone doesn't feel comfortable or safe in their role or job, that will likely affect their sense of Security. A construction worker who feels at risk of being physically injured because his foreman's primary focus is on getting things done fast and cheaply would likely feel low morale related to security. This morale factor is also consistent with one of the universal human needs that the humanistic psychologist Abraham Maslow identified in his hierarchy of needs—safety. If a member of your team is being harassed or bullied, either physically or verbally, their sense of safety or security will be affected.

Imagine that one of your direct reports feels concerned and preoccupied about the likelihood or even possibility of losing their job. How secure do you think they feel showing up to work every day? Security, or lack of it, can take many forms.

Justice or Fairness

Simply put, if someone believes that they're being mistreated or screwed over, Justice or Fairness is the morale factor most affected. A perception of unfairness may be created by the boss, a coworker, or the organization itself. Mistreatment, like all morale factors, could be real or perceived—yet the result is the same. An unfair job classification, work assignment, or workload may also trigger low morale. Or it could result from a disparity (real or perceived) involving pay or other work benefits.

Meaning or Achievement

Although you might be helpful as a boss, the "meaning" of one's job is something each individual has to uncover or discover themselves. Everyone has up and down days. However, when we continually question the Meaning and purpose of our work, morale is affected.

If your staff member regularly dreads Mondays and looks forward to Fridays too much, this Achievement factor may be at least one of the four morale factors in play. A "same stuff, different day" mentality can be an example of a mind-set adopted by a direct report perceiving that there's not enough meaning for them in the job they are doing. This negative mentality eventually leads to having a lousy time at work if it isn't addressed.

The ability to achieve an acceptable work-life balance can also affect morale. When there is a perceived imbalance—say, too much work and not enough play or personal time—low morale can become associated with the meaning/achievement factor.

Participation

A team member who doesn't feel a sincere connection to a boss or coworkers may develop a sense of isolation. This is a Participation factor. If your boss rarely asks for your input by asking a version of "What do you think?," your morale may eventually be affected by your lack of participation and involvement in "how" you do your work.

This can also happen when a direct report doesn't feel involved in the decisions that affect his or her work. As the boss, when you don't allow your team members to have reasonable time to talk with each other and socialize informally at work, that lack of social participation may cause a morale issue.

Remember the most common prescription for low morale that I outlined earlier? If you diagnose that the team is overworked and doesn't get enough time together, a team lunch or dinner may be the right prescription. However, just remember that it won't improve morale if any of the other three morale factors are perceived to be low.

It's your responsibility as the boss to continually track and assess the morale of each of your direct reports. Suppose you wait too long to notice a dip in any of the indicators described above? In that case, you'll likely have individual and team performance problems that can become more difficult to handle and take longer to correct.

Addressing a team's morale issues often requires more than a single approach, given that any one or more of the four morale factors may be affected. Continue to be proactive. Be willing to put in the time and effort to regularly connect with your individual team members so that you can keep reasonably current on all aspects of their morale.

Once you determine a dip in any single morale factor, you can decide how best to step in and respond to the team, whether individually or collectively. When you get lucky, you might decide that "Team Go-Kart Night" is the easy fix!

(Now, can you determine which elements of Sue's and Alex's morale were affected in the example above?)

Use the "Employee Morale Worksheet" (*Figure 8.7*) to consider each of your employees and identify the elements of their morale that may be currently affected.

Employee Morale Worksheet

Employee Name	Security	Justice/ Fairness	Meaning/ Achievement	Participation	Follow-up Actions

Figure 8.7

Leveraging the Boss Triad

When you consistently focus on the three indicators that represent the Boss Triad—Trust, Needs, and Morale—you will have fewer blind spots as you continually look for effective ways to be successful at both management and leadership.

When you focus your time and attention on the first two indicators—being trustworthy and then doing your best to meet the needs of your direct reports—the likely result will be high individual and collective morale for all of them!

Accept the fact that you won't always be able to give people what they need, such as more time. However, whenever you can't satisfy a need, remember to tell them why.

The 12 elements and factors that are part of the Boss Triad are the most important and useful metrics to keep high on your dashboard as a boss. Take them seriously, and don't ignore or deny what you see (or don't see). Be willing to dig deeper to verify what's working and not working. To be a better boss, always choose to be impactful with what you can control or influence, and be a true advocate as needed.

Chapter | **9**

Three Perspectives
for Leaders

The better bosses can lead and adapt to changing situations by using sound judgment, skill, ability, and desire. These bosses flex their style and approach to get positive results from the people they want to lead. They understand what they should be seeing *and* doing for their team, or an individual, in different situations and circumstances. They effectively Lead at the Front, at the Side, and at the Rear.

Here's a breakdown of what happens when you are leading from each perspective (*Figure 9.1*):

Three Perspectives for Leaders

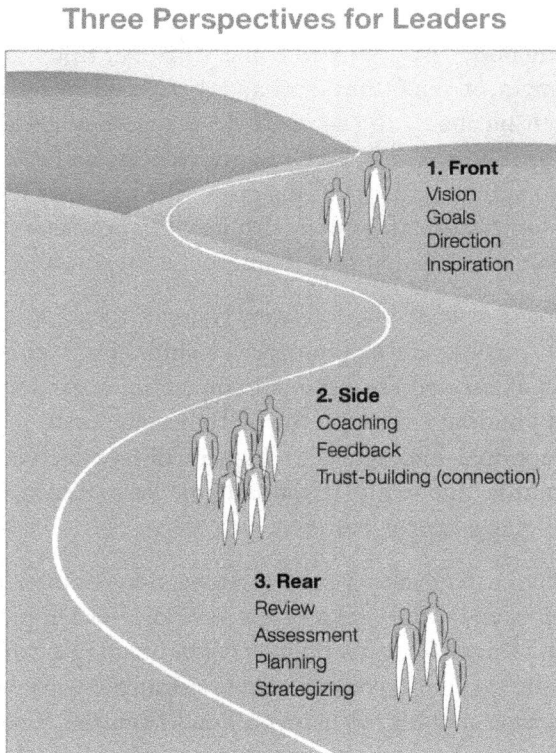

1. Front
Vision
Goals
Direction
Inspiration

2. Side
Coaching
Feedback
Trust-building (connection)

3. Rear
Review
Assessment
Planning
Strategizing

Figure 9.1

When you Lead from the Front, you usually begin by standing alone, sometimes literally. From this perspective, your first objective is to attract at least one follower. Remember, for you to become a leader, you only need one person to follow you!

Leading from the Front can involve communicating the big-picture situation and purpose to a group. When you Lead from the Front, you make an effort to get people willing and motivated to move in a common direction toward a goal or objective. Even inspiring a single person to buy into your plan is Leading from the Front.

Near the beginning of the movie *Jerry Maguire*, Jerry is leaving his big-time sports agency job. On his way out the door, he looks around the large, open-floor-plan office to see if he can encourage others to leave with him to start a new agency. With a few dozen people nervously eyeing him, he begins to Lead from the Front. "Okay. If anybody else wants to come with me, this moment will be the moment of something real and *FUN* and inspiring in this god-forsaken business, and we will do it together! Who's comin' with me? *Who's coming with me?!*" Dorothy Boyd is the only person to speak up. "I'll go with you!" she cries. She becomes his first follower, and Jerry leaves the room with her. Dorothy was Jerry's first follower. Because of her, at that moment, he became a leader.

Once you have at least one follower, you can then Lead from the Side, which involves developing relationships. From this perspective, you focus on making personal connections, getting to know people, and building trust with them. To become really good at this requires emotional intelligence, which involves effective interpersonal communication skills. If you struggle here, fortunately, emotional intelligence can be learned.

After you begin to develop personal connections and relationships, you can then step back to get a better view of the "big picture" you started with. This is what you do now when Leading from the Rear. From this vantage point, you can be more strategic with your thinking and decision making. When you Lead from the Rear, you can also see team members who are struggling, either in understanding the goal or trusting you and the team well enough that they are motivated to follow along. You can also be more objective when you Lead from the Rear. Sometimes when Leading from the Front or Side, you can be too close to a situation or a person. Moving to this third perspective helps you to maintain your objectivity and stay out of the weeds.

Effective leaders understand which actions they need to take, and when, based on the information they glean from each of the three perspectives. As time unfolds and changes to your situation and circumstances occur, your goal or goals may also have to change. When this happens, you'll have to decide if it's necessary to go back to Leading from the Front to communicate the change or changes to your team. Then, if you want to keep others following you, you'll also have to continually foster relationships by Leading from the Side.

I've found that many leaders can *naturally* operate from one, or maybe two, of these three perspectives, but rarely from all three without some development. For instance, some leaders are really good at communicating with groups at the "front of the room" and inspiring them toward action by using their personal power. However, when it comes to forming personal relationships or making longer-term strategic decisions, these charismatic leaders are not always effective.

Other leaders are more personal and are good at building rapport with individuals and helping them grow, develop, and perform. However, these relational leaders may not have the natural ability to communicate a clear, inspiring vision along with well-defined goals. They may also miss recognizing the shifts in morale because of an inability to clearly see and understand the big picture.

Finally, some leaders are quite skilled at seeing the big picture, making strategic decisions, and planning accordingly. Yet, these leaders may tend to stay cocooned in their workspaces without being regularly visible and inspiring to the team. Or they don't invest the time to connect with their individual team members so they can build relationships and trust.

If you're sincerely committed to learning, then build on your strengths and enhance your natural abilities. When you are indeed an effective leader, you can naturally move consciously and unconsciously from the Front, Side, and Rear as needed.

In the following chapters, I'll describe the skills, approaches, and tools you can use to lead from each of the Three Perspectives—and be a better boss.

Chapter | **10**

Leading from the Front

Part | 1

"Leaders help others see
what they can't see on their own."

Showing **the Way**

Imagine that it's summer and you're out in the woods, ready to begin a week-long hiking and camping trip with a group of friends and new acquaintances. Because you're the one with the most out-door experience, you've been given responsibility for guiding the group. By the way, there's no set plan for where to go or what to do. Everyone has left that part up to you. It's now your job to manage everyone's week and make it worthwhile and safe.

Let's assume that you've done your research looking at maps and online sites, and have determined that there's a cool lake down the trail, over a hilltop. It's a spot where you believe you can all set up tents, swim, and hang out. Even though you haven't yet been there, you decide that reaching the lake should be the group's goal for the first day. Fine.

Your first move in this situation is to step up and Lead from the Front. Your objective is to get your group to *want to* follow you to the lake. You begin with a message that includes a clear description of the lake that you have in your mind, with all the benefits they'll find there so that they can begin to "see" what *you* see. Here's a tip: When you're Leading from the Front, you should give the same message to everyone simultaneously, if at all possible.

Leading from the Front should also involve giving people a compelling reason "why." Your potential followers may need to change their thinking or their actions in order to follow you. In this example, with you as the trail leader, why should they change where they are and move ahead toward a place where they have never been?

The Vision Thing

As the leader, you need to see an image of what's possible. This "possibility" can form in your mind even though you may not have experienced it before. As the trail leader in the example we began with, the image of arriving at the lake becomes your vision—the possibility. When you decide to make a vision become a reality, and you genuinely believe in it, you should then share it with the group in a way that it can become *their* vision, too.

When Leading from the Front, aim to get at least one initial follower to believe in your vision. After getting a follower, your work as a leader will eventually include helping others—your potential followers—to understand *why* they should also want to follow you. To get others to follow takes patience and the investment of time and effort in leading from the other two perspectives—the Side and the Rear.

A primary reason leaders are necessary is to help others to *see* what they can't see on their own. If your group could *see* the lake for themselves or were already motivated to go there, they wouldn't need you to lead them there.

I came across an entertaining and very insightful video on YouTube titled "First Follower: Leader Lessons from Dancing Guy" by Derek Sivers (an entrepreneur and musician). The video initially shows a shirtless guy dancing by himself at a music festival. The dude quickly inspires one other person to join him, then another, and so on until the entire hillside is filled with people dancing around him. This all takes place in about seven minutes! The key message is that the first follower, by choosing to follow, had the *most* impact on creating the whole scene—not the shirtless guy (leader) who started it.

If you can get at least one follower to see your vision and go along with you, that person can now step up and help share the lead position on the trail with you. Your first follower or followers can have a positive impact on the rest of the group. They can help you lead them, mainly because some members of your group may be reluctant or unwilling to follow you initially. In fact, your other team members may be more willing to follow your first follower rather than you! That's okay as long as they are moving in the same direction you want them to go.

Vision and Mission

A vision statement and a mission statement are not the same. They can both be useful and should be created for different reasons. Let's go over the differences so that you can see how you can use them effectively.

The Mission

A mission statement is really a purpose statement. It describes why your organization exists, what you do, and whom you do it for—both currently and for the foreseeable future. It might begin with, *"We are…"* Mission statements don't typically change unless what you do now significantly changes.

A compelling and relatable mission statement can help attract people to your organization, inspire them, and keep them motivated. Many people, particularly in the nonprofit and government sectors, are passionately mission-driven. This means their work is focused on their purpose. When motivation decreases, a compelling mission statement can help remind everyone in your organization why they are there and, more importantly, why what they do matters.

With a powerful and attractive mission statement, some people may not need leaders to be wayfinders. The mission guides them forward. However, when there is uncertainty about the future and what it may mean, a vision can help provide the focus for "what could be." Influential leaders most always use a vision to Lead from the Front.

The Vision

The vision statement describes what you or the organization *want* to be or become. It's future-focused and can change or be revised if or when the vision is realized or needs to change. A vision should be clear and include a big-picture description of where you're going as a team or organization. It should also focus on possibilities—what things could look like when you get there. It might begin with, "*We will be...*"

A vision statement can be extremely useful if it's clear and concrete. I believe that too many organizations develop visions that are nothing more than flowery, generic-sounding declarations that are mainly used for the website or put in a nice frame for a lobby or conference room wall. Waste of time.

Vision statements, whether formal or informal, should be taken very seriously and be used as a guiding tool for leaders and "wannabe leaders" to focus on what could *be* as they begin to lead others. Your vision statement should be in plain language that is easily understandable and imagined, whether spoken or written. The vision may or may not be communicated outside of the organization or your team. Where it is used beyond the group it's intended for should depend on whom you want to see it and why.

As a leader, you are the vehicle for driving your organization toward the vision. A clear vision should be easily communicated and repeated so that it can be easily remembered. When people can see in their mind's eye where they're going and where you want them to go, that also helps them understand you and your intentions. Your people can then develop reasons why they should follow *you*. Once you have followers focused on your vision, you can also describe how they can get there and what you know (or don't know) about what's ahead. This could include what to look for and what to watch out for. Don't forget that if you want to inspire people toward a vision, you have to first inspire yourself—and genuinely believe in it!

Here are a few examples of vision statements:

· "We will create a sustainable group of best-in-class companies that are the envy of the marketplace."

· "We will become the most trusted real estate investment company on the West Coast, focused on relationships, innovation, execution, and continuous improvement in all aspects of our business."

· "To be the place that people go to when they want to watch any TV show or movie."

· "To become the world's most loved, most flown, and most profitable airline."

· "To provide better health and well-being for all residents, now and for future generations."

· "To be an empowered workforce known for safety, reliability, transparency, diversity, and responsiveness. We will deliver modern and integrated services in collaboration with the community and others."

A vision statement for the organization may have a time line that extends over years. Many books and online resources offer more detail about crafting a vision statement for your organization. Regardless of your management level, you'll find it useful to develop a vision for *all* projects and initiatives you are leading, regardless of their duration. Continually be developing and refining your vision, and whenever you can, do this with others. But when you have to, update your vision alone, if necessary, to keep your vision relevant.

Leaders should be communicating the vision to others whenever they have the opportunity. Staff meetings, employee recognition events, and training sessions are all appropriate forums for keeping people focused on the future. When you are effective at Leading from the Front, you use your vision (and your mission) to help inspire people and give meaning to their efforts—as well as yours. Work hard at this so that your vision becomes *their* vision.

Willing followers want to frequently know where they're going and why they're going there. Whether it is long- or short-term-focused, what the vision communicates must be clear and neither ambiguous nor fluffy. You'll find this to be an important and most effective first step when you are Leading from the Front.

The next step to take is setting clear goals.

Goals Focus Effort

Once the mission and vision are in place, goals are developed for focus. Goal setting should provide a clear purpose for effort with a description of a measurable result. Be aware that goals can be ineffective and not very useful when they're too fuzzy or unclear, like many mission and vision statements are.

In my work with organizations, I still encounter many busy people who don't appreciate the value of the goal-setting process. Many of these managers and individual contributors pay lip service to the importance of goals, and I still hear countless complaints that goal setting is "too time-consuming." These same people claim they're getting work done without investing any real time determining *deliberately* what they're going to focus their effort on, and why. Most are indeed busy. So they must be busy doing the right things. Yes?

Not really. Unfortunately, many of these people are bosses with responsibility for the efforts of other people. What do you think happens when a boss isn't clear about what the goals are? Most often, this manager just assumes that everyone who reports to her will figure out on their own what's important to focus on, as they try to do their best work. Too often these people fail to achieve effective results. Does this sound familiar?

The Road Trip

Imagine that your boss left you a voicemail and assigned you to drive to the Midwest to meet her for an important meeting sometime this month. Assume for now that you were unable to reach her and that her message was the only information you had to use. Where in the Midwest would you go, and when would you get there?

Suppose you drive to Cleveland (yes, it's in the Midwest!) and arrive there next week, only to find that your boss was in Minneapolis two days earlier waiting for you. Even if we assume that your boss had a pretty good idea of what she meant by Midwest (in this case, it was specifically Minneapolis) and knew when she thought you should get there, the fact is she wasn't clear. The result is that you didn't arrive at her expected destination and time. Beyond that, you would likely feel extremely frustrated, and your boss would probably doubt your ability to follow directions! Have you ever received vague direction from a manager that seemed like this example?

Too many managers don't invest enough time working with their direct reports to clearly define the goals and the expectations associated with those goals. These bosses are "wishing and hoping" types. They spend their time wishing and hoping that the results they want from their direct reports will just happen automatically. The fact is, there *is* no magic to getting consistent results. A good boss purposefully invests real time and effort in goal setting with their people.

Let's start fresh with a new trip. This will be a cross-country road trip with your team. Your specific destination is the goal. For this example, let's make it Baltimore. The road or roads you'll take from Las Vegas (your starting point) to reach your destination represent your plan. Once you establish the goal (Baltimore), as the leader, you would support your followers by helping them to navigate the route and manage their plan for getting there.

Let's also add this piece of information: *why* you're going there. The purpose of your team's trip to Baltimore is to meet with another team that is willing to share their experiences and best practices for implementing a billing system that your own group will be implementing over the next year. You'll also need to let your team know when the meeting is scheduled. Now your team has clear information about where, why, and when.

On a road trip, the destination typically doesn't change unless there's been a significant change in the trip's purpose or other circumstances. You already know intuitively that most of your time and energy managing a road trip would be spent determining the team's route (planning) and then sharing the driving to reach each milestone you set for the day (execution). You would look at the

GPS directions and make daily, maybe hourly, adjustments to the route based on weather, road closures, or to take advantage of other opportunities that may present themselves along the way.

This is a simple, straightforward process to reach a desired result. Decide on your particular destination, determine when you need to arrive, plan your route, and then just drive. And make adjustments as needed along the way. For goal setting, the process is similar— except the "where" now becomes a "what."

Goal setting is an essential activity of Leading from the Front. It's critical to being effective, because goals focus on supporting the mission (what you do) and realizing the vision (what you want to become). They can be set at the individual level and at the group or organization level.

A clear goal includes TWO parts: the goal statement *plus* the plan for achieving it. The odds for success go up sharply when both parts of the goal are in place. When you actively involve people in developing the goal statements and action plans, you get even better results by sharing ownership. Remember the road trip example. Be clear about the destination (goal) and also be clear about the route (plan) to achieve the desired results by design, not by accident.

SMART Method

A goal statement should describe the primary action, why it matters, and when it will be accomplished. The SMART method is the most effective approach I've encountered for developing a goal statement. George T. Doran, a consultant and former director of corporate planning for the Washington Water Power Company, published a paper in 1981 that first described the use of this acronym for goal setting. Since then, a few variations have cropped up. This is this version I find most useful (see *Figure 10.1*):

SMART Goal Method

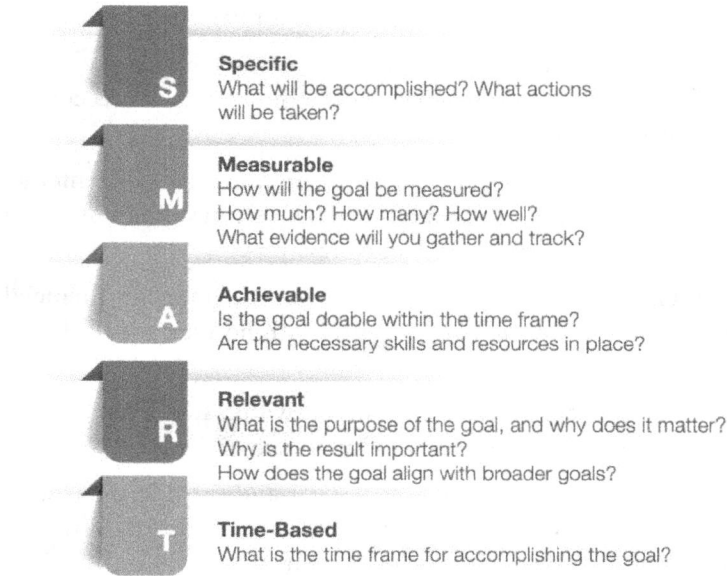

Specific
What will be accomplished? What actions
will be taken?

Measurable
How will the goal be measured?
How much? How many? How well?
What evidence will you gather and track?

Achievable
Is the goal doable within the time frame?
Are the necessary skills and resources in place?

Relevant
What is the purpose of the goal, and why does it matter?
Why is the result important?
How does the goal align with broader goals?

Time-Based
What is the time frame for accomplishing the goal?

Figure 10.1

SMART Goal Template

Goal Statement	What makes it SMART
Do _____	Specific action taken
in order to _____	to accomplish Measurable, Relevant result
By _____	Within certain Time frame

Make sure it's Achievable: (realistic time frame, sufficient resources, feasible target)

Figure 10.2

Here are some instances of SMART goals for various jobs:

- "Provide high-quality customer service on an ongoing basis resulting in a 90% customer satisfaction rating on accuracy, timeliness, and courtesy measures."

- "Provide direction, support, and oversight to the call center so that 95% of hotline calls are answered within 1 minute, and fewer than 2% of calls result in complaints."

- "On an ongoing basis, reconcile the department financial reports by the 15th of every month with no increase in reconciliation errors."

- "Manage the department budget to stay within appropriations and accomplish 85% of service results by the end of the fiscal year."

- "Coach and support my direct reports and provide them with clear expectations, meaningful feedback, and fair performance evaluations by the end of the fiscal year."

- "Plan and oversee the office's relocation to the new facility such that the office and all systems are fully functional by September 30, 20XX."

- "By January 1, 20XX, design and pilot a new outreach strategy using social media to increase by 25% the usage of our programs by our teen clients."

- "By July 31, 20XX, develop and conduct a training program to support the transition to a new automated case-management system with minimal effects on customer service such that all staff can accurately process 30 cases per day within three months of the training."

Your goals should describe the overall results or outcomes you, or your team, are responsible for. They should be specific and clear, with a measurement that indicates when you or your group have been successful.

"Why" Matters

An essential piece of information that often gets left out of goal statements is the "why." Too many bosses assume that the "why" is implicit and easily understood and accepted. Be careful to avoid this omission, as this often happens to a "wishing and hoping" type of manager.

Remember that goals should focus effort. Many distractions by less-important things will compete for your followers' time. As a leader, then, you will frequently need to help your followers stay focused. When you establish goals, always ensure that the desired result or outcome of the effort is made clear. Build-in an answer to the "so what?" question. In other words, why will the effort spent on achieving or meeting this goal matter? Don't assume it's known or understood. Goals should describe the results and outcomes that matter most.

When people understand the underlying reasons for their effort (the why), they can be more self-motivated. When people feel motivated, they apply more initiative and use better judgment to resolve problems.

Here's an example of a goal statement that a new manager at a public agency initially shared with me:

"Develop a quality improvement process for the department by the end of the fiscal year that satisfies the state's mandated requirements."

Technically, this goal statement fits the SMART format. However, there is no clear *why*. In this situation, I coached the manager by drilling down with questions to get the goal-setter to describe *why* the state mandates their requirements since they were the basis for his goal. What is the purpose? Why were the mandates established? What problem or problems is the state trying to address by its requirements? Those who developed the state's mandated requirements thought they were important. *Why?*

Without getting and understanding "why" information, the quality improvement goal, as written above, may not do much to inspire people to stay focused on achieving it. It will likely only be looked at as a "check box" activity.

Look, I get it. Sometimes there is no clear "why," especially if you didn't come up with the goal entirely on your own. My point is that you should invest a reasonable amount of time seeking to understand the goal's underlying purpose if need be, especially if you want to get others to follow you.

Action Planning

In addition to being too fuzzy, another significant reason why goals aren't consistently achieved is that little to no thought is given to the "how." The action plan describes *how* the goal will be accomplished. Without a plan for "how," a goal is mostly an aspiration, an intent. Yet, even if it is not entirely developed with great detail, the mere addition of the plan increases the likelihood that the goal will be achieved successfully. An effective plan includes the specific steps that need to be taken and due dates for each step. Depending on the goal's complexity, the plan may also include the assignment of specific responsibilities, resources needed, and so forth (*see Figure 10.3*).

Action Plan Example

	Action Steps	Primary Responsibility	Due Date	Resources Required	Potential Barriers
1	Developing new working procedures to support separate check-in	Janet	January	• Regular hire staff	• Money • Time
2	Complete renovation projects to make libraries customer-friendly and increase the opportunities for self-service	Damon	June	• Branch Managers • Money	• Money • Existing space • Community partners • Newspapers, articles
3	Develop Merchandising Plan	Donna	October	• City Plan • Innovative ideas	• Space • Money
4	Explore relocation of the Bookmobile	Damon	November	• Money • CAO • Architects • DPW	• Money • Space

Figure 10.3

Once your action plan is developed, you can use it when you Lead from the Side, working one-on-one with your directs. Don't bury the plan in your computer or stick it on a shelf. Review and monitor the plan regularly, depending on the duration and the complexity. Catch things that slip as you investigate what's working and what's not. Acknowledge successes along the way, and learn from and note mistakes. Make whatever adjustments or reassignments need to be made. Always be proactive, look ahead, and anticipate, just as you would on a road trip.

When you're effective in Leading from the Front, a clear SMART goal statement with a realistic action plan can be a powerful tool to provide your followers with the information they need to believe with increased confidence that the vision can be realized. Learn and practice how to develop compelling goals and communicate them clearly, and in various ways, such as in large and small group meetings, email messages, video messages, and newsletters. Remember: goals focus individual and group effort and help to ensure that desired results are achieved.

Role Model the Way

When you're Leading from the Front, you have multiple opportunities to show people the way forward. As a boss, you are a focal point for your team. Remember that the objective here is to gain followers, *then* to get them to move forward with you toward the vision and goals.

At the front, you will likely see that some people simply don't have the knowledge, skills, and abilities they need to continue to move ahead. They need to learn more. Others may be reluctant to change how they are thinking or how they've been doing things. They need to be guided. You can help people learn and deal with change when you Lead from the Front. The best bosses do.

When people feel highly motivated to learn something new or to change their behavior, training and coaching can be very useful. However, one of the most powerful and effective approaches for influencing others to learn something, or to change their behavior, is to model it yourself. You already know that "actions speak louder than words."

People respond better to training and coaching and absorb learning at a more visceral level according to what they observe. Observational learning tends to stick better in the mind and be more memorable than content absorbed only from reading or attending presentations. Remember the two forms of impact we covered earlier, control and influence? As a leader, focus more of your time and energy on what you can impact. Good bosses are good role models. Whenever and wherever you can, do more "showing" and less "telling."

Although role modeling is a powerful and practical approach, it can be double-edged with an undesired effect if your actions are incongruent or inconsistent with what you say or claim to be important. In other words, when you don't "walk the talk," you'll create a credibility problem between you and others.

What you do and how you do it is likely remembered more than what you say in person or in an email message. A disconnect between your words and actions can eventually be considered hypocrisy if it becomes a pattern. This serious disconnect can derail what you're trying to accomplish.

Despite your positive intent, you can fail as a leader, manager, supervisor, peer, friend, parent, spouse, partner, or whatever, if you're not careful always to avoid hypocritical behavior. In other words, this is true for all of us. "Hypocrite" may sound like a strong word that we are reluctant to attach to ourselves or others, but it may be the appropriate descriptor for when actions don't match words.

Hypocrisy is more than just annoying. When the stakes are high, it affects the degree to which we trust each other, our organizations, and our institutions. When a manager says it's important that the team members support each other, and then that same manager bad-mouths one member behind the back of another, that's blatant hypocrisy—and that's a problem.

We're much more conscious of what we are thinking, along with our intentions, than we are of our behavior and actions, which actually impact others. Your good ideas alone are usually not enough to influence and lead others in the direction you want them to go. The best ideas and positive intent become meaningless when individuals or organizations act hypocritically. The result can even be a setback in credibility and trust (meaning integrity) that can take a long time to recover from, if recovery is possible.

Unfortunately, high-profile examples of hypocritical behavior can be observed daily coming from politicians, business leaders, sports figures, celebrities, and many others. Use these examples as reminders of what *not* to do.

Are you getting the results you want from the relationships you have? If not, does your behavior contradict what you say is important? If you sincerely care about being an effective role model and preventing hypocritical behavior, work on being more self-aware.

We'll cover some other approaches for role modeling in the Coaching section contained in the chapter on Leading from the Side. For now, recognize that role modeling is extremely impactful and that "you're always *on*."

Part | 2

"Simplify the complicated."

Managing Information **and Transparency**

As work becomes more decentralized, team-based, and virtual, most everyone relies on timely and useful information to make better decisions and solve problems related to their jobs. Successful organizations are becoming more open and transparent with information. The endless advances in our personal technology also provide many potentially useful methods of sharing information more widely and quickly than ever before.

Managing Information

It's clear that more information is available to more people in more ways, with more speed than ever in our lifetimes. This truth can be double-edged. Unfortunately, the checks and balances we once had on the information we consume in our society have fallen away as we tend to gravitate to fewer sources for news and opinions. And it doesn't help that practically everyone is constantly connected to their personal devices, typically in more ways than one. The recurring problem is often an overload of unvetted information—and nonstop working.

Organizations, beginning with senior leadership, can always do a better job of managing this abundance of information as it relates to their business. By "manage," I don't mean block or censor. Well-managed information (data) in the world of work is accessible, sensible, and actionable.

Accessible

Information that is *accessible* is readily available for use. As a manager, you are typically privy to more information than your team members—at least, to the type that flows from the top of your organization. So, practice openness and promote information sharing within your core circle. When you're a senior leader, also *be* accessible and share appropriate information at all levels in your organization. Effective bosses are generous with information and don't hold it back just to flex their power.

A smart CEO I work with makes it a point to hold regular staff meetings to share successes and setbacks his company has experienced. He makes it an expectation for his managers to also share information similarly with their team members. In fact, he will spot-check the information flow within his company to ensure that there are no bottlenecks. When he finds an information blockage, he holds the senior manager accountable for correcting it.

Sensible

Leaders should also take the time to determine the accuracy and validity of the information they have. Regularly ask, "Does this make sense?" A good boss thinks about how, why, and even *if* the information may be useful to the recipients *before* hitting the send button or scheduling a meeting to discuss it. When you possess sensitive information, also recognize the importance of discretion. Be aware of both the content and the context of what you are sharing for the receivers. A good rule to follow is to fully understand your purpose for sharing information and consider the potential consequences—*before* you share it.

Leaders need to be both open *and* prudent with information that relates to change, like potential restructuring. Responding to change is always personal and usually triggers some level of emotion. Unfiltered information shared without being mindful and deliberate can create unnecessary anxiety, mental distractions, and even fear because of the different ways people react to change at a personal and emotional level.

Sharing any and all information all the time with people is not always practical. Understand your audience and the situation—the context. Consider timing, current events, and the prevailing level of morale to determine how and what to share about what is known and what is *unknown*—and when. "If in doubt, don't."

Actionable

Leaders can also help manage information by showing their team members how best to use and apply it. Actionable information provides people with insights and perspectives that matter and have value for how they think, feel, and approach the work they are doing.

Some good questions to consider before communicating important information are:

- Is the information you have the most current?
- Is it valid and accurate? How do you know?
- Why should you share this information?
- What are the benefits? The risks?
- What is the best method for communicating the message?
- When is the best time to deliver this message?
- What questions may arise and do you have answers?
- How do you want people to feel after receiving the message?
- What do you want people to do after they receive it?
- What difference would it make if the information wasn't shared?

What It Means to Be Transparent

A useful definition for *transparency* is "clear, open, and honest communication that is delivered authentically with accountability for the message." Being transparent builds trust because it can positively and directly affect the Trust elements of Concern and Integrity.

Here's an approach for being transparent with one person—or one thousand or more! Whenever you have significant information to share, particularly the kind that may require people to change their thinking or actions, use the following format:

1. Here's what I know...

Tell them as much as you can about the subject, using your judgment and discretion. Anticipate their questions and concerns, without waiting for them to ask you directly. Prepare thoughtful answers based on the best available and shareable information you have.

2. Here's what I don't know...

Let people know what you *don't* know about the subject. Follow the same approach as above, anticipate what they may be thinking, and prepare your message. Have the courage to look people in the eye (literally, or figuratively if in an email), and tell them what you don't know—particularly about any elephants that may be in the room (say, a potential need for layoffs, or other bad news). This could also include decisions that you anticipate being made that haven't been decided yet.

Too often, leaders avoid this approach and wait until they have all the shareable answers or information before communicating. Realistically, when an information vacuum develops, people often fill in the blanks with their assumptions (often incorrect) about what they think is really happening, or not, based on what you *didn't* say. Once that assumption is made, it often gains momentum and is difficult to shift or change. So get out in front and acknowledge and address what is, or may be, most on their minds.

3. Here's what I can't share with you—and why...

This information can be the most difficult, awkward, and uncomfortable. As a manager, you will have some information that's not appropriate to share with others—say, certain decisions have been made that can't be shared due to timing, corporate secrecy, personnel or legal actions, medical conditions, and the like. In those instances, tell people as much as you can without disclosing anything inappropriate. Use your judgment and discretion. Here's an example: "I know you are wondering why 'so and so' left suddenly this morning. I'm not able to discuss why at this time. However, I'll let you know more as soon as I can."

Whenever it's appropriate, sharing this third piece of information can also help build trust. Being honest and telling people that you can't share specific information also signals that you believe you can treat them as adults. By treating them as adults (if they are reasonable), they will likely accept that you can't share every piece of information with them.

No matter what you're communicating, always target your message and approach for an audience of "reasonable" people. Don't stoop any lower just to appeal to those who are unreasonable—until you really have to.

As with virtually all you do, set a good example. Encourage others in your team or organization to thoughtfully manage the information they have to share. Using collaboration tools can help (you can find them on the web). As you sift through what information to send, use good judgment and always be sensitive to the needs, capabilities, and capacity of the recipients of your messages. Finally, always be mindful and understanding of the context in which your information is being communicated.

See the big picture.

Simplify

I saw a quote attributed to the poet Criss Jami some time ago that stuck with me regarding information and communication: "The role of genius is not to complicate the simple, but to simplify the complicated."

Life is filled with all sorts of complexity that affects each of us similarly and differently. From how our computer software operates to how to navigate a big city's multi-modal transit system, life can be complicated. Don't make your communication any more so than it needs to be.

When messages and concepts are simplified, it's easier for a person to relate them to what they already know. Learning and retention is more successful when people build on and expand their existing knowledge base. Invest time upfront to simplify your messages (instructions, directions, and the like) by choosing clear language, straightforward analogies, and familiar examples that can be easily understood, repeated, and remembered.

According to Albert Einstein, "If you can't explain it simply, you don't understand it well enough." The notion of keeping things simple is the key to the acronym K-I-S-S (Keep It Simple, Stupid!), which was used by the U.S. Navy as far back as 1960 to describe a design principle. This reliable principle should apply to the design of your communication, for both verbal and written messaging—especially when you're the boss.

Power of Repetition

A Harvard business professor named Tsedal Neeley conducted a study investigating how managers use redundant communication, so she could learn the effect it had on getting the desired response from the message. Her team studied managers who needed to communicate with their team members to deliver projects on time and on budget.

Neeley found that managers who sent a message multiple times and through different methods got their projects completed more smoothly and on time than those who did not. Examples of various methods included face-to-face communications, emails, and text messages.

Related research by psychologist Robert Zajonc indicated that people show a preference for a thing, an idea, or a message, *if* they are familiar with it. As communicators, repeating a message leads to familiarity, which likely leads to a preference. Sending a message more than once may be more effective in getting someone to act, because they develop a preference for (or comfort with) what's been repeated.

Here's another logical reason to repeat significant messages: There's too much noise in everyone's head! We're all bombarded with messages in all forms throughout the day and night, through our phone and computer screens and through our earbuds, leading to stress and distraction. You're often going to have to work hard to cut through the noise experienced by your recipients by repeating your message.

And one more thing. When you give important direction to a group or an individual, also remember that communication is imperfect. This means that you'll likely have to check, more than once, that your message was received in the way you intended. So repeat it often, in different formats. Messages that are repeated multiple times tend to get through to people more effectively. Get it?

Go Slow to Go Fast

Early in my professional training, I was intrigued when I heard the phrase "Go slow to go fast." I don't know who said it first, but I do know that it's a powerful statement that I've thought about and shared with others countless times.

We're all part of an action-celebrated culture. Mantras that echo Nike's slogan, "Just do it," can be seen and heard throughout our media. Organizations, stockholders, and stakeholders typically reward and admire action because they like to see immediate results. Don't we all?

When you decide to lead people, especially through change, don't cut corners by ignoring the psychology that drives all of us. Remember, each day of our lives is focused on getting our needs met. For sustainable change to any behavior to occur more quickly, first make every effort to help people get what *they* need before you begin to expect them to change the way they do things so they can suit what *you* need. Don't lead people *to* change. Lead them *through* change.

Effective leaders take the following two key steps to address the critical needs people have in order to move through change. Too often, these steps are neglected.

Step 1 - Be sure that the language and terminology are understood.

The related need here is Information. Believe it or not, we usually think before we do or act! Unless we are in "fight-or-flight" mode, we first process the thoughts and ideas that we have in our brains by using language. We use the language we know and understand best. The author and consultant Peter Block has frequently written about the power of language and how change first occurs by changing the language. Semantic misunderstandings are often unknown, yet they can be significant obstacles to taking effective action.

So, before moving forward with any initiative that requires someone to behave or act differently, be sure that they understand the specific language and terms used to describe what it is (for example, what "merit-based performance" really means).

When you begin a change effort, unless you are completely confident there will be no misunderstanding with anyone involved, take the time and care to clarify the meaning of your words. Check for understanding and then restate or rephrase the message if necessary. Don't rush it. Go slow to go fast.

Step 2 - Focus on their thinking before moving them to action.

Help provide others with an answer to the fundamental question targeted at understanding motivation, "What's in it for me?" (the acronym WIIFM). Consider which ideas, assumptions, or beliefs they need to change for any desired action or new behavior to occur. This applies whether the change you are leading them through is one they chose voluntarily or not.

Don't assume that others will immediately buy in to a change just because you believe in the power of "the idea." Many initiatives with great potential fail to get implemented effectively—or at all—because leaders can overlook the fact that people are not always motivated by reason alone. Despite how logical, rational, valuable, and timely you may think an idea is, a brilliant idea is not always enough to move people through change.

You can increase your potential for success by investing time to plan your approach before you begin. Strategize ways to help change the way people think about the situation or the merits of an idea before pushing the implementation of new methods, procedures, systems, and the like. Give people time to think and process—mentally as well as emotionally—the anticipated impacts (such as, what will be lost? what will be gained?) of acting or behaving differently. If you don't allow people sufficient time upfront to understand and consider the potential consequences of the change, you'll likely be spending a lot more time dealing with their resistance to change *after* you've rushed into it. Go slow to go fast.

I believe a common reason that many people spend less effort upfront to address language and thinking issues related to making a change is their long-standing reluctance to plan. Planning takes time and doesn't usually involve action that you can see immediately. So, it often receives much less attention and gets short shrift.

For many managers who are strongly influenced by our action-oriented culture, planning is not usually "fun." It can be tedious and can even delay the action they can't wait to begin. They would rather jump in and "Just do it." Is that true for you, too?

I'm confident that if you don't rush the two steps above, more often than not, you'll get better results much more quickly—and with less angst for everyone involved, including you.

Slowly plan for faster action!

Leading from the Front (Summary)

Here are some important tips to remember:

- Leaders help others to see what they can't see on their own.
- You only need one follower to become a leader.
- Followers may attract other followers more directly than you can—and that's okay.
- A clear goal includes both the goal statement and the plan for achieving it.
- One of the most powerful and effective approaches for influencing others to learn something or change their behavior is to model it yourself.
- Well-managed information (data) in the world of work is accessible, sensible, and actionable.
- Always strive to simplify your messages (say, instructions and directions) so that they can be easily understood, repeated, and remembered.
- Repeat your messages to have them stick.
- Give people time to think and process—mentally as well as emotionally—the anticipated impacts (for instance, what will be lost or gained) of acting or behaving in a different way. Go slow to go fast.
- Keep your ego in check.

Chapter | **11**

Leading from the Side

True leadership gets personal. You build relationships (and trust) more quickly and deeply by genuinely interacting with people one-on-one. If you want to lead effectively, then establish and nurture *personal* connections. This effort and attention will help inspire people to want to follow you. Do this by learning more about your people and what they're thinking—and feeling. Care enough to find out who they are. Leading from the Side involves developing and strengthening relationships.

When you personally connect with your direct reports, you can also learn what they may need (Resources, Information, Support, and Control) in order to follow you and reach the goals you've set. You're also available to provide them with individual help (such as coaching, encouragement, and many other forms) if and when they seem to be struggling to keep up or to get started.

Remember the example with the group on the trail? When you have at least one follower to join you and help take the lead toward your goal (the lake), you as the primary leader should have gained more freedom and ability to move away from Leading from the Front. You can then invest time to personally connect with the individual members of the rest of your group.

From this Side perspective you connect "shoulder to shoulder" with people, especially those who may be reluctant to follow you. Along the way, you can target, tailor, and reinforce your vision and goal messages to those individuals who need to hear it from you again—and then again.

Depending on the group's or team's size, it may be difficult or impractical to form a personal relationship with each individual. However, the more personal connections you make, and the better the quality of each, the more effective you'll be as a leader. Each follower you develop can also become someone who can help you lead others.

Having a personal relationship with your team members doesn't necessarily mean you hang out socially. Nor should it. When you're the boss, you need to get to know people—as people, not just "tools" to get the work done. Don't wait for your direct report to reach out.

If you want to lead them, take the lead. Even if you're an introvert, step up and pay attention to them. Ask questions and really listen. Find some common ground to talk about that doesn't make both of you feel awkward.

Have you ever traveled to another country where the spoken language was different than your own? How about meeting a new neighbor, shop owner, or coworker here at home who didn't speak your language? Chances are you took the time to learn a few phrases to connect and begin to communicate. You probably made an effort to adjust and learn. That same approach might be required to connect with someone from a different generation or someone with a very different communication style than yours.

Everyone has a "language" they use or prefer. So, make an effort to flex your own communication style, especially when you are the boss. Try to learn people's "language" and determine how best to sincerely share your thoughts, ideas, and directions in ways that they can best understand you and your messages. If you pay attention, you may notice that collectively even your *team* can have its own preferred language.

Just make sure that you don't try too hard or come across as patronizing. It shouldn't take too long to find clues from your team members that will help you to connect, providing that you make a sincere effort.

Even if your work group is relatively small, making personal and authentic connections with its members will require some time and attention. What's most important is demonstrating your desire to connect. Don't give up trying, even if you find you can't make a connection with everyone.

I've coached more than a few leaders who were highly effective when making group presentations and Leading from the Front. However, as individuals they were introverted, and some were even a bit awkward around people, which affected their ability to gain more followers. Making personal connections (that is, Leading from the Side) was hard for them because it meant they had to get out of their comfort zone, and they often dreaded having to make authentic one-on-one connections with their followers or would-be followers. I convinced them that being good at social interaction is a skill that can be developed by both extroverts and introverts.

Here are recommendations for improving your sociability and ability to connect with people at work:

1. First, get a sense of what 3 minutes feels like.

2. Each day choose one person in your team or group whom you don't know well and start up a 3-minute conversation by asking them a question or making a statement about anything other than work. Listen and ask a sincere follow-up question. At the end of 3 minutes, find a smooth breakaway from the conversation and move on. (Examples: "Good catching up with you!," "Well, I'm on my way to my next meeting," or "Have a good day!")

3. Make a brief note in your journal (I advise all my coaching clients to use journals to record their learning) about what was easy, what was hard, what if anything was tricky about the exchange, and what you would say or do differently if you had an opportunity to redo the conversation.

4. Be willing to practice and stick with it.

Remember my earlier point in the book about "liking people" as a key leadership characteristic? If you happen to naturally like "people" and are usually comfortable with them, Leading from the Side will happen more easily, and the time and effort to make connections will not feel like work or a drag for you. For the rest of you, you'll have to make more of an effort to be sociable to be effective at Leading from the Side. I believe the ability to genuinely connect with people is a critical requirement for being a better boss.

Regardless of your personality, as you genuinely connect with and understand who the individuals in your group are, you will be able to help them commit to your vision and goals. When they buy into your message—even a little—they are following. And you are now leading!

Part | 1

"The single biggest problem
in communication is the illusion
that it has taken place."

George Bernard Shaw

Communication–The Very Basics

Your ability to communicate affects the quality of your connections with other people. And the quality of those connections affects their trust in you. The level of trust people have in you will ultimately define the quality of your relationships.

Since leadership involves achieving positive relationships with others, communication skills are critical to your success as a leader. Communication is the critical circulation system for all organizations. And the quality of communication also determines its health.

Despite our sincere hope that our email exchange, presentation, meeting, or phone call communication we had was perfect, it never is—because it can't ever be! Communication is imperfect because we're human beings, not machines.

Communication Model

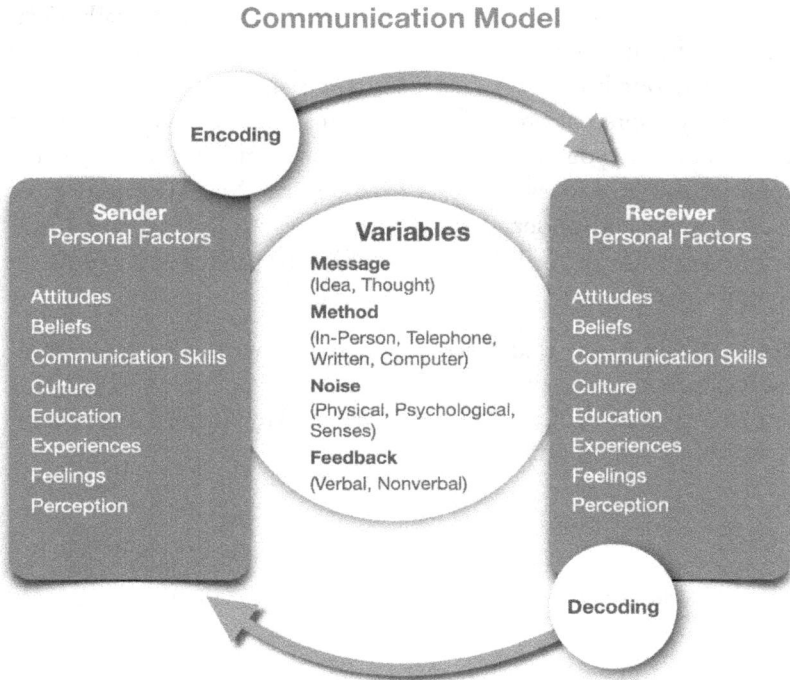

Figure 11.1

Let's briefly break down the process of communication. Communication involves both sending and receiving messages. We do this by encoding and decoding thoughts, ideas, and feelings between ourselves and others every day, and often unconsciously (see *Figure 11.1*). The codes we send to each other and decipher are more complex than a computer's simple machine code. The codes within human communication involve more than objective facts. They contain subjective opinions and emotions, which can be complex. It's often said that, "the perception of a message is more important than the message itself." Remember that both the sender and the receiver are limited by their knowledge, skills, and capabilities. Consequently, it's easy for communication to go wrong. You only need one side of the exchange to either use the "wrong code" or inadvertently misread, misinterpret, misunderstand, overlook, or even willfully ignore all or any part of the human communication code.

Unfortunately, our communication with others is not easily decipherable by any reliable codebook. Whenever we wish, hope, or deny away our limitations as humans, we usually get into trouble with our personal or professional relationships. To become a skilled communicator, you have to be more conscious and aware of the communication process while it's happening. You also need to be more patient and understanding of how easy it is for communication to go sideways, either on the sending or the receiving end—or sometimes even both!

You've likely heard that it's important for there to be open communication between people. Along with the imperfections of being human in general, here are some reasons why keeping open communication can be difficult.

Optimal Middle Continuum

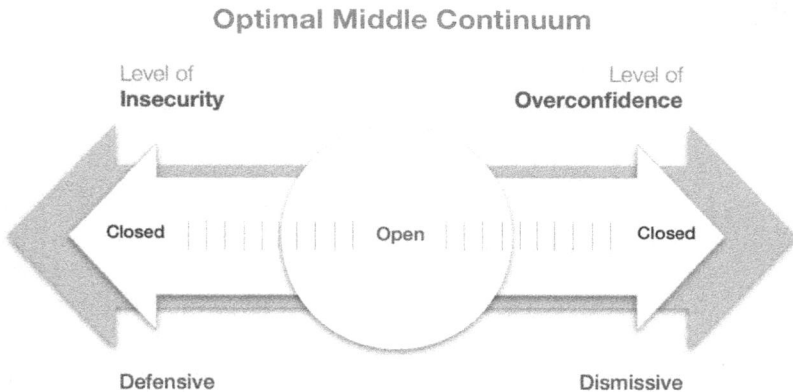

Figure 11.2

In every interpersonal relationship, whether it's between individuals or within groups, each of us stands somewhere on the Optimal Middle Continuum between being insecure and being overconfident (see *Figure 11.2*). When we are highly insecure, and at one end of the continuum, we tend to be defensive and protective of ourselves and our ego. The effect this has on our communication is that we become more closed off and less open to receiving messages. Since we're more self-conscious when insecure, we can also be slower in deciding which messages to send or decipher. Even a short delay in messaging can be misconstrued.

On the opposite end of the continuum, when we are overconfident, we tend to believe we "know it all" about a given topic or message. Our listening narrows or stops altogether as we close off and focus more on our internal thoughts and beliefs rather than what's being communicated to us. This narrow or even nonexistent listening can also occur when we are indifferent about either the message or the speaker.

Even though they are at opposite ends, what both behaviors have in common is that the sending and receiving of messages (that is, communication) is narrowed or closed and not open. For effective, two-way, open communication to occur, first manage yourself. Remain somewhere in the optimal middle. That means you need to manage your insecurities as well as your hubris.

The Very Basic Principles of Communication

1. People are imperfect and complicated. Therefore, communication is imperfect and complicated.

2. Somehow, in some way, we are always communicating with each other. We can't not communicate if we have any sort of relationship with, or connection to, someone.

3. We can't take back something we said or sent. We can only try to smooth over any damage that may have been done to the relationship.

4. The context of the communication (as in the setting, timing, medium, expectations, the relationship between people, and so on) significantly impacts the messaging—and the outcomes.

Assumptions and Intentions

One of the primary reasons communication gets derailed is mistaken assumptions about other people's intentions. An intention is the inner "why" that motivates us and determines how we behave, especially when communicating (or trying to!). Our intentions are internal to us. No one can truly know our intentions. Others can only know our behavior.

Everything we do, say, don't do, or don't say is behavior. Until the time comes when people can literally read our minds, the people we communicate with can only perceive and know our behavior and assume to know our intentions.

We can indeed speak (or write) and choose precise and deliberate language to describe our intentions (that are internal to us) to others and explain our reasoning, and so on. However, we must accept the fact that no matter how clear and correct we think our chosen words are, speaking and writing is "behaving." And our external behavior is all that another person will be able to observe and interpret in order to try and understand us and determine what they think we mean—at least for now.

Do you see what I meant when I said earlier that communication is imperfect and complicated because people are? Your communication, interactions and relationships will benefit greatly if you are willing to check your assumptions when you are unclear or may be put off by what's been communicated by another person.

Here's an example of a direct approach to checking an assumption. "Bill, when you spoke up at the meeting I got the feeling that you were frustrated by the way I handled the customer. Were you?"

Direct and Indirect Communication

Skillful communicators can be aware of different communication styles and can flex their personal style to fit the person they are communicating with. The most fundamental differences in communication styles can best be categorized by Directs and Indirects. These differences may become even more pronounced on multicultural teams. The direct communication style is most associated with Western cultures, like Americans, Australians, Germans, and Anglo-Canadians. Direct communicators typically speak what's on their mind, leaving little to infer.

Indirect communicators are commonly from Eastern cultures, like Japanese, Chinese, Indians, and Saudi Arabians. Indirect communicators are more subtle, leaving more room for their listeners to have to interpret the message. Keep in mind that even though there may be cultural commonalities, you'll still find both direct and indirect communicators within the same culture. As I said earlier, it's complicated!

Your success as a communicator will depend on how well you can adjust to the differences between people when you need to. There is no "best" way, only your way, their way, and the way that works to get you connected.

Continuing to develop a broad range of communication skills is essential for your ongoing learning, no matter your role. There are many articles, books, videos, podcasts, and other resources dedicated more specifically to communication, especially speaking and writing skills. I encourage you to absorb the many useful tips and techniques you'll discover in them.

In this book, I want to focus on the most useful and powerful communication skill you need to develop to be a good manager, leader, boss, or human. That is called active listening.

Active Listening

Listening is the foremost communication skill because it is the most effective way to build connections with people. When it's sincerely practiced, listening is often reciprocated, and that leads to building relationships and trust. Unfortunately, compared with speaking, listening is taught the least. This lack of emphasis on listening usually starts when we're young. In grade school, I was taught to be quiet, not how to listen.

Consider this typical experience that often happens during a child's first year: their first words. "Frank, come over here! Jimmy just said his first word!"

How often do you think this happens? "Peg, come over here! Jimmy hasn't said a word. He just looks at me and nods his head. What a great listener!"

Good listening is rarely celebrated with any awards. Face it: we encourage and validate speaking skills over listening skills early on in life, which usually continues into our adult and professional lives. Fortunately, today there is an increasing emphasis being placed on the importance of listening as a critical communication skill. For you as a leader, I want you to focus on *active listening*, which is a particular type of listening that's most important for any boss to practice.

The purpose of active listening is twofold. Number one, it involves hearing *and* understanding the content being communicated. Number two, and perhaps more important, active listening also involves communicating back to the sender that they are sincerely heard. This type of listening also signals respect for someone by demonstrating the importance of connection as well as the content.

Active listening usually takes more energy than speaking. If you've ever been an interviewer and listened to multiple candidates throughout the day interviewing for a job, you probably spoke about 20% to 30% of the time—or at least should have! I'll bet that you felt exhausted at the end of the day. Active listening for long periods can be mentally draining because of the focus required to do it well.

Active listening is not simply waiting your turn for the speaker to finish so that you can say what's on your mind—that's waiting to talk. Active listening is also not "polite listening," which is when you tune in and out as you give someone a bit of time and space to talk but make no real connection.

Clearly, at times throughout the day all you really need is the content from someone. In other situations, the relationship may be more transactional. For instance, if you need directions from someone when you're in an unfamiliar neighborhood, building a relationship with them is not that important.

Don't be too quick. Even when you may only be looking for an interaction with someone, you may have an opportunity to develop a real relationship—*if* you're ready to listen actively. I've developed more than one long-term client connection after exchanging small talk on line at a coffee place. How many people do you think have met their future spouses or even business partners through a random encounter in which both actively listened? Have you had a similar experience with someone who is now an important part of your life?

Active listening is *hard*. When you really lock in and connect with a speaker, it takes focused mental energy, even when less talking is involved. To do it well, you need to engage your ears and your mind and also use your body (appropriate physical gestures) to encourage another person to speak if necessary. This level of effort helps to maintain the connection with them. Whether or not to actively listen is a choice. In any verbal communication with someone, you each have to decide if it's worth your time and energy to do it. How important is the relationship?

Does the Relationship Matter?

When my kids were young, one of my responsibilities as "dad" was to grocery shop and prepare dinner for the four us. This was always a stressful and rushed part of the day. By the time I got home and began to prepare the food, it was usually 7 or 8 p.m., and we were all hungry—especially me!

One of the highlights of that time in my life was to have my then three-year-old daughter meet me at the door with a kiss and a bear hug and then follow me into the kitchen and hang out next to me while I quickly put the meal together.

I can distinctly remember one evening when I was typically rushing around the kitchen, and she was chattering on about her day at preschool. I was sort of listening to her as I was trying to multitask and pull dinner together. Typical of a three-year-old, her story was a bit disjointed, but enthusiastic. I believe it involved cupcakes and "Teacher Judy."

At one point, as I was more or less following her spirited chat, something clicked for me. I suddenly realized that she was there with me to share more than the *content* of her story about the cupcakes. What she really wanted was to *connect* with me! So I stopped chopping garlic, squatted down to her level, looked her in the eye, and locked into her every word.

I can remember her smiling and becoming even more animated as she discovered that she had my full attention. As she was speaking we were connecting—because I was actively listening. I was fully present, and she knew it.

From that time forward, many of our dinners took a little bit longer to get to the table. But the connection between us grew stronger. The loving relationship that I continue to have with my now-grown daughter was worth every minute I invested actively listening and focusing on her and not just dinner. (Fortunately, my son and I also share a close relationship, I believe for the same reason. I made a conscious effort to actively listen to him, too.)

If you believe a given relationship is important, decide to invest the time and energy necessary for active listening. It shouldn't be a surprise that a true leader treats their relationship with each follower, or potential follower, with this high level of importance.

Active listening not only builds connection, it can also help others make their thought processes more visible. For instance, many of us are extroverts, so when we speak, we're also thinking out loud. For some listeners, this can take a lot of patience, especially when the content itself may already be known, be well understood, or be considered to be irrelevant or even trivial. Whenever you make the effort, the positive result of active listening is *connection*.

Active Listening—Best Practices

If and when you decide to listen actively, try to remember two essential things:

1. Pay fierce attention to the speaker. Make them feel like they are the only person in the room. Focus on them.

2. Find and maintain the *flow*. Flow occurs when you and the speaker, as well as the conversation, get into a natural rhythm. Don't just focus on doing this as a technique; be authentic. Being authentic means to do "you." As an active listener, do what you can to make adjustments to follow the other person's speaking and listening style and pace. If the relationship truly matters, do everything you can to make the speaker feel comfortable and natural communicating with you so that they will ultimately feel heard and understood—and *connected*. If you set a good example, the other person may help the conversation, and your connection, by reciprocating.

Below are some more specific active-listening best practices.

Be Very Present

Active listening requires a real focus on what the other person is communicating—verbally, physically, and emotionally. It also involves being aware of your body language and using your whole self to communicate (nonverbally) that you understand and are open to hearing more.

At some social events, you might politely listen and wait for the other person to finish speaking so that you can tell *your* story. In those situations it might be okay to do that because you determined that the relationship you have with the speaker is already firmly established, or may even be unimportant to you. However, don't fool yourself by thinking that you can fool others by pretending to listen. It rarely works.

How often do you wait to talk rather than listen? When you're multitasking or making a mental "to do" list, you're not actively listening. Most people can tell if you're tuning in or tuning out. Can't you tell if someone is really listening to you, even when you're on a phone call?

If you are reasonably sure that you received and understand the speaker's message as they intended, use any "extra time" when listening to pay more attention to the nonverbal signals—both theirs and yours. If you don't actively listen, you may be missing some relevant messages that they're sending, beyond their words. You may also be missing opportunities to send related nonverbal messages (such as nods and other gestures) that can help build and reinforce the connection between you and them.

Be aware of what distracts you, and be disciplined in avoiding these distractions *before* you decide to actively listen. You might start by putting your phone or laptop away and out of sight, or even turning it off. Focus on the speaker and find out more about their intentions. Most of your texts and emails can probably wait—don't you think?

Respond to Emotions

Recognize when there are feelings or emotions linked to the content or message of someone speaking to you. Tap into your emotional intelligence before moving too quickly to the logical part of your brain to problem-solve. When you show empathy to a person who appears to be emotional, you actively show Concern, which is one of the essential Elements of Trust.

I once consulted with a lead manager on a project team who came to me extremely upset and frustrated because his boss was not using any of the ideas he had suggested. I knew this person reasonably well and was aware that his presentation style came across as blunt and arrogant. He had come to me for some direction and help in how to move forward.

Although I had some advice that I really wanted to share with this manager, it became clear to me in the first two minutes that he was way too emotional to be open to any input from me, or anyone else. What he needed first was some space and time to vent. I gave him that and held back my recommendations. When he worked through his emotion with me actively listening, he eventually got to a point where he could be receptive to some new approaches. I didn't rush him. I paid attention to his emotions before I stepped in to try and help.

Never try to use reason when someone is being unreasonable (emotional). Remember that timing is everything. Guide people through their emotions if that's what they need from you at that moment. In those situations, stop talking and listen. You can help deal with their problem later, if and when they get into a less-emotional state of mind.

Don't Interrupt

Most of us have been raised to understand that interrupting can be rude. However, within the context of active listening, try and learn to differentiate an "interruption" (which stops communication flow) from what's called an "overlap." An overlap can occur in a spirited discussion when people interject comments and build on each other's ideas or intentions. That can be just fine. Remember, find the flow.

Let people *solo* without your charging in too soon with a response. A common understanding in law enforcement, investigation, and even psychotherapy is that the first thing people bring up when they have something to say often *isn't* the central point they will eventually make, whether they know it or not. With that in mind, don't jump in too quickly with your thought or position at every opening in a conversation, especially after the first comment made. You may shut the other person down, or miss out on important information, and even eliminate the other potential benefits of listening. Be patient and give the speaker enough time to finish what they're really trying to say.

Use tact when an interruption is absolutely necessary, like when you are running out of time. Otherwise, use pauses to indicate that more of a response is expected from them—without creating an awkward silence.

Adding a pause when conversing can be used in a similar way that a composer adds a notation for a "rest" in a piece of music, along with other musical notes. A rest indicates the absence of sound. Even when you are unaware, the placement and length of the silence in music is just as significant as the sound that's created. If you're not familiar with it, check out the opening of Beethoven's Fifth Symphony for a great example of how musical notes and rests work together to form a masterpiece.

A pause, with nothing being said, can be highly significant in a meaningful conversation. Find the flow and use your judgment when deciding when and how to use a pause. Generally, a good practice is to wait for three beats...before responding verbally.

Wait Before Offering Unsolicited Advice

When someone comes to you (in-person or virtually), focus and find out what they want from the communication. Do they want direction, or feedback, or do they simply want to vent? Even when you are well-intentioned and the trust level is high, it's usually a good idea at the start to ask or look for what the speaker intends or wants out of the conversation with you. This includes whether they're seeking ideas and advice or only someone to listen and be a sounding board. I often ask, "Do you want some feedback, or do you just want me to listen right now?"

When you're the leader, you're likely the top problem-solver in your group. However, if you jump in too quickly and give unsolicited advice or solutions, a person might feel judged at a time when they may be feeling less confident and when your input can be perceived by some as "I'm right, you're wrong." Most likely, this is *not* the desired outcome you want from their interaction with you. Keep your focus on their needs at the time. As always, remember that timing is everything.

Manage Your Biases, Stereotypes, and Preconceptions

It's tough and nearly impossible to be completely objective all the time—we're human. And unfortunately, we can create problems for ourselves and our relationships when we allow our biases and filters to prejudge what a speaker will say or what they mean before they've finished speaking. Sometimes you guess correctly. However, when you're wrong, you potentially lose more than the value of some saved time. When you make a habit of prejudging and not really listening, you may also miss important information—both the spoken and the unspoken. Perhaps more important, the relationship may suffer as trust is eroded.

Slow Down

When you slow down your listening, you can better "digest" the meaning behind each word and pick up on important nonverbal cues and messages. You can be a better decoder when you're patient. You can also be more prepared to ask better and more purposeful questions that link your thoughts to what was just spoken.

When you're impatient and are concerned about forgetting what you might want to say, if possible, discreetly jot down ideas on a notepad to refer to when it's your time to speak (if that isn't awkward to do). If you're getting anxious for the person to finish or it's not appropriate to scribble notes, take a deep breath and remind yourself why the relationship is important. Focus on the purpose of the conversation, concentrate and make mental notes, and recommit to listening intently.

Some people can have a challenging time with patience. They can absorb information and process words at a rate that can be three times as fast as another person can speak. All of us make judgments, however, some people tend to make lots of judgments very fast. Although many times they may be correct, too often, these judgments can trigger unhelpful biases that can form a barrier to listening. This processing and thinking speed can be a real strength in many situations for managers and leaders. But when it comes to active listening, this kind of speed can also slow down honest communication. If you're one of these people, be more patient.

Be Curious

Being curious is the *most* potent listening approach that can produce immediate results. Being curious sharpens your active listening skills. And I really do mean *being* curious, not *acting* curious. When you're curious, it's much easier to focus. And when you're focused, you can lock in and connect—verbally, nonverbally, and even emotionally. When you are curious, all the best listening practices described above become more natural and effective.

Curious people naturally ask good questions. They also ask questions to learn—and to connect. Being curious also involves listening to how your questions are answered and building on the responses to gain a deeper understanding of what's been said. Just be careful not to ask too many questions. That might make someone feel as if they're in an inquisition, which can be creepy and annoying.

Impact of the Follow-Up

Another significant way you can demonstrate that you are really listening to someone is to ask a sincere and straightforward follow-up question in response to something they have shared with you.

You: "Tell me about how the meeting with the management team went."

Them: "I guess it went okay. They wanted to know more about why the project was delayed."

You (follow-up): "Did they have any specific issues or questions about the budget impacts?"

Sometimes a follow-up question can be related to something you already know about the content or the situation. Other times it can take the form of an understanding and empathetic response or even an acknowledgment. If you're *connected* to the speaker, a good follow-up question can emerge naturally for you as a result of being curious.

I recommend that you try to notice whether or not someone asks you a follow-up question the next time you are in a conversation. If they do, how does it make you feel?

Acknowledge the Other

To improve your ability to acknowledge, slow down and check your understanding of what's been said and possibly unsaid. Be willing to ask about the speaker's intentions before you jump in and assume that you know what they are trying to say. When you're patient and wait for an answer, it gives them a chance to say or signal, "…that's not what I meant."

Remember that the main objective of active listening is to make the speaker feel understood as well as to increase your understanding of the other's point of view. William James, an often-quoted nineteenth-century psychologist and philosopher, wrote, "A deep principle in human nature is the craving to be appreciated." I believe he might also have added "and to be understood."

Acknowledgment doesn't always require words—it could be a nod, or some other form of supportive nonverbal language. And acknowledging is not necessarily agreeing with either the feelings or the content that someone communicated. You can acknowledge the importance of specific feelings or content while disagreeing with the substance of what is said.

Remember that communication is imperfect. By consistently applying these active listening approaches, you should eventually experience smoother communication in your work relationships as you Lead from the Side. When you invest time in active listening, you also make better and more personal connections. This is a critical way to build trust and maintain solid relationships in all areas of your life. As with any other skill, developing active listening skills requires commitment, focus—and always practice.

Part | 2

"Feedback accelerates learning and illuminates blind spots."

Importance of **Feedback**

Providing useful feedback is a critical skill to develop to be successful when Leading from the Side. Feedback is critically important because it accelerates learning. Anyone who wants to improve personally or professionally needs feedback both to know what to change and to understand what they are doing that's working. Remember, the most successful people and organizations are always learning.

If people in organizations could give and receive feedback more effectively and also could actively listen, I believe overall communication would be dramatically improved. When individuals and teams get better—and more consistent—with giving and receiving feedback, many common and counterproductive communication problems that exist often decrease. Unwarranted workplace conflicts and other misunderstandings might even be eliminated. Work could truly be more enjoyable if everyone just got better at handling feedback. What do you think?

The primary source of feedback we continually rely on through-out our lives is of course the mirror. It reflects visual information about our exterior—our physical presence, size, shape, features, and expressions. We use that information to shape our basic self-image and develop our self-awareness. Our self-awareness is also signifi-cantly influenced by the direct and indirect feedback we get from others throughout our lives. Feedback is like a mirror that can illu-minate our blind spots—and we all have blind spots.

Beginning at birth, feedback is given by touch, gestures, and words. We learn to interpret the feedback we receive as we grow and navi-gate our world. We feel safe, unsafe, or something in between. From our parents, family members, teachers, friends, bosses, coworkers, strangers, and many others in our lives, we are taught when to go and when to stop, what is okay and what isn't, and what works and what doesn't. If we're fortunate, we'll learn from and incorporate the *useful* feedback we receive from others as we continue to grow into adults and move on throughout adulthood.

Like it or not, we will always have blind spots regarding the impact our actions have on others. Little or no feedback can result in our becoming too self-confident or overly self-critical. This happens because we are mostly aware of our intentions (which are internal to each of us), but we are much less aware of the impacts our behavior (including our work performance) has on others.

Many managers intuitively know that feedback is necessary for good job performance, yet they avoid giving it, or they wait too long before they give it. Instead, they "wish" and "hope" to justify their avoidance of giving feedback. What they wish and hope for is that their team members will either continue to do the right things or magically figure out on their own what they need to do to change—without getting feedback.

How clear are you about how well you are performing in your job? Do you receive regular feedback from *your* boss? When I interview people as part of organizational assessments, I often hear that many are starved for feedback. How about you?

"No news" is not necessarily "good news." Reasonable people, especially those who are millennials and Gen Z, want to know how well they're doing at work. They generally welcome timely feedback because they want to be more aware and understand what they can do to improve to grow, develop, or stay the course—on purpose.

Here's a sailing example to illustrate a point about staying on course. I'm sure you'll understand how this lesson applies even if you've never set foot on a boat.

I've lived in the San Francisco Bay Area for many years and have sailed boats on the Bay since I first moved here. About 30 miles west of the Golden Gate Bridge lie the Farallon Islands. Imagine you are now on a sailboat passing through the Golden Gate headed for these "sea-stack" islands off in the distance. It's a typical foggy day and you're not able to see more than a few miles offshore, and the islands are not yet visible. However, you do have a compass and a map, and you've accurately plotted your course and heading. (You've left your GPS device at home!) So you point your boat westward, set your sails, and steer toward your compass heading.

Since the Farallons are some 30 miles away and you're in a sailboat, you can assume that the trip will take a few hours. Even though you can trust your compass heading, and knowing that the islands rise up away in the distance, would you recheck your compass after you began sailing toward your destination? (Of course you would.) Would you only check it once? (Of course not.) Even if you're not an experienced sailor, I'll bet that you would instinctively check your compass often during the trip to make sure that you are still on course.

Each time you check your compass, you're getting feedback—either positive feedback that indicates you are on course, or negative feedback that lets you know you are off course. Depending on the feedback (information) you get from your compass, you would maintain your course or change it to remain accurately headed in your desired direction. What would happen if you never checked your compass after you began sailing? Do you think there's a high probability that you would reach the out-of-sight Farallons without getting regular feedback on the direction your boat was headed? The answer is no.

So how come so many people don't receive regular feedback at work? Why do some managers believe that their team members will do what's expected and achieve their goals without feedback from them? Maybe they believe that the initial direction given (even if clear and accurate) is sufficient for their direct report to be able to achieve results without any further assistance. Some people might get lucky, and reach their "destination" without any feedback. I think the odds are better with feedback. What do you think?

One of the challenges with giving and receiving feedback is the word itself. Often, just hearing the word "feedback," without getting any other clues about the context, can signal a negative connotation about what may follow before any content or information is delivered. Did you ever have a boss approach you and ask if you wanted feedback? How did you feel at that moment? What type of message did you think would be delivered to you—something positive or something negative? I thought so. This negative association with the word is a common reason why feedback is often hard to receive and why it can also be hard for some people to deliver.

Praise and Criticism

Although praise and criticism are two common forms of feedback, they are not examples of highly *useful* feedback. Praise and criticism are usually based on subjective opinions and feelings and lack meaningful specificity. Consequently, there usually isn't any real value for the receiver. Most often, neither makes clear what should be continued or changed.

Praise *can* be useful for a short, quick message signaling that more details will follow in another interaction. An example could be when a supervisor says to their direct report, "Nice work with the client this morning. Let's talk more this afternoon." If that supervisor follows up with more specific information about what the person did well and why what they did was effective, that can be useful and valuable feedback.

Although it sounds good, if the supervisor only shares the "Nice work..." comment without any meaningful follow-up information, there isn't enough for the employee to clearly know what they should specifically continue doing in the future. They can feel good and still be left guessing.

Praise is like candy. Candy tastes sweet (and most of us like sweets) and can provide a short-burst sugar rush, but it isn't sustaining and valuable for the longer term like a healthier protein or carb. Praise gives a positive yet short-term burst but isn't sustainable. More information is needed for praise to be valuable.

Criticism is similar to praise, in that there is limited to no real long-term benefit for the receiver unless more information is revealed. Having a manager say, "How *could* you make that mistake? What were you *thinking*?" will probably get a team member's attention—because it stings. However, after the criticism is delivered and the sting still lingers, it may not be clear what *specifically* needs to change or be done differently—or why.

Some people are just hotheads, or worse, and need to blow off steam and criticize when they see someone screw up. If you're that type of boss, understand that your criticism may make *you* feel better, but it isn't very useful feedback for the receiver. And it won't make you a better boss.

Stop Using the Sandwich Model!

Can everyone please stop delivering the "S--t Sandwich" for feedback? There's a time for positive feedback and a time for the negative kind. Don't "sandwich" the messages. That can send mixed signals about your intentions and can definitely distract from the impact of your feedback.

Here's why the sandwich model is flawed. Consider a situation where a manager (Grace) doesn't deliver frequent feedback to her team member (JD). Grace wants to correct an approach that she observed JD taking with a client. If manager Grace follows the sandwich model, she'll typically start with something positive, because she wants to show that she is supportive, even though her primary purpose for the feedback is to deliver a negative message. Grace might open with, "JD, I want to talk with you. First of all, I appreciate all the efforts you've made these last few weeks..." Now, if JD hears something positive from manager Grace, who doesn't typically share positive news, it would be natural for him to think, "It's about time she noticed..."

Now imagine if Grace, in the same conversation, tags on negative feedback immediately after providing the positive feedback. Something that JD did or didn't do, "But...last week, JD, when you talked with the client, you should have...." (How would *you* react to being told about a mistake you made *right after* you received some rare positive news from your manager?)

To make matters worse, manager Grace continues to dutifully follow the sandwich model and tags on something positive at the end. "So, JD. I hope you're clear about what I need you to do differently, and I want you to know again that I appreciate having you here... [blah, blah, blah]."

Although the Sandwich Model has been around for a long time, I believe there's a better approach. I call it Value-Added Feedback.

Levels of Feedback

Before getting into a description of what Value-Added Feedback is, let's consider how it fits within the four levels of feedback in the workplace (see *Figure 11.3*).

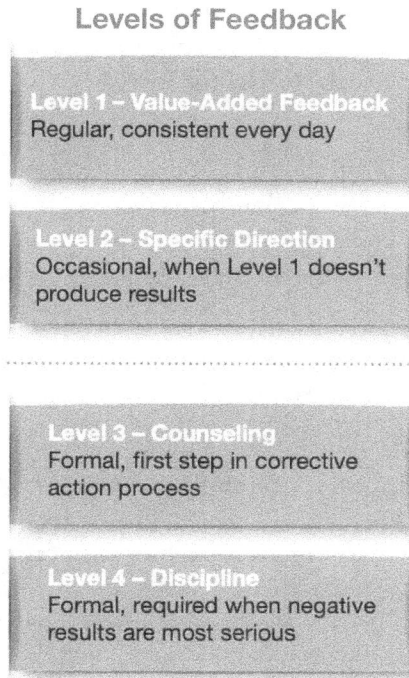

Levels of Feedback

Level 1 – Value-Added Feedback
Regular, consistent every day

Level 2 – Specific Direction
Occasional, when Level 1 doesn't
produce results

Level 3 – Counseling
Formal, first step in corrective
action process

Level 4 – Discipline
Formal, required when negative
results are most serious

Figure 11.3

Value-Added Feedback is Level 1 feedback. This is the type of feedback that every solid and competent employee should be receiving regularly. For most employees, the 80/20% rule should generally apply: that is, you should be able to focus on what people are doing right, and reinforce that positive behavior about 80% of the time. Be on the lookout for what's working—and why—and explore ways to continue that behavior with your employees. About 20% of the time, even your competent staff will likely do something that should be corrected or changed so they can continue to do good work, achieve their goals, and so on, to stay on course. That negative information may still sting, yet successful professionals in any field need and want it. Is that true for you?

Level 2 feedback involves specific direction. With any luck, this is only needed occasionally when you've tried Value-Added Feedback (Level 1) and determine that it's not getting through to the person.

Feedback that starts with something like "We've discussed your recent experience with your last three projects. When you start a new project, I need you to change how you..." is an example of Level 2 feedback.

If Level 2 feedback still doesn't produce the results you need from your direct report, then a line gets crossed. This can be the line between a solid, competent team member and one who may be experiencing more significant performance or conduct problems.

If you're not able to consistently give someone roughly 80% positive feedback versus 20% negative feedback, then you likely have a problem employee that you're dealing with—or need to. "Problem" employees may need an elevated level of feedback.

At this next level, Level 3, more-formal counseling may be appropriate, which is typically the first step in a corrective action process. I encourage you to learn more about how your organization specifically handles corrective actions so that you can follow the appropriate guidelines and use the tools and resources that may be available to you when giving this type of feedback.

Level 4 is the last, and typically final, level of feedback. When counseling doesn't work, more-formal discipline may be required, which might even lead to termination. Unfortunately, when employees cross the line into Level 3, and certainly into Level 4, it's often difficult for some to get back into the solid and competent group without real focus and commitment. That doesn't mean you should give up. It only means that you should be paying close attention to them and actively managing their performance.

Typically, bosses who effectively provide Level 1 (Value-Added Feedback) have less of a need to escalate to the other levels. In practice, and perhaps paradoxically, you'll find that when more *positive* feedback is sincerely and regularly delivered, it usually becomes easier for *negative* feedback also to be delivered—and received.

Let's look at what Value-Added Feedback is and how it should be delivered.

Value-Added Feedback Model

Effective feedback should be used to encourage future behavior or development, especially when you are the boss. It should help the receiver understand what they did well and what they didn't do well—and most importantly, *why*. If the information (feedback) provides no real value for a person, why share it?

Value-Added Feedback doesn't focus on correcting the past, because the past can't be changed or altered. Such feedback should be based on direct observations and current information. This type of feedback is most effective when describing the behavior or results you are recognizing as specifically and immediately as possible. Value-Added Feedback is for *everyone* on your team.

Remember the earlier section on the impact of the word "feedback"? Let's keep it simple. There are only two types of feedback: positive or negative. Can we agree that the term "positive feedback" is universally understood to be what it is? It's news about something that is going well or went well that should continue or be reinforced. Given that definition, the opposite of "positive" is "negative." When you have news about something that needs to change or be improved, that's "negative feedback."

If I could start fresh with my own terminology, without any regard for the existing connotations held by others, I would call the Value-Added Feedback Model this: "Constructive Feedback." Unfortunately, I can't do that now because constructive feedback already means "negative feedback" in too many minds. Do you agree?

A direct report's performance is either "on course" or "off course." You can maintain or correct someone's performance (behavior) by giving them one of two types of valuable information: positive or negative feedback. So let's not get hung up on terminology and focus on delivery.

The steps in the Value-Added Feedback model below can and should be used for either type of feedback, positive *or* negative. Giving feedback using this approach doesn't have to take very long. Ideally, getting through the first three steps should only take a few seconds, maybe 10 to 20.

Although this is a direct type of communication, it can still be informal and doesn't have to come across as harsh. Value-Added Feedback (*Figure 11.4*) is intended to be clear and straightforward so that misinterpretations and misunderstandings can be avoided.

Value-Added Feedback Model

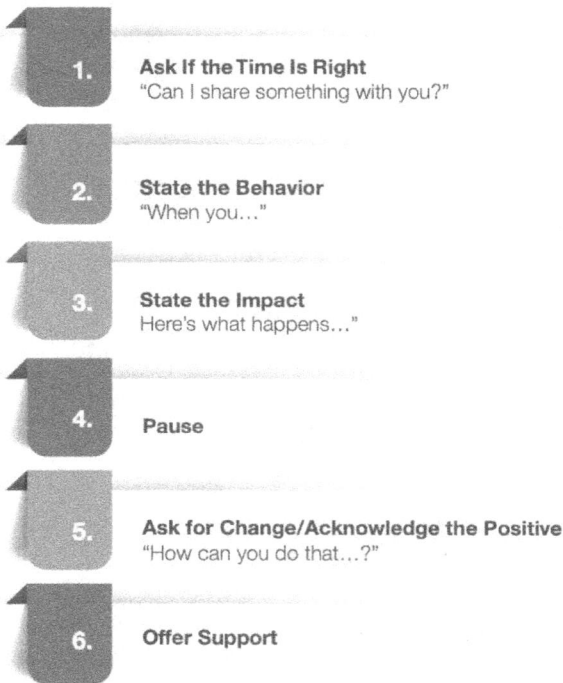

1. **Ask If the Time Is Right**
"Can I share something with you?"

2. **State the Behavior**
"When you..."

3. **State the Impact**
Here's what happens..."

4. **Pause**

5. **Ask for Change/Acknowledge the Positive**
"How can you do that...?"

6. **Offer Support**

Figure 11.4

Step 1 – Ask If the Time Is Right

Don't push your feedback on somebody who is too busy or distracted, just because *you* feel ready to deliver it. Remember, "Timing is everything." You want your message to be heard, don't you? Since feedback is about encouraging another person's future behavior, it's not worth taking the time to deliver it (positive or negative) if the other person is not ready to hear it.

Begin by finding out if the time is right. If the employee tells you that the time is *not* right, you should find another opportunity to go back and ask again. You may not even have to ask. Just notice what they are doing and decide for yourself. If someone seems extremely busy, even positive feedback may not be received as effectively. Find a time when they are less busy.

Here are some questions you could ask to check on timing:

"Can I share something with you?"

"Can I talk about something that just happened?"

"When would be a good time for you to talk about...?"

"Can I give you some feedback?"

You want to be best prepared to calmly deliver your feedback. If you determine that the behavior represents a performance problem that needs to be corrected immediately, choose a time when your emotions (and theirs!) are under control. This will likely be necessary when your feedback is negative.

Remember that this sensitivity and respect for timing will not necessarily apply if you need to deliver feedback at Levels 3 and 4. It would be appropriate for *you* to choose the time in those more serious situations and not necessarily the person on the receiving end.

Step 2 – State the Behavior

Before providing feedback, identify the specific form of behavior that you observed. Behavior can be something someone did or didn't do.

Behavior takes the following forms:

- Verbal communication (the words that are said and how they are said: tone)
- Nonverbal communication (facial expressions, body language)
- Work products and service delivery (quality, quantity, completeness)
- Other actions or inactions

This next step begins with a statement that describes the specific behavior:

"When you…" or "Here's what happened…"

"You did a very complete job of following the work order instructions that Sue gave us last week."

Remember to describe the results or behavior you are recognizing as specifically and immediately as possible. Don't *wait* too long, and don't *take* too long to deliver the feedback.

When delivering negative feedback, try to avoid focusing on "attitude," because that's difficult to accurately identify and pin down. Attitude is something we make a judgment about. It can't easily be described in clear-cut objective terms. Instead, describe what you actually observed. "Mario, when Nia finished speaking you rolled your eyes…" Even though we may feel we are experiencing someone's attitude, in fact it's a conclusion or judgment we make after observing his or her behavior.

If your feedback is strictly about characterizing attitude, understand that it can generate defensiveness and might even be interpreted as a personal attack, depending on the level of trust you have with the receiver.

Step 3 – State the Impact

This step must follow Step 2 and involves clearly describing the effect of the behavior on you or others. The impact could be consequences, conclusions, results, and so forth. Be factual and descriptive, not judgmental. The impact should describe why the behavior "matters."

Begin with a statement that clearly describes the impact:

"It causes this…"

"Here's what happens…"

"It makes me feel…"

"The benefit is…"

Or it could follow the behavior described above. "*You did a very complete job of following the work order instructions that Sue gave us last week [behavior]. She told me that she would recommend us without hesitation [impact]."*

When delivering the information in Steps 2 and 3, be clear, be straightforward, and quickly get to the point.

Step 4 – Pause

The "Pause" is the most potent and pivotal step in the Value-Added Feedback model. Deliver the Behavior and Impact messages, and then stop talking. Think of the Pause like a stop sign at a road intersection. You can still proceed forward as you may have planned, or you could take a right or left turn and modify your direction—but only after waiting. Because you came to a full stop, you have options. After you deliver feedback, you can decide what to do next after taking in the information you see and hear at that "intersection."

During the pause, pay attention to the receiver's body language and check that your feedback was received as it was intended. Be willing to change your approach if you don't get the desired result or reaction from the receiver. Sometimes you may have to repeat Steps 2 and 3 if the message didn't quite get through. When you pause, you allow time for the person (receiver) to offer either additional information (explanation) or a solution.

If the receiver argues or acts defensive after you deliver feedback, close out the conversation quickly and move on. Since the purpose of feedback is to encourage effective future behavior, it probably won't be productive to push your feedback on the person at that moment, especially if their emotions are running high. If you're the boss, you still can address their performance in other ways of your choice. However, with Level 1—Value-Added Feedback, it's usually better to avoid a conflict at that moment and instead follow up later if you are still not getting the desired performance results.

Step 5 – Ask for Change/Acknowledge the Positive

In many cases, the receiver will know what behavior must change or should continue after you complete Step 3 (State the Impact). In those circumstances, if you agree, it's not necessary to go to Step 5 (Ask for Change). Validate their solution and move on. Otherwise, ask meaningful, open-ended questions to guide the person toward understanding which behavior you think they need to change *and* how to go about it.

If the person doesn't present an acceptable solution to you, work collaboratively to develop one to achieve the desired outcome. Go into coaching mode and ask a form of the following questions:

"How can you do this differently?"

"What would be a more effective way of handling that situation?"

"What ideas do you have for improving your performance in this area?"

Remain steady and objective and keep the focus on them and what you want them to change or continue.

Step 6 – Offer Support

Ask the receiver what specific support or direction they may need from you to change their behavior. An example of this could simply be a sincere question like this: *"Please let me know what I can do to help."*

Because most people don't enjoy receiving negative feedback—even though it may be needed—offering support signals to the person that you still care about them despite their having done something that you think needs to be corrected. This step (Offer Support) is a simpler and better way to close out the feedback on a positive note without using the Sandwich Model.

Although I believe you'll find that following this Value-Added Feedback model is highly effective, it still requires preparation and practice to deliver it sincerely.

Feedback Preparation and Delivery

Know Your Intentions

Before you deliver any kind of feedback, be clear about your intentions. Giving feedback, especially as the boss, is too important for you to "wing it," so take your time to think about it and make a plan if necessary. Do you want the person to maintain their course of behavior or to change it? If you decide to provide negative feedback, know what you want the person to change or to do differently—*before* you open your mouth.

Use a Script

For negative feedback, it's always a good idea to prepare a short script that can help you to concisely State the Behavior (Step 2) and State the Impact (Step 3). Once you script the language you plan to deliver, consider running it by a trusted peer or colleague to get their reaction to any trigger words in your feedback that they may pick up. You don't want your feedback to create any unintended consequences.

Having a script can also provide you with more focus to help you anticipate and be ready for possible reactions that you may need to deal with. Of course, use the script as a guide, not something to read during your feedback!

Check out the Value-Added Feedback Preparation Worksheet in *Figure 11.5*.

Value-Added Feedback Preparation Worksheet

Purpose: What behavior are you trying to reinforce or correct?

_____
_____
_____

State the Behavior: What did the person specifically do or say, or not do or say? When did it happen?

_____
_____
_____

State the Impact: What was the consequence of their action or inaction?

_____
_____
_____

Ask for Change/Acknowledge the Positive: What could the person do differently (or continue doing) to bring about the desired results?

_____
_____

Figure 11.5

Keep the Feedback Brief

Getting from Step 1 to Step 4 (Pause) following the Value-Added Feedback model should only take around 10 to 20 seconds. This is particularly important for delivering negative feedback. If you go on for too much longer, the receiver's natural response may be a defensive one, which can create noise that may block out their reception of your message. Despite even your best effort to provide context and justification for your feedback, most people will begin to be distracted by *their* own internal voice if you talk too much. That voice typically leads them to wonder what you're going to say next or begin to question your motives. Or they may start to prepare a response (defense) to your feedback without fully listening to the rest of your content. The point is, if you talk too long, your message may not be heard as you intended—or at all.

Be Mindful of Your Tone

Your tone (or body language) will be the first "message" they process, and it will influence the receiver's overall assumption about your intentions. You can really screw up well-intentioned feedback by using the wrong tone. Think like a good teacher or coach before you speak.

If you're angry or frustrated, it will be reflected in your tone. The timing might not be right. So pick another time when you're less affected by your emotions.

It's One or the Other

Don't use positive feedback as an opening to negative feedback. I hope you've begun to forget the "feedback sandwich." If you are making a real effort to use the 80/20% (positive versus negative) approach, you shouldn't have to blend the two types of messages in order to soften their response to negative feedback. There should be a time for positive feedback and a time for negative.

For negative feedback, always be discreet. If you protect someone's self-respect and dignity, you'll likely be trusted, and your feedback should be better received. Even if it stings.

Catch People Doing the Right Things

To give effective Value-Added Feedback with any real success, remember that you'll likely have to reframe and reprogram the way your direct reports think about and respond to the word "feedback." The best way to start is by focusing on positive messages first.

Notice what's working, and let them know *why* you appreciate what they've done. With a few exceptions, of course, people tend to trust the intentions of those who take the time to recognize their positive behavior. This is another way for you to show Concern (one of the Elements of Trust). When people feel that you, as their boss, show concern for them, they will find it easier to receive and accept the negative message or news they need to hear when they hear it.

The Value-Added Feedback model is a strategy. It's most important that you deliver it sincerely, using your own words. Be willing to practice until you get more comfortable delivering both kinds of messages to each of your team members. You may even find that you become more open to receiving feedback yourself!

Getting Feedback from Others

You, as the boss, also need accurate, timely, and useful information to be successful. You can encourage this by creating a safe climate in which people feel that it's okay to share their thoughts, questions, and feedback with you without fear of any negative repercussions.

Your goal should always be to have people feel comfortable saying what's on their minds to you directly. If they avoid you and only share what they're thinking with a coworker or a colleague out in the lobby or in the parking lot, you are failing in this area. Remember, you set the tone.

Here are some straightforward questions I picked up from Peter Block that you could ask a group or individuals after *you've* shared significant information with them (for example, a new program, a major change, or the like):

- What did you hear?
- What is the impact (on you, your thoughts, feelings, and so on)?
- What questions do you have?

These questions could help solicit thoughts, ideas, and feedback, particularly if the information you shared was controversial. After receiving any information (feedback) from your team members, you can then decide how and when you'll follow up with more information, explanation, or action. Always be reliable and follow up with any promises or commitments you make, so that you can continue to be trustworthy. This should lead to more information being consistently shared with you.

Avoiding Blind Spots

When you get busy, you can't possibly keep an eye on, or out, for everything. A blind spot occurs when you lack information. It can also happen when you become overconfident and think you know everything there is to know. It usually occurs when your attention is spread too thin.

One of the biggest challenges for leaders is avoiding blind spots. If you don't have the best information, you can't make the best decisions. When your people are engaged, they are more likely to share information with you, the boss—*and* with each other. Focus on getting your engaged followers to share the information they have with you in a timely and open fashion.

Here are some examples of important information your followers may have to share:

- What they see happening at their level and vantage point—with your customers, with your employees, and with your competition.
- Ideas for how to improve work processes. (They are probably in a better position to know where the real waste is in time and resources.)
- Problems with the implementation of decisions that were previously made (including yours).
- How effective you are as their leader, and how you could improve.

A couple of useful ways to avoid blind spots are to:

1. Check in regularly with at least one team member who sees and thinks differently than you. Ask them questions. Be sure to actively listen to what they say, even when you may disagree.

2. Dig deeper and ask for specific feedback from those you trust—people who you believe are fair, honest, and credible. Again, be sure to listen actively, especially when that feedback stings. Ask questions like "What could I have done better to...?" and "What do you need from me?" Whatever you do, manage your ego and emotions, and don't get defensive. If you do get defensive, you'll likely shut down future feedback, and you won't get the valuable information you need to illuminate your blind spots.

When your team members share honest and relevant information, you will be better positioned to know what they need and can use that info to lead them effectively. Remember the Security Morale Factor from chapter 8? It's normal for employees to be reticent about speaking up to their manager. You have to make people feel safe giving you information, because you have more power as the boss.

Part | 3

"Support and encourage people
to think and act like owners."

What Employee **Engagement Means**

It seems that almost every company I work with or hear about is concerned about employee engagement—and, of course, they should be. Studies and other workplace analyses consistently show that when people don't feel engaged with their work, there is more stress, absenteeism, accidents, and involuntary worker turnover. What there is less of is job satisfaction *and* productivity. Do you need any more justification for paying attention to employee engagement? To modify a phrase used by the political consultant James Carville, "It's the people, stupid."

One popular definition of employee engagement is attributed to Kevin Kruse, an entrepreneur and thought leader. He calls employee engagement "the emotional commitment the employee has to the organization and its goals." Makes sense! When employees feel committed to their work, to their organization, and maybe even to their manager, they are engaged. However, in my view, "committed" is not *actionable* enough.

I think a fundamental problem for many managers is a lack of shared understanding about what "employee engagement" or "commitment" looks like. If you don't know what it looks or feels like, you can't take effective action to improve it. Employee engagement needs to be defined more clearly so that you and other bosses can see what it looks like in order to help your team members be committed.

Countless dollars are being invested every year in administering seemingly endless surveys to employees worldwide, attempting to gauge how satisfied and *engaged* they are at work. The most noteworthy and widely referenced employee survey example is the Gallup Q12 survey. Although employee survey questions may be comprehensive (often too much so), the response rates may not be high enough to accurately represent the overall employee group. This is a big problem. Despite all the communication and explanation and digital safeguards built into online surveys, some employees may still avoid taking them because they don't trust that the feedback is truly confidential. Then there are others who get turned off by the number of survey questions and their repetitiveness.

Some people also have a strong tendency to focus only on recent events, rather than think about the entire year (or time period) being measured—this is called "recency bias." Because so many employee surveys are being administered at certain companies, often employees and managers understandably get "survey fatigue."

A client and valued colleague of mine is an experienced HR/people professional who calls employee engagement surveys "employee entertainment." Like entertainment, the surveys are subjective and not always enriching. The survey feedback can distract and hold everyone's attention for a while, yet doesn't typically result in any fundamental changes—just like entertainment.

Managers usually struggle with this question: "How do I actually *improve* employee engagement and employee satisfaction?" Once the data is collected, analyzed, and fed back to management and others, few real answers are supplied as to what to *do* with the employees' feedback. Although many competent survey companies outline steps that may be helpful, they are usually generated algorithmically and are therefore generic, not at all customized to the affected individuals' specific needs and challenges in the unit, department, or organization.

Sometimes a well-intentioned "Employee Engagement Committee" is formed that can lead to some progress. However, too often the truly "disengaged" continue to feel neglected, while many of their managers continue to feel dejected. These managers keep reading survey reports that indicate "issues," without ever seeing any real improvement in the engagement survey ratings. The cycle continues with yet another survey that shows little to no significant change in employee engagement. Does this sound familiar?

Although there are many sensible approaches and techniques that relate to improving employee engagement, what's usually missing are actions focusing on changing the employee's mind-set. Like most behavior, "being engaged at work" starts with how you think (and feel)—not what you do.

———

As the boss, the first action you should take to improve employee engagement is to begin focusing on how *you yourself* think about your employees. This will influence how you treat them. In turn, how you treat them will directly affect how they think and feel about the time they spend at work with you as their boss—in short, how "engaged" they are.

When employees are engaged, they think, feel, and act like *owners*. A person who is engaged at work has an owner's mind-set and behaves like a reasonable adult in their role.

Thinking and acting like an owner can apply to every person at work, regardless of whether the employee is in a government job or in the private sector. Someone with an owner's mind-set, regardless of position or rank, takes personal responsibility for looking out for others, as well as for everything that's being done (or not done) that involves their team or organization.

Positive Actions for Developing an Owner's Mind-set

So, you might ask, "How can managers actually cultivate, support, and maintain employee engagement?" Simple: Treat employees like owners! Begin by having an owner's mind-set yourself. Then treat others with care and respect by focusing on their needs *before* encouraging and expecting them to have an owner's mind-set, as well.

An owner's mind-set is not limited to "50/50" thinking regarding sharing responsibility. The problem with 50/50 thinking is that it's individually oriented and not team oriented. It's focused on "me" and not "we." Regardless of your role, when you think 50/50, you'll likely act 50/50 and will only share responsibility for your "half." Meaning that, as soon as you're done with *your* work, you believe that your job is "done." True as it may be that *your* tasks are completed, there may be a wide gap in attention paid to the overall team or organization's needs and goals. When a gap like that exists, collective performance can slip through the cracks due to a lack of shared responsibility—and of real engagement. This is especially problematic when the boss has a 50/50 mind-set.

An owner's mind-set is "100/100." The best example of 100/100 thinking can be seen by watching how any championship-level sports team performs. Take basketball. On a team that uses 100/100 thinking, when a ball is "stolen" at the defensive end of the court, the player with the ball hustles down to the other end to attempt a layup or a dunk. That's their *task*. Often, in that situation, they're successful, and they score by themselves and the team benefits by the points. A basketball player with a 50/50 mentality will simply watch their teammate (or not) sprinting down the court and hope that they'll score on their own.

A teammate with a 100/100 mind-set will most often trail behind or beside the player with the ball, down the full length of the court. That person is there just in case their teammate is defended at the rim and needs to pass the ball out of trouble. Nine times out of 10, the trailing player thinking 100/100 may never get passed the ball; however, they *will* make an effort to run down the court to be in a position to help, in case they're needed to share responsibility for scoring.

To gain an owner's mind-set yourself, always think 100/100. That means take 100% responsibility for ensuring that results are produced and that other coworkers and team members are supported—especially when they're struggling. This has to start with you as the boss.

A good boss should encourage others to look around to see who needs help and not merely wait to be asked or told what to do. Be a positive and consistent role model and show others how to take responsibility for seeing and doing what's required, not simply focusing on matching a job description. This type of 100/100 thinking *and* doing defines actionable commitment. Frankly, that's the type of commitment that matters most at work, regardless of your role.

Here's another example of a 100/100 mind-set. Imagine that you and one of your colleagues decide to start a business—any type of business. You are each co-owners, with equal ownership shares in the enterprise. However, you each agree to fill a separate role and responsibility for managing the various parts of the business. To streamline decision making, you both agree that one of you will take the role of CEO and the other of CFO, even though you both remain co-owners. Each of you has more or less control in running different parts of the business. Yet as owners, you each accept 100% responsibility for the success of the overall business.

If you are the CFO, you may step in to assist your co-owner (teammate) with managing the business when they are buried in work trying to negotiate a new client contract. In turn, your CEO co-owner would assist you when you may be slipping behind producing a financial report.

When you think and act like an owner, your commitment and attention to your team or organization are the same, regardless of position, role, or assignment. When a boss promotes and expects this type of shared "ownership thinking," it's much more likely that tasks, duties, responsibilities, and the like, will not be overlooked or slip through the cracks. When you think and act like an owner, you also look out for everyone else as you keep in mind the organization's overall mission. In turn, the vision and goals of the organization are more likely to be achieved. Everyone "wins" when there is 100/100 ownership on any team!

Granted, this sets a high bar for a level of responsibility that's not easy to accept or adopt, or practice for that matter. But that's what real ownership looks like. By expecting and accepting anything less than this level of 100/100 ownership thinking, at best you'll get a lesser version of employee engagement within your team or workforce.

Three Key Questions

If you're truly serious about guiding your employees to be engaged by thinking and acting like an owner, the three key questions you should continually ask them are as follows (*Figure 11.6*):

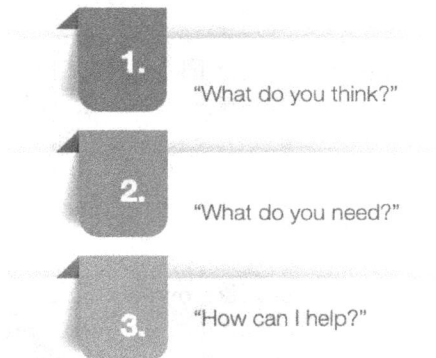

1. "What do you think?"

2. "What do you need?"

3. "How can I help?"

Figure 11.6

"What do you think?"

This straightforward question, when sincerely asked, can be compelling and impactful. Successful owners ask each other this question all the time. All owners should! When you sincerely ask this question as boss, it shows that you're interested in and respect your employees' thoughts and opinions. Moreover, it can also result in some valuable input and feedback from them—*if* you actively listen to the response you get.

"What do you need?"

Remember the Four Employee Needs (R-I-S-C)—Resources, Information, Support, and Control? Successful owners never take it for granted that their partners have what they need to do their jobs. They find out or confirm it by *asking* them—and then they assist or follow up however they can. As the boss and even as a coworker, sincerely ask people what they need regularly. Being attentive to and providing for your team members' needs is a significant part of any job when you have a 100/100 ownership mentality. This is especially true when you're the boss.

"How can I help?"

By following up with a "How can I help?" question, owners make themselves available to provide for the needs others have, whenever possible. When you ask this question of your team, and then when you step in to sincerely help, it shows that you care (Concern) and that you are Reliable (these are Trust Elements). This will contribute to your trustworthiness. Be aware, though, that if you don't follow up or follow through (Reliability) with your offer to help, it can also erode trust in you, regardless of your role.

The Parent Trap

Some people don't think and act like owners because their managers don't expect them to. Too often, and even unintentionally, managers tend to adopt a parental approach and treat their employees like "teenagers" even though they are adults—at least chronologically. As a result, their employees respond by holding back any potential commitment or ownership mentality they may have and simply comply with what they perceive the boss wants.

Developmentally, teenagers often need more direction and monitoring to ensure that they follow through with what is expected of them. Typical parents of teenagers provide needed oversight. Because parents are not always confident of a teenager's judgment or reliability, they often step in and micromanage to be sure that their kids' homework gets done before they leave the house with their friends. For a teenager, a parent's focus is often on compliance.

Most child psychology professionals would agree that this can be an age-appropriate approach—at least, for a parent dealing with a teen. However, as a management method, it almost always leads to dysfunction and disengagement when applied by a boss responsible for adult employees. The reasons why a manager can default to this "parent–teenager" dynamic can be complicated.

When people are first put into a position of power and control, maybe as a new supervisor or manager, they often logically tap into their early family experiences. This can occur for you, as well, either consciously or unconsciously. When you become the boss, it's not unusual to channel the first authority figures you became aware of. If you are like most people, that authority figure was your mother or father, or maybe a grandparent. Those early role models have an initial influence on how you will likely behave when you are first given power over others as a boss. It all depends on you and how you were affected by your familial role models.

Depending on the relationship a new boss had with their parents (or primary caregiver), how they exercise power and authority can imitate their parent's behavior. Or they could actively avoid that parent's behavior. For instance, a new manager raised by an over-bearing parent might become a bully-type boss when given that first promotion. Or they might deliberately resist that role model and adopt a type of nurturing management style that is the opposite.

Remember that your family unit was the first organization you were part of! Whatever type of family you were in, you had the oppor-tunity to observe and learn about authority and the use of power. If you had a typical upbringing, you also experienced an effective or ineffective approach to goal setting, applying rules and regulations, task assignment, and the meting out of rewards and punishments. There can be valuable lessons learned from those experiences, both what to do and what *not* to do. These life lessons may be most appli-cable as a future parent, and they can sometimes be helpful even as a boss—*if* you don't go too far.

Unfortunately, some managers can too easily slip into, and stay in, a parental mind-set when supervising or managing people, regardless of their team members' chronological ages. They act like parents and not bosses. When you say, "Do this my way…," you can usually get people to do things and strictly follow your direction because, well, you're the boss. When you do this most of the time by over-using a "Hub and Spoke" leadership style, I call this playing the "mommy" or the "daddy" card.

Managing people should not be practiced the same way as parenting them, even if there are some similarities in the power relationship. Like all actions, managing others starts with how you *think*. If you mostly think about your direct reports like you think about your kids (if you happen to have kids), you'll likely fall into this parent trap too often—and maybe stay there.

Just know that when you take a firm parental approach, you are probably focusing more on getting them to *comply* and not on *committing*. Your team members may do what you direct because they "have to," not because they "want to." If you take more of a parental approach, you are just managing and not leading.

The eventual impact of continuing a parental approach is that employees who are consistently *treated* like teenagers can then revert to *acting* like teenagers—who never grow up! This can be de-skilling when adults lack opportunities to exercise their judgment and to solve problems independently. This "parent trap" is one reason why otherwise competent people become overly dependent on their bosses and eventually disengage at work.

Sometimes you'll have team members who can't, or won't, behave like reasonable adults. In those situations, you may have to stress compliance to get the work done. But don't fall into or stay in the trap of *always* thinking and acting like a parent. If you do, you will be encouraging all your adult employees to be disengaged dependents. And if they continue to be disengaged and overly dependent on you, you'll have less time available to lead and develop your team—and your organization may suffer.

Create Reasons for People to Stick Around

When you reach a certain age, you realize more and more that life is short. During our working years (for many, that's about 50 years of our life) we spend some 35% of our waking hours at work. Does anyone really want that time at work to suck and feel like a prison sentence? No matter their age, I think it's safe to say that most people want to work someplace where it's fun, even if the work itself isn't. How do you feel when you're having fun? What happens to *how* you work when the place where you work feels fun? Is what you produce or deliver better, worse, or the same when you're having fun? Hopefully, having fun at work matters to you—especially if you want to be a better boss.

Realistically, finding fun at work may not happen all the time, everywhere. However, if fun at work is rare, people generally won't stick around for long—at least not those with other options. Those who do stick around anyway may not necessarily be the workers that you *want* to stay. They may be the ones who have nowhere else to go, are most negative, and are keeping everyone else on the team from having fun.

When you're the boss, pay attention to how people feel and act when they're at work. It's up to you to make it okay and safe for others to have fun. To have fun, encourage people to *find* fun. Fun can be found at and in any type of work. When work is fun, it can increase energy, reduce stress, bring out more creativity, and often strengthen relationships.

Of course, if you work at a resort or a theme park, it might be *easier* to find fun (although not necessarily if you have an a-hole boss). You don't have to look very far to see that a lot of work that needs to be done throughout the world can be dangerous, dirty, difficult, or just plain boring—not "fun" for many people. However, I believe that regardless of the type of work, most people still have the potential to find fun in their interactions with coworkers—and ideally even with their clients, customers, and their bosses. Is that unrealistic?

As the boss, create opportunities for your team to share informal time together and make connections—at work and outside of work. Casual face time can lead people to having fun. You don't have to organize team-building weekends or zip-lining activities, unless that's what your team wants. Be aware that some team members may work remotely or have family or personal obligations or interests that affect their ability to hang out after work hours, so try not to organize every one of your events at a time that leaves them out.

What's most important is to give people real time and space to socialize and talk about things other than work, even if it's during "work" time. Help make it safe for people to reveal more of themselves if they want to. It might take a while for some, but given regular, consistent opportunities, most people soften up, lighten up, and eventually come out of their protective shell and connect with others.

If your team doesn't already connect very much naturally, start simply. Take everybody to lunch or bring in lunch or some other appropriate refreshments. Give it time.

Keep in mind that some people may have issues with socializing with certain coworkers and others that you're not aware of and can't control. So don't force it.

To be clear, getting people to socialize at work can also be hard if they have to work with a-holes or have an a-hole boss. Still, sometimes workers bond more closely together when they have an a-hole boss. Having a common "enemy" often unites people. Since you've gotten this far in the book, you're probably *not* an a-hole—so you'll have to look for other, more positive ways to get your employees to lighten up and connect!

You can start by remembering to loosen up yourself. Be authentic and keep things light, even if you are doing serious work. If you have a natural sense of humor, tap into it often, as long as it's appropriate. Look for what makes people smile or laugh. Humor can be personal and subjective, so one approach may not work for everyone. (Sound familiar?) You do have to be careful with humor at work because what one person thinks is funny could be offensive and discriminatory to others. That doesn't mean that you should avoid humor. Simply use good judgment. A good rule of thumb is, if in doubt—don't.

As the leader, you don't have to be the clown. You only need to encourage others to bring out more of their playful, informal side. You set the tone—right?

Especially if the work you and your team do is demanding and stressful, try to get people to relax when they can. When people are relaxed, they are more open to humor and having fun. They also feel more motivated to look out for and help their coworkers—*and* their manager.

Having fun and being relaxed in the workplace also contributes to better physical as well as mental health. By now, I'm sure that you've learned that constant stress usually leads to a long list of problems. Fun is an antidote for stress. So don't forget that when you're the boss.

Look for how you could "gamify" some of your group's work by creating some friendly competitions within or between your teams. Find something that fits the team's personality and the type of work they do. People generally like games and good-natured competitive challenges.

Consider how to create celebrations around larger wins that the team or teams can all share in. These recognitions can also be casual and informal. Use these opportunities to acknowledge effort and accomplishments, both large and small. Loosen up and build some fun into these events. Make things interesting. But again, don't force it. If people feel that you are working too hard to create fun, you might end up coming off like Michael Scott or David Brent from *The Office*.

Involve your employees directly in figuring out with you what *they* consider to be fun. If their ideas are reasonable (and affordable), help make them happen. After all, you're the boss!

Producing results is a manager's number one priority. Doing work, and having fun at it, don't have to be mutually exclusive. Creating a fun place to work should also be a top priority. Talented people have choices, and where they choose to work will likely include where they find meaning, accomplishment—and fun. Sometimes the best thing you can do to encourage more fun as the boss is to *lighten up!*

Do what you can to give all your valued team members a "sticky" reason to stay loyal. Give them good reasons to *want* to stay and work with you and your organization

Part | 4

"Help people develop knowledge,
skills, and abilities to solve problems
or improve performance on their own."

Coaching Fundamentals

Why Coaching Matters

Helping people develop includes guiding them to learn in as many ways as possible. Edgar Schein, an icon in the field of organizational development, makes clear that helping is "at the heart of all social life, whether we are talking about ants, birds, or humans. It would seem then that if we can be more effective as helpers, it will improve life for all of us." Do you agree?

Think about the best coach you had at any point in your life. What qualities did (do) they possess? What did they do when they were coaching? How did they treat you? How did they make you feel? The better bosses are good coaches. Agreed?

These sections on coaching contain some very effective and highly actionable approaches that can be immediately applied. However, they are *not* intended to be the definitive source for all things related to the topic. Coaching is covered here at a fundamental level because it is part of what you, as a boss, should do when you are Leading from the Side.

Coaching as a well-defined skillset was not always included in corporate management training programs or formal business higher education. Now an increasingly diverse workforce not only thrives on coaching, they *expect* it from their managers and from the companies where they work. I'm certain that the ability to effectively coach employees will be an essential requirement when the most successful organizations select their next generation of leaders.

Current workplace surveys administered by Gallup and other respected sources show that the best leaders are almost always good coaches. Good coaches foster trust, not fear, and help those they lead find positive, compelling reasons and motivation to move toward a change or improvement. Organizations that encourage and support a coaching culture with skilled leader/coaches will most often attract, develop, and retain the best talent in the long run.

Shifting from 20th Century Methods

Although the modern coaching approach practiced by today's most successful leaders is appropriate and effective, it wasn't always that way.

I worked at a busy advertising agency when I was in my twenties. The big boss was the majority owner of the ad firm, and he always made that clear to everyone who worked there. If somebody in the agency screwed up—most anybody!—he would yell and try to strike fear in them. He would rarely say anything positive unless he was kissing the ass of a client or someone else he needed. You know the type. He believed that no news was good news. Most of us did what we could to avoid him. He's now considered a classic, old-school boss. Even though I really liked that job, I left it primarily because of him.

Unfortunately, there are still plenty of experienced and even newer bosses who still practice old-school management approaches. Theirs is a 20th-century command-and-control, "my way or the highway" style. Some of these bosses continue to believe that many management and leadership practices taught and practiced today are too *soft*. They resent having to "coddle" people because *they* had a different experience. Most reasonable people of any age don't want to be yelled at, pushed around (even verbally), or intimidated by a hothead boss who uses only fear to get people to do what they want. This approach is *not* effective leadership.

I will acknowledge that an authoritarian style *may* produce results in some limited instances and within some industries and workplace cultures. However, it typically doesn't produce the long-lasting and positive results needed in the 21st century world of work. There is mounting evidence that the "old school" way of demanding or expecting quick fixes to personal weaknesses or limitations without providing coaching support doesn't work today. As a manager, you don't always have to be a "nice" boss, but you definitely shouldn't be a jerk—or worse. There are more effective approaches to getting results.

You'll recall that the most successful people and organizations are always learning. And, the most significant risk to successful people and organizations is complacency. At various times your team members, regardless of their role or the type of organization they work in, will need or benefit from coaching. The reason is that coaching is an approach to *actively* support learning, growth, and development.

Expect Some Resistance

For all the potential benefits of good coaching, you can face an unexpected challenge now and then when you try to incorporate it as a boss. That is, everyone may not view being coached as a positive thing.

I was reminded of this recently while working with a senior manager on skill development. We were discussing the topic of performance management and the supportive role of coaching. I asked how coaching was viewed in her organization, and I was told that the word "coaching" was associated with correcting problem performance. This narrow view of coaching can limit the potential benefits. You can help change this thinking by adding coaching skills to your manager's toolbox and by practicing it with your direct reports.

Coaching Preparation

Preparation is the key to success for most activities requiring skills—including coaching. If you want to be a better boss, think and act like a good coach. The first step is to prepare.

Be Self-Aware

To prepare for coaching, begin by focusing or refocusing on the development of your emotional intelligence. By developing your emotional intelligence, you'll increase your coaching skills, which are part of good leadership skills. Self-awareness is the gateway to emotional intelligence, which is most critical to being a better boss—and an effective coach.

Observe

Learn to read people. People are always giving you some type of information about themselves. Usually, they send verbal as well as nonverbal clues to how they are thinking and feeling. The challenge for you is in accurately deciphering or decoding the meaning of the information, feedback, or clues they are giving. When you get good at reading people, you can be far more effective as a coach.

Here are some things to look for:

· Watch their reactions to your communication. Gauge their response to what you are doing while you are doing it. Are they open to your approach, or are they tuning you out?

· What messages are you getting from their nonverbal cues? Is their eye contact or body posture signaling something that would be helpful for you to know? Pay attention to your gut reactions, and determine if you should adjust your approach accordingly.

· How does the person learn best? How do you know? What are the clues? (See the Learning Styles section for more ideas. Figure 11.7)

· Are you enough in sync with them to be able to predict what they will say or do before they do? Is the communication between you in "flow"?

- Which patterns of "what" or "how" they do what they do (their behavior) are helpful to them and their performance? What are they doing that gets in the way?

- Once you begin coaching, which approaches work best with them?

Self-Manage

Self-management is yet another aspect of emotional intelligence. Remember to keep "you" in check. One key to self-management can be best described by the axiom "go slow to go fast," discussed in chapter 10. It's extremely challenging to be a successful manager, and especially a successful leader, if you can't effectively manage yourself. Sometimes you simply need to slow...down.

For example, if you insert your views, options, or direction too quickly or forcefully, you risk triggering a defensive reaction or having the "coachee" turn off or tune out. At that point, the learning stops, and your intentions to help will likely be questioned.

Be willing to get out of your comfort zone if it helps guide your coachee in the right direction. Stretch and expand your habits and behaviors. Remember what the word "effective" means—it means "doing what works." Do what works for *them*.

If you're not used to active listening, be willing to try harder at remaining focused and practice *being* curious. When you are in coach mode, always maintain your focus on what your coachee wants and needs. Use your experience, creativity, and judgment to help them learn and grow.

Be patient. When you see things differently, you can still communicate your views to a team member in other ways that don't come across as too directive. Keep your cool. When you feel frustrated, disappointed, or even annoyed, gain control of your emotions or take a break. In other words: self-manage. Do everything you can to resist shutting down and shutting them down, if you really want to be helpful as a coach.

Possible Cues or Triggers for Coaching

Coaching doesn't have to occur only in a one-on-one meeting (although that can be an excellent time and place for it). Other spontaneous opportunities will appear to you when you are thinking and acting like a coach.

Pay attention when employees are:

· Starting a new project or accepting a new responsibility

· Approaching or just completing a milestone (event, meeting, deliverable, and so on)

· Experiencing a setback or failure

· Coming to you with a problem

· Starting to lose motivation or enthusiasm

· Asking for additional opportunities or challenges

You can find time to provide regular coaching as part of:

· Annual check-ins (expectation setting, "stay" interviews, and such)

· Pre-project or event planning sessions

· Postproject or event debriefing sessions

You may also find other good opportunities throughout the day, week, or month when coaching might be helpful and appropriate for your direct report—*if* you're prepared to look for them.

Coaching Approach

Good coaches understand their coachee as a person, so that they can customize and adjust their coaching style to do what works. Each coachee has their own personality and individual needs that will vary from person to person. Your coaching approach should always be focused on the person being helped.

Good bosses recognize that effective coaching practices and approaches are not unlike those that foster good relationships in general. It's most important to manage your ego so that it doesn't get in your way *or* the way of the person you are trying to help. I can't overemphasize this.

Since coaching involves helping people develop knowledge, skills, and abilities, it's about helping people learn. Just as we have different personalities and communication styles, we also have different learning styles. Understanding and adapting to your coachee's preferred learning style will help you be a more effective coach.

Learning Styles

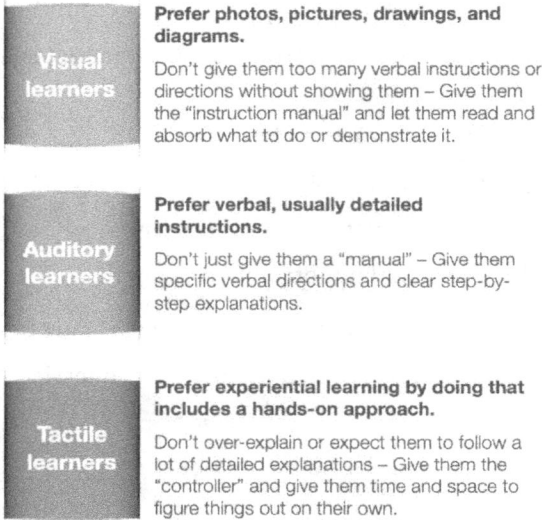

Visual learners

Prefer photos, pictures, drawings, and diagrams.

Don't give them too many verbal instructions or directions without showing them – Give them the "instruction manual" and let them read and absorb what to do or demonstrate it.

Auditory learners

Prefer verbal, usually detailed instructions.

Don't just give them a "manual" – Give them specific verbal directions and clear step-by-step explanations.

Tactile learners

Prefer experiential learning by doing that includes a hands-on approach.

Don't over-explain or expect them to follow a lot of detailed explanations – Give them the "controller" and give them time and space to figure things out on their own.

Figure 11.7

Many learners prefer a combination of two of the three styles in *Figure 11.7*. If you're not sure about your coachee's learning style, try different approaches so that you cover all three learning modes. As with all coaching approaches, pay attention to what works and what doesn't, so that you can be more effective the next time. Continue to practice as you find your own coaching style and voice that best fit you in your role as a boss.

Direct or Indirect Approach

Deciding between a direct or indirect approach should be determined by whether or not you believe your coachee is best served by being given the answer *or* by receiving help to find it. The decision you make about which approach to take should depend on your assessment of the purpose (intent), problem, risk level, time available, skills, experience, and your feel for the overall situation at that moment. Of course, you'll have to use your judgment. Easy, right?

Providing an immediate solution, instruction, or even direction may be the best approach when the person you are coaching truly can't find an answer because they lack experience or knowledge. They may also need a solution to a problem right away because time is an issue, or soon will be.

Some examples when this direct approach might be appropriate are:

1. When one of your unit members comes to you and says, "I'm stuck. I tried to deal with this problem three different ways, and nothing worked," or words to that effect.

2. You might also use a direct approach when a team member is really stressed out because of their workload or personal challenges. For instance, if they have an upcoming deadline to meet and they are just too overwhelmed to think clearly about what they need to do next.

In both of these situations, the best approach may be for you to step in and help with a specific direction or solution.

Be careful, though, because it's very easy to slip into a habit of providing more answers and solutions than are necessary. Some people are more than happy to have their boss continually tell them what they should do, rather than put in the effort to figure it out for themselves. Although it may be faster and easier for you to just give people answers, be careful not to fall into this trap as a boss. If you do this habitually, it can lead to your team members' becoming overly dependent on you and unable to act with confidence on their own without your direction. When you create this type of team, you can even unintentionally end up micromanaging and have less time to focus on other priorities.

Although you may be the premier problem-solver in your unit or business, when you are in coaching mode, help them to *think* and *do*. Even though it's easier to deliver answers to someone, there is usually better buy-in when an idea comes out of their own brain. The solutions tend to "stick" and stay in their mind and memory better. When a thought or insight "sticks," a person is more likely to act on *their* solutions or retain the knowledge *they* discovered over a longer term.

An indirect approach can be most effective in helping a person grow and develop, especially if time is not a limiting factor. Whenever possible, invest time and effort to work with your direct reports to help them form their own conclusions and find the right answers on their own. You can always step in afterward and assist them when needed.

Coaching Strategies

Remember that coaching is a Leading from the Side practice that involves positively connecting with others to help them on their terms. As a boss, choose the right coaching strategy that works best for your team member and their specific circumstances.

To Be a Good Coach, Be a Good Guide

Guiding helps the coachee develop, apply, and trust their knowledge, skills, insights, and judgment. It can be an effective, indirect strategy that involves working collaboratively with the coachee. When you guide, you use and share your experience to help them learn. You challenge and use questions to help them think. And you use encouragement to help them take appropriate and practical actions that can lead to more effective results.

Share

Depending on the person and their needs, one helpful approach to guiding is to share with your coachee what you know, see, and have learned based on your experience and position. Find appropriate opportunities to "tell the story" of what shaped you over the course of your career (and life). Know your audience, and only share personal stories that you think might be helpful before launching into one. Your stories and related experiences—the early ones, as well as your most recent ones—can provide insights and relevant learning that can make a powerful difference for someone now and in the future.

Some examples of "stories" to share are these:

· What you see from your place in the organization, and how that perspective might be helpful to them

· How you've handled similar situations that they may be struggling with at the moment

· The criteria you use when making decisions

· What you've learned from your experience (as it relates to them and their situation)

· Why you think an issue is important and how it impacts the "big picture"

· What you wish someone had told *you* when you were in their position

· Which organizational values are most important to you

· How your experiences shaped your beliefs

· What failures or setbacks you've encountered, and what you learned from them

· What motivates you to come to work each day

· What you look for in your interactions with others

· How you want to be treated as a manager

Another way to share what you know is to have your team member shadow you in real time when you are in problem-solving mode. Consider doing this whenever there may be an appropriate learning opportunity for them—which is probably often. Get into the habit of thinking about who could come along with you when you are in a customer meeting, negotiating with a subcontractor, providing direction or feedback to a vendor, brainstorming ideas and solutions, or in other relevant situations. Never squander what might be a potential learning experience for your coachee or team member. If and when it makes sense and won't be awkward, have someone join you to observe *what* and *how* you do what you do.

Challenge

Some people learn and grow best when they feel challenged. A challenge could be in the form of a new assignment, a new task, or another responsibility that requires them to stretch outside their comfort zone.

Here are some ways that you can challenge someone:

- Push them to look deeper to see underlying issues and not just the symptoms of problems. Expect them to explore the problem as well as the impact.

- Assign them a stretch assignment that will help them toward a development goal. Choose something that is a little more than they think they can handle.

- Make it an expectation for them to develop solutions and recommendations, not merely report problems. Emphasize the "2 solutions approach" (Direct them to bring 2 potential solutions to any discussion related to the issue they want help resolving).

- Ask them to consider other perspectives (of coworkers, clients, policymakers, or others).

- Emphasize the importance of planning ahead and thinking long-term to anticipate impacts over time.

- Show them how to express disagreement by being assertive or by using tact and diplomacy (if they are too soft or too harsh).

- Push them to broaden assumptions about their personal limits. Ask questions like "Why can (or can't) you…?"

A colleague of mine, Steve, shared a story with me from his early career experience. Steve and his boss had prepared for a presentation that they would co-deliver to their organization's board. Although it was a fairly routine presentation, Steve had never given one before at this level. This assignment was going to be a new, stressful and challenging experience for him.

Steve's boss was very supportive and worked closely with him to develop the overall content and become familiar with all of it—from start to finish. As a result, Steve felt thoroughly prepared for his section, as well as his boss's section of the presentation. They agreed to meet at the scheduled time outside the board conference room for their joint presentation. When Steve showed up on time, his boss was nowhere to be found. Steve waited a few minutes, and still no boss in sight.

A board member soon appeared and ushered Steve into the conference room to get started. Steve had no choice but to deliver the presentation to the high-level group by himself. The presentation went very well, and Steve left the conference room and returned to his office to look for his boss. When he arrived, he saw him standing in the hallway. The first words that came out of the boss's mouth were "I knew you could handle it!" His boss had intentionally not shown up for the meeting! He wanted to give Steve the experience and opportunity to shine.

Now, I'm not recommending that you push your employees like my colleague was pushed! I wouldn't have handled it that way—but it worked. In Steve's case, the positive experience helped increase his confidence, because he was ready for the challenge. If Steve had failed, his boss's decision might have been considered the wrong one.

As a coach, you need to use your best judgment in determining how far you can challenge someone. If there is a possibility of failure, be sure it's survivable and doesn't cause the type or level of negative and unintended consequences that may set back the coachee's learning—or even damage your coaching relationship—or worse. Know the individual you are coaching.

Question

Too much emphasis is placed on knowing answers and solutions. I think the real talent and skill for a coach (and a boss!) is in knowing the right questions to ask. Questions are like master keys for a lock. If you can find the right "key" (question), it can unlock the right answer. This is basically the Socratic method (named after the Classical Greek philosopher Socrates).

Asking and answering questions can stimulate critical thinking and draw out ideas and assumptions for a coachee. Good coaches are creative and open-minded as they focus on generating the right questions, for the right person, in the right situation, at the right time. Guiding people through questioning can provide several benefits for the coachee, including:

- Improving their critical thinking skills
- Energizing thinking
- Facilitating the learning that comes from mistakes
- Encouraging more self-sufficiency and self-confidence
- Keeping responsibility, ownership, and accountability with them

Here are some tips to keep in mind to be an effective questioner:

- First, be an Active Listener to learn about the person's needs and the situation.
- Listen for underlying meaning, and build on the answers with follow-up questions.
- Be patient. Remember, the first thing people say is often *not* their ultimate central point.
- Don't always fill the silence. Stay with it and be comfortable with the pause. Increase your talk:listen ratio. (This means talk less!)
- Use open-ended questions to get them to engage and share more.
- Avoid questions that can be answered with a simple "yes" or "no."
- Unless time is critical, try to respond with *more* questions, even when the coachee is looking for answers. (Just don't be annoying!)

Here are some examples of effective questions that can be used for different purposes:

Questions to Uncover Ideas, Insights, and Experiences

- What do you think?
- Why is this issue important?
- What do you want to change, improve, speed up, or make easier?
- What are you trying to accomplish?
- How would you describe the issue to someone else?

- What assumptions are you making?
- Is this the problem or actually the solution?
- What's in the way? What's stopping you?
- What does this information mean to you?
- What are you responsible for here?

Questions to Recover Ideas, Insights, and Experiences

- Is that a story you heard, or the factual truth? How do you know? How can you find out?
- How can you learn what you need to know about this?
- What have you already tried and learned?
- When have you been successful in similar situations?
- What approaches did you use?
- What skills did you develop?
- How would you coach someone else facing the same issue?

Questions to Discover Ideas, Insights, and Experiences

- What will happen in the long term if this situation is not resolved?
- What can (or can't) you control in this situation?
- What can you do now that you couldn't do before?
- How would you like it to be?
- Have you ever experienced something like this before?
- If you changed your belief about this, what would be possible?
- How can you learn from this problem so it never happens again?

Encourage

Everyone can use a regular dose of positivity and acknowledgment from their boss (coach). Sometimes the best strategy for a coach to use is to encourage what the coachee is already doing. It shows that you are paying attention—and that you care. It's another way for you to provide Support, one of the Four Employee Needs. Remember R-I-S-C?

Here are some ways that you can encourage someone to think independently and also take reasonable risks:

· Let them know that you have confidence in their ability.

· Show empathy for his or her challenges or insecurities.

· Show your appreciation for his or her ideas, contributions, and effort.

· Back them up and be positive, especially when they take reasonable risks and make intelligent mistakes.

Focus on Strengths

There are numerous, well-intentioned, self-improvement and health-related programs that too strictly focus on why we need to change who or what we are, rather than why we should maximize who or what we are *already*.

The difference in this initial focus or approach may appear to be subtle, but it really isn't. Although there are some exceptions, when many of us start with what we want to "fix" first, our fight-or-flight response can be triggered, which can lead us to behave defensively or to quickly find excuses to avoid the effort because it's HARD. We then get uncomfortable, and we are less open to feedback and soon lose any real commitment to addressing the limitation or making the change. In other words, we avoid the hard work that change can require and just give up trying.

Several useful concepts regarding change and the role of coaching are detailed in a book by Daniel Goleman, Richard E. Boyatzis, and Annie McKee called *The New Leaders: Transforming the Art of Leadership into the Science of Results*. Their research suggests that personal change occurs more effectively and sustainably when focused on a positive emotional attraction (PEA) rather than a Negative Emotional Attractor (NEA). Focusing on the positive means building on strengths, which allows one to be more open to possibilities.

We often choose or are led down a negative (deficit) oriented path designed to fix what's wrong with us. That usually isn't very effective.

Here's an example: I worked with a coaching client, named Kim, whose boss had previously coached her to change her approach to her direct reports. Although Kim was considered a high-potential manager, she was told that her direct communication style was too abrasive for her staff and that she needed to improve her interactions with others. Her well-meaning manager apparently spent many months working with her and pointing out each of her missteps. Although Kim seemed open to improving, she began to lose motivation for changing because she felt that all the attention she was getting was focused on how she had "screwed up," to use her phrase. She was feeling dejected and stopped responding to her boss's coaching. Despite her apparent desire to improve her communication approach, she never felt positive enough to believe that progress was being made during the coaching process with her boss.

Coaches can help the personal change process by identifying the positive reasons for making a change *first* and then building on individual strengths to achieve some small wins. Once those small wins are achieved, motivation can build.

Find a way to focus on your coachee's strengths before doing anything else. It's much more motivating to have them start the process with what they're good at. When they gain some traction by maximizing a strength, they can then build some positive momentum and be more open and motivated to learn more about what they need to improve afterward.

Be willing to take the time and make the effort to understand each employee's innate talents (like establishing quick rapport with people, as one example). Have the patience to find ways to help each team member cultivate their broader talents as a person, rather than focus solely on their technical skills and work-related knowledge. Those are more obvious to observe and can also be learned more easily.

Here are some coaching questions that might be useful in identifying a person's overall strengths:

·   What are you really good at?

·   What do you like to do?

·   What have you learned to do quickly?

·   What gives you the most satisfaction at work?

·   What do others see as your strengths?

Once you get a reasonably clear idea about your direct report's strengths, ask them to consider what the consequence is, has been, or might be if that strength is overdone. For example, if someone identified speaking skills as a strength, have them think about when that can be overdone (as in "talking too much"). They could discover that a consequence might be that they don't take enough time to listen to others. This discovery could provide you with an avenue to explore as you coach them.

Change/Growth Force Field Analysis

The chart (*Figure 11.8*) is called a Force Field Analysis. The template was developed by Kurt Lewin, a social psychologist, to study and think about the impact of change on organizations and individuals. It's a standard tool used in the field of organizational development that I've adapted and applied many times in coaching. It helps to create a visual description of an individual's strengths that support the change, growth, or improvement they want to develop, along with their corresponding limitations or weaknesses that may be slowing down or preventing their progress.

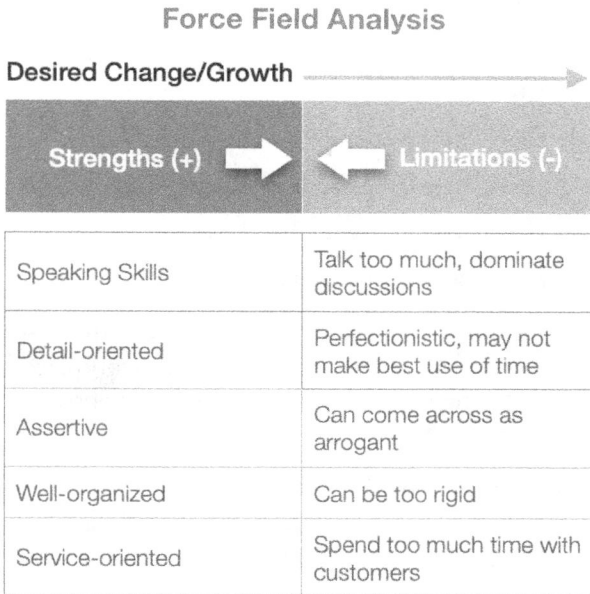

Force Field Analysis

Desired Change/Growth ┈┈┈┈┈┈┈┈┈┈┈┈┈┈➤

Strengths (+) ➡	⬅ Limitations (-)
Speaking Skills	Talk too much, dominate discussions
Detail-oriented	Perfectionistic, may not make best use of time
Assertive	Can come across as arrogant
Well-organized	Can be too rigid
Service-oriented	Spend too much time with customers

Figure 11.8

To complete the limitations side of the force field chart, first work with the coachee to identify the corresponding behaviors or consequences related to their overdone strengths. Then follow up and add any growth opportunities, other limitations, or blocks that have been recognized by the coachee, by you, or by others.

Use Other Role Models

In some coaching situations, you may not have personal examples to share, or you might feel that the other strategies described above are not appropriate for guiding your coachees forward to achieve a desired result. You may find as a coach that using a role model (real or fictitious) can be every bit as instructive and helpful (maybe even more so) if the role model has the skills or qualities that can help the coachee develop.

Pay attention and use your creativity to help find the best role model for the person and their situation. Involve the coachee in this strategy. Encourage them to observe and listen to others. Point out other familiar people who are successful in certain situations, and discuss the following:

- What kinds of words do they use?
- How do they adjust their communication style?
- What differences do you see in their approach?
- Why do they do what they do in those situations?
- How do they react in similar situations?

If your coachee wants to learn to be more direct and assertive, see if there's another person inside or outside your workplace that they can observe to see how they handle certain situations that call for assertive behavior.

Effective role models can also be fictional. Maybe a movie or TV character portrays the desired skills that the coachee can also develop, with some knowledge and practice. There's no reason why they can't use a fictional character's behavior as a role model and study it more closely on the screen for tips that could help them handle a challenging personality or another type of situation that they are facing.

It's worth repeating that *each person is different, with unique strengths (talents), behaviors, motivations, and needs.* Focus on the individual and pay attention to the best coaching strategy for them, not you. Find a way to help build up people's strengths first. It's much more motivating to have someone start with what they're good at. When you help people maximize their strengths, they can build positive momentum toward changing and developing. Then they can be more open and motivated to address their limitations.

Good coaches manage their own ego needs. They don't require credit for helping their coachees to learn, develop, and succeed. They gain satisfaction from seeing the results produced by their team members.

To be effective as a coach, you also need to continue to learn. Be open and attentive to what works and doesn't work—for *them*. If you're unsure about the verbal or nonverbal messages you're getting from them, check your assumptions before moving too far ahead with your coaching. For example, if you saw your coachee change their expression or posture after you discussed a topic, you might want to ask a question or give them some value-added feedback.

Effective coaching takes time and patience to achieve real results. Human "software" can't be programmed for instant change like computer software...at least not yet. Despite knowing what you know about what works best in 21st century organizations, you'll still be faced with a dilemma: "How do you find the time and patience to apply to coaching when both seem to be in short supply?" Maybe the better question is, what happens if you *don't*?

Coachee Readiness

Ever wonder why some people respond to good advice, recommendations, or suggestions, and others don't? It may have more to do with how "ready" they are than with the quality of the ideas, content, or coaching they are given. This is true regardless of who is trying to help them—you *or* your favorite coaching guru.

Before moving too far ahead with exploring ideas for growth and improvement with someone, assess their readiness. For the coaching process to be effective, Five Readiness Ingredients are required for success.

Readiness Ingredients

1. Motivation
2. Focus
3. Content
4. Commitment
5. Follow-through

1. Motivation

People who respond best to coaching have a sincere, compelling, and personal answer to the question "What's in it for *me*?" The motivation that produces lasting results must be inner-directed. Although you can tell someone that they should do something, it is only when *they* tell themselves to do it that real motivation kicks in and has a chance to stick with them. For the most part, people motivate themselves. Leaders can help by creating the conditions for motivation to happen.

Numerous motivational theories have been offered, all with some level of validity. Self-Determination Theory (SDT) is a popular one that grew out of research done by Edward L. Deci and Richard M. Ryan. Their work suggests that there are two main types of motivation: intrinsic (internal to self) and extrinsic (external to self). Both types are powerful motivational forces that shape how we behave.

Monetary compensation (an extrinsic motivator) is often the focus of tangible workplace motivation. However, it usually only works for a short time before people need additional incentives to increase or even maintain their commitment and effort. It's not because people are inherently greedy or ungrateful; rather, it's just that most need more-intangible (more-intrinsic) motivators for motivation to last over a longer term. We may not even be conscious of these needs—we just know when something's missing.

Each coachee needs to respond to their own motivational message. This might involve understanding what could be gained by learning or changing their behavior, and what might be lost if he or she *doesn't* learn or change. Sometimes the potential loss for them may be their job.

Regardless of whether a person's motivational messages relate to a potential gain or a potential loss, the dopamine in their brain carries those messages—not a coach. According to research done by John Salamone, Ph.D., the head of the Behavioral Neuroscience Division at the University of Connecticut, dopamine is not only involved with our feeling of pleasure. Dopamine also encourages us to *act*.

Clients often ask me to provide coaching to individuals who are uniquely valued or depended on by their organizations. Sometimes their value is owing to their superior technical ability. In other cases it may be because their senior manager is overly dependent on them and the work they produce. One of the first questions I'll ask the client sponsor is: "How willing is the individual to learn and change?" Unless I get a strong, positive, and honest response at the outset, I'm not very hopeful that I can help that individual as a coach.

One of my early regrets as a coach was accepting an assignment from a CEO to work with her CFO, on whom she was highly dependent to keep the organization's finances in order. This CFO had anger issues that he was frequently unable to manage while working with his direct reports and colleagues. The CEO wanted him to stop acting out his frustrations with others because he was a real disrupter. She asked me to work with him to help get him to behave more appropriately because she was not willing to consider terminating him at that time. Even though I soon discovered that he lacked sufficient motivation to learn and change, I continued with the assignment to try to please the client.

Futilely, I kept trying new approaches to get him to change his behavior. In hindsight, his CEO most needed me to keep his behavior in check—not to help him change that behavior, which, deep down, we both knew *wouldn't* change. Sometimes he would improve for a short while. Then he would slip back to old habits. He would then apologize to me and his boss and promise to try harder. However, he wasn't really motivated. When he slipped back and berated people, word eventually got back to me that his colleagues were holding *me*, his coach, responsible for his lack of improvement. The CFO finally quit the organization and, despite my best intentions and efforts, the client stopped using me as its executive team's coach.

The lesson I learned? Figure out if the coachee is genuinely *ready* to be coached. In this example, my right choice would have been to end the coaching assignment on *my* terms after realizing that the CFO really wasn't ready to change his behavior. Despite my client's unspoken desire for me to "keep him under control," deep down I knew it wasn't going to be possible because the CFO wasn't sincerely motivated to change. I fell into the common trap of "wishing and hoping" for change to occur in someone who wasn't really motivated. (I believe this can happen to spouses as well as to bosses!)

As a manager, you don't have the same ability to easily walk away from working with a coachee as I might, since that person will likely be your direct report. You *do* have choices, though. One is to determine whether that individual is motivated enough to respond to your coaching. If they aren't sufficiently motivated (ready), you can try a more directive approach to changing behavior and producing a better result.

Coaches can help inspire and can assist with lighting and fanning the "flame," yet the coachee has to find their own reason for building desire for change and development within themselves. That's the only real motivation that sticks.

Leaders have always been challenged to find ways to motivate their workforce. Motivation is the key to achieving meaningful and lasting results for the coachee. You can't easily coach someone to be motivated. If this first factor—Motivation—doesn't exist for the coachee, then they're not ready to move forward.

2. Focus

One of the reasons we all start many more projects than we finish is that we lack real focus. Even when we *are* motivated, too often we decide to do way too many things at once. People will usually succeed more often by setting and prioritizing just a few goals. If your coachee has more than two or three significant goals or priorities, it can be easy to lose focus, get distracted, and eventually even give up.

When someone is distracted or unfocused, they can't invest enough time and energy to keeping the motivational fire going. Then they get discouraged because they don't see sufficient progress. They stop trying, and the little remaining effort they apply to achieve the goals is only fueled by wishing and hoping—which gains them nothing.

You can help by working with your coachee to craft goals using the SMART method outlined in chapter 10. The SMART methodology has been a best-practice goal-setting approach since the early 1980s because it *works*.

3. Content

As a coach, when you are also clear about what a coachee's goals are, you can help guide them to find whatever they need to know or learn to improve virtually any desired skill or ability. Content is usually the easiest ingredient to find or develop. When your coachee is motivated and focused on a goal, they're much more ready and open to finding, accepting, and absorbing whatever knowledge or information (content) is required to achieve the goal.

Relevant and useful content can exist almost anywhere—on websites and in books, videos, podcasts, and journal articles. It can also be found in the coach's or even the coachee's own experience. Your skill as a coach is marked by how you use your ability to diagnose a real need and then apply your judgment and creativity to help the coachee absorb the *right* content for them at the right time.

4. Commitment

Without commitment, goals can be achieved by "accident," but rarely by design. When someone is committed, they decide to act on what motivates them. Motivation fuels commitment. When someone is committed or dedicated, they consistently apply effort to their focus. When they find the right learning content, it usually requires a change in their behavior or a need to practice a skill or approach so they can internalize it and make it a habit.

Achieving a specific goal, or developing a new habit, usually requires practice—sometimes daily, depending on what the habit is. The compounding effect of focused, daily practice on anything is immense. Whatever the practice cadence is, the coachee needs to have the discipline and desire to find a routine that they will diligently follow for any real learning to stick.

5. Follow-through

You'll remember that follow-through is part of the Reliability element of trust. A coachee needs to begin with the proper routine for applying new knowledge, along with having a sincere commitment to following it. However, getting to the desired result requires consistent application of the routine or habit—follow-through. When disciplined and focused follow-through is practiced, the likelihood of positive results being produced is virtually guaranteed. Remember, there are more starters than finishers in life, as in many marathons, too!

A successful coaching relationship can be challenging and isn't always possible. Although coaching can be beneficial as a positive and active approach to learning and development, it won't fix every performance and conduct issue you'll likely have to deal with throughout your career as a boss. Don't let that discourage you from trying.

As a good coach, you can help guide your coachee through the coaching process. Be attentive to each of the five readiness ingredients along the way so that you make the best use of your time and effort. Whoever you are coaching may *express* a sincere desire to accept new ideas, methods, or approaches. However, despite their professed sincerity and your best efforts, they may be emotionally bound to their old habits. How (and when) they choose to deal with letting go will determine what they *will do* to follow through with what they *need to do* to truly change.

Help to Get Around the Blocks

Before focusing your attention on helping someone determine what and how something could or should be done, as a coach spend time uncovering the emotional roots of the coachee's old ways that may block new learning. These may be the real obstacles to acceptance that reinforce their habits, not your lack of teaching skills or their lack of understanding of the potential benefits.

As those blocks are removed, the coachee can then replace them with new and improved habits. To help as a coach, you don't need to be a therapist. You *do* need to be skilled at using targeted questions creatively and appropriately to help identify what the blocks are and what may be keeping them there.

Some good questions to ask are:

· How is what (or how) you're doing working for you?

· What problem or problems do you see in the way you are doing things?

· What would have to happen for you to consider changing how you are doing things now?

- What are you unsure about when you think about making a change?
- What are your doubts and concerns?
- What happened the last time you tried a similar change?
- What are the current (or anticipated) demands on your time and attention?
- What new knowledge or skills do you need to develop to be more effective?
- What change or changes could you make that would increase your effectiveness, and the like?

People's willpower, previous history, and personal circumstances can strongly influence how readily they accept and adopt any new approach, regardless of its actual merits. The more you can learn about their life experiences and how they may influence their current choices, the more effective you can be as you try to help.

Remember, how we behave is shaped by what has already worked to get us what we want and where we are. Conditioning (that is, forming habits) is a powerful outcome from what we learn. Coaches often must help people unlearn old habits and behaviors (programs) and replace them with new ones.

If you want to help people get different results, try to understand the individuals you are coaching at a deeper level. Work with them to learn why they believe what they are currently doing has worked or will continue to work for them. Try to crack that code with them. Help them, if you can, to find whatever may be blocking their ability to change. If significant blocks are not uncovered, you may waste valuable time working to guide them to develop new knowledge, skills, abilities, or habits that really won't stick, or stick for very long.

If someone is not truly ready to listen and respond to your coaching, first try to find out *why*. When your team member truly decides that what they are doing (how they are behaving) is *not* getting them what they really want or need, they are then ready for change and growth. For coaching to be effective, the coachee needs to be ready and open to receiving it.

With that said, don't give up too soon, and don't let *them* give up too quickly, either.

Part | 5

"The delegatee is responsible for the action; the delegator is accountable for the outcome."

Delegation—Ready or Not

Delegation is another example of Leading from the Side. To *delegate* means to entrust something to another. It involves giving someone the responsibility to do or manage something that is not typically part of their job. Delegation provides someone Control—one of the Four Employee Needs. Remember R-I-S-C? That is the authority and freedom to make decisions and use their judgment related to their delegated responsibility. Typically, delegation shifts decision making vertically from one organizational level to another—usually from a higher level (boss) to a lower one (direct report). However, it can also be accomplished horizontally, from one team member, or one team, to another.

Giving a team member work that is part of their specified role and duties is technically a task assignment and is not true delegation. A task and a responsibility are not the same things. Responsibilities tend to be broader in scope and sometimes more complex, requiring personal judgment and problem-solving. Responsibilities often involve completing more than one task to achieve a broader end result. Tasks are more specific "to do's" with a narrow focus that typically involves follow-through with an action to completion. Tasks are more like "check box items." You finish them, and you move on.

If you assign a person to "design a survey for the staff about the work flow," that's a task. If you direct that team member to "analyze the work flow and get back to you with recommendations," that's a responsibility. An assignment of a new responsibility is delegation.

Readiness

Readiness applies not only to coaching; it's also necessary for effective delegation. For delegation to be successful, *both* the delegator *and* the delegatee need to be ready. If you're not prepared to let go of a responsibility, or if your direct report is not ready to take it on, you can bet that the likely result will be some sort of a breakdown, or even failure. So let's look at what it means to be ready.

Your Readiness

First, consider how ready you are to *let go*. If you're not willing or able to give up a responsibility or a sufficient level of control, you may easily slip into unproductive and time-consuming micromanagement. For delegation to be effective, you have to accept (and sincerely believe) that giving someone else one of your responsibilities will free you up to focus your effort on another priority that may be a better use of your time.

To determine your readiness, some questions you might ask yourself are:

- Am I accomplishing what is most expected of me?
- What is the highest and best use of my time?
- Who can do the job instead of me?
- Who can do the job better than me?

- Who can do the job at less expense than me?
- What will be the benefit to me if I give up the responsibility?
- Could I use delegation to support the training and development of someone else?

When you're ready, you have to be willing to accept the reality that what you delegate may not be completed in the same way, with the same exact result, as if you had handled it yourself. Can you also deal with the consequences if the responsibility you delegate to someone else fails?

Here's a readiness example to consider. Monica has to submit a bid proposal for an important new client that will take many hours. She's also pressed for time to deal with other priorities and commitments. One of her team members, Jose, is familiar with the bid process and has produced a few successful proposals on his own. However, if Monica gives Jose responsibility for this bid, she's not confident that it will be done to her satisfaction level.

Monica is very concerned that if Jose misses an important detail, the result would likely be the loss of potential business. Do you think Monica is ready to delegate this responsibility to Jose?

If you can't let go and accept the result and the consequences of someone else handling a responsibility, you're not ready. When that's the case, look for other options. Instead of delegating this bid responsibility to Jose, Monica could consider delegating some of her other duties to him so that she would have more available time to work on it herself. Or she could temporarily reassign some of her workload to others so she can complete the bid proposal on time. Delegation is rarely effective for either party when the delegator is not ready.

Their Readiness

Before you delegate a responsibility, you also should consider the delegatee's readiness to accept it. Then, when you do delegate, you will have a better chance of increasing their chances of success *and* reducing your level of stress.

To assess their readiness, first consider your direct report's overall potential to take on new responsibilities, noting:

·   Strengths, skills, likes and dislikes, and life-and-work experiences

·   Career and learning objectives

·   Next steps on their career path

·   Responsibilities that would be a good fit with a reasonable amount of stretch

·   Tasks they are performing that can be discontinued, streamlined, or shifted to allow for more time to take on the new responsibility

Start by finding out more about their general background. Be curious, but first let them know *why* you want to know. Otherwise, you may be considered to be nosy—or worse. You might ask about their very first jobs, then listen and learn about what they did and why. Any job or other experience can shape, and contribute to, a person's knowledge, skill, and ability. All life experience can potentially be tapped by someone when they need to.

If you don't know much about your employee beyond what they are doing now, spend some quality time finding out! Use their résumé as a starting point to guide your inquiry. Show some sincere interest and have conversations with them so that you can truly get a better understanding of at least their professional history. But try not to come across like an overly inquisitive prosecutor.

Some relevant questions to consider are:

·   What are they good at?

·   What was their first job?

·   What previous jobs did they have that they liked? Disliked?

·   What did they learn to do when they were young?

Other questions that relate to delegating a responsibility could include:

·   What can be learned on the job that would help them achieve their objectives?

·   What have they done as part of their work, and also outside of work, to prepare for this responsibility?

- What are they doing now that has minimal impact? Can it be dropped? Who else could handle it?
- What do they most enjoy doing, and why?

Don't hesitate to find out what your team member really likes to do as you learn more about them. It's true that many jobs (and responsibilities) are far from fun. To a point, what's "fun" is subjective. Some jobs are considered to be more fun than others. When you know what people like to do, you'll be more successful matching them up to the responsibilities you have to delegate—and probably with less resistance.

Remember that every person carries with them their unique life history and experience, as well as their potential. Don't be limited by a job title or what you only see your employee knowing and doing in their current "job."

Ask them questions like these:

- What do *I* do that you could help me with?
- What do *I* do that you could do if I gave you some help?
- What do *I* do that you could do by yourself?

Be curious, and keep an open mind. Think broadly about how they might be qualified and ready to handle a responsibility, and encourage them to do the same for themselves.

Although a challenge can be motivating, be careful that you don't stretch a person too far or overload them with too many responsibilities. If you do, negative consequences may crop up in the results and the overall quality of their work. You could also create longer-lasting issues and problems that may impact their morale—and yours!

Remember that delegation can be most effective when you are ready to give up a responsibility and when your team member is ready to take it on.

Delegation Approach

Whether you are assigning responsibility (delegating) or providing direction for an assignment (leading), be sure that you provide clear expectations or standards of performance at the start. One of the most common problems with delegation is incomplete information upfront.

The key questions you should provide answers to are as follows:

· What is to be done?
· How much?
· How well?
· By when? (Be realistic.)
· With whom?
· What are the limits on their decision-making authority (control)?
· When should they ask for help?

Use the Delegation Planning Checklist (*Figure 11.9*) to help you consider the most significant delegation factors.

Delegation Planning Checklist

- ☐ What is the assignment/responsibility being delegated?
- ☐ What are the expected results?
- ☐ What are the performance standards—qualitative and quantitative?
- ☐ What is the time frame for completion? What are the milestone due dates?
- ☐ Who else can the employee work with to complete the assignment?
- ☐ Is this the right person for this assignment? Why? How do you know?
- ☐ Is the employee interested in the assignment?
- ☐ Does the employee have the required skills and/or experience?
- ☐ Does the employee's current workload allow them adequate time to be successful?
- ☐ Does the employee need any specific training to be successful?
- ☐ What resources are needed?
- ☐ What information is needed?
- ☐ What support is needed?
- ☐ What control (authority) is needed?
- ☐ What decisions can they make?
- ☐ What related decisions do you want to make?
- ☐ Can the risk(s) be managed if the employee fails? What is Plan "B"?
- ☐ What do you expect the employee will gain from completing this assignment (i.e., new skills)?
- ☐ How and when should the employee come to you with problems or issues?
- ☐ Is it clear to others that this assignment has been delegated?
- ☐ Are others clear about the level of authority the employee has to complete the assignment?
- ☐ How and when will the employee report on progress?
- ☐ How and when will you provide feedback and coaching?
- ☐ Does the employee clearly understand all of the expectations for the assignment/responsibility? How do you know?
- ☐ Did the employee openly commit to taking on the responsibility along with the due dates?

Figure 11.9

Clarify your instructions and always solicit feedback from your team member. Review the objectives of the responsibility as well as their proposed plan of action, any potential obstacles, and ways to avoid or deal with these obstacles. Be sure your direct report understands the desired results (*what* to accomplish, not *how*), the guidelines to follow, the available resources, and the consequences to expect at the end (both the positives *and* the negatives).

A delegated responsibility does not have to involve completely giving away responsibility. Depending on the levels of readiness (yours *and* theirs), it may be best to start slow and easy. When possible, it's okay—and even advisable—to provide a direct report with only some of the responsibility you have to give, until their competence and your confidence both increase. You can then give more responsibility to them in stages when both of you are more ready (see *Figure 11.10*).

Delegation Ladder

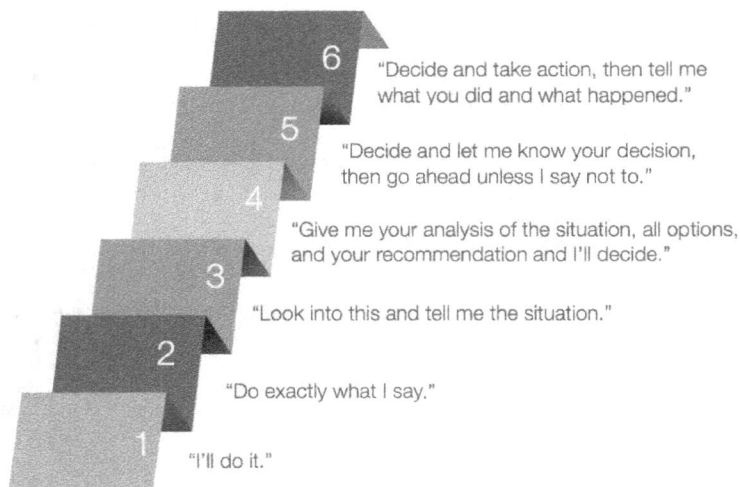

6 "Decide and take action, then tell me what you did and what happened."

5 "Decide and let me know your decision, then go ahead unless I say not to."

4 "Give me your analysis of the situation, all options, and your recommendation and I'll decide."

3 "Look into this and tell me the situation."

2 "Do exactly what I say."

1 "I'll do it."

Figure 11.10

One of your objectives for effective delegation should be to help your direct report learn and build their capacity. Remember to encourage them to use their judgment and problem-solving ability. Avoid making decisions that they can make themselves. Support their decisions regarding the methods they choose (the "how"), even if they differ from yours, if you believe they will produce the desired results. Always focus on the results, and try to stay out of the way.

When handled effectively, letting go of a responsibility can be a much more effective use of your time and resources, allowing you to reallocate where you focus your attention and effort. Do what you can to delegate significant responsibilities and whole projects to the lowest possible organizational level that makes sense from a readiness standpoint. Once you delegate, allow your team members to make and fix mistakes whenever possible. If you do, they'll learn more and build greater confidence to take on future assignments.

Regarding resources, be sure you make every attempt you reasonably can to provide what's needed by your delegatee. Resources include time, materials, equipment, space, budget, and maybe even staff if required. Remember that you're also a potential resource. Be available to provide your support and guidance, as necessary.

Follow-Up

Remember who is ultimately accountable for your delegated responsibility. That's right, *you* are! Your delegatee is responsible for the action; you are accountable for the outcome. You own it. Remember and accept that fact, especially if they fail.

If you blame your team member for a failure related to a responsibility that *you* delegated, you'll lose both their respect and the respect of your boss—if your boss is principled. And you will have proven that you aren't a good boss, either. Conversely, if you generously give your direct report credit for a successful outcome, you'll gain respect and probably their loyalty as well.

As part of your delegation process, work with the delegatee and agree on a feedback loop. Make clear what you have to be informed of. Follow up regularly on the progress of the delegated responsibility. Set realistic milestone times or dates so that you can be ready to make adjustments in response to any unforeseen problems without having to be reactive. It's always a good approach to "trust but verify." In other words, follow up.

How often you follow up should depend on:

- Complexity of the responsibility
- Importance and risk level of the responsibility
- Your experience with the individual (for example, if they have a proven track record of completing similar projects, then you may not need to follow up as often as you might with someone else)

Be sure that you provide positive as well as negative value-added feedback along the way. Let your team member know what they're doing well and what they could do to improve—long before the end result. Remember, feedback accelerates learning, so use the experience of taking on a delegated responsibility as a learning and coaching opportunity for your direct report.

Becoming a skilled and effective delegator will also help you be more productive and successful as a manager or leader. It's well worth learning to be patient and learning to let go if you want to be an effective boss. Even though you might be able to do things better than your direct report, delegating a responsibility to them can help them develop and grow by increasing their skills, abilities, experience, and confidence.

As your team members develop, so too will your capacity to take on more. You can then decide if you want to use that added capacity to take on a more-expanded role yourself, pursue a promotion, or do something else. You can also choose to use any extra time to focus on other priorities you may have been putting off.

Delegating doesn't come easily to every boss. Still, it's always worth attempting delegation when you Lead from the Side, as long as you consider readiness and refer to the Delegation Planning Checklist questions. If you're new to managing, expect your delegation approach to not always result in immediate success. You'll learn from your experience, just as your delegatee will learn from theirs. Don't be discouraged as you're learning the best approach to take. Be willing to practice at it and positive results will follow.

Part | 6

"The one-on-one is the most important meeting you have."

One-on-Ones **Are #1**

Without a doubt, the one-on-one meeting should be the most important meeting you have at work. This applies whether it's the one-on-one you have with your direct report or the one-on-one you have with your manager. These meetings should be regularly scheduled, dedicated times that allow for meaningful communication between a manager and their employee.

If you believe, as I hope you do, that the manager-employee relationship is fundamental for a healthy and high-functioning team and organization, maintaining effective one-on-one communication should be a top priority. Conducting productive and regular one-on-one meetings is one of the essential actions you can take as a boss. You can start by putting your smartphone away when your meeting begins!

Although this meeting should be primarily for your team member's benefit, as the boss you must commit to ensuring that the one-on-one meeting actually happens! In your position, you can approach your direct report whenever you wish, throughout the day, week, or month. However, for your direct report, the one-on-one meeting may be the only opportunity they have for consistent, focused time with you. Make that time a priority for both of you.

The one-on-one meeting is also an effective, impactful approach to Leading from the Side because it involves relationship-building, which really means trust-building. The time you allocate for one-on-ones will likely be one of the best time investments you can make.

Purpose of One-on-Ones

An effective one-on-one meeting is different than an informal "drive-by meet-up." The drive-by is when you decide to go to someone's workspace or reach out to them to give direction, ask a question, or share information. There's nothing wrong with drive-by communication by the boss. And no doubt a lot of productive day-to-day work is handled in this casual, spontaneous way. But when it's the *only* type of contact a direct report can expect to have with their manager, that may eventually become a problem.

The one-on-one should be a more-formal meeting that you have with each one of your employees—individually. "Formal" doesn't have to mean stiff and stuffy. The meeting can have a casual and comfortable tone and can also occur in an informal location (even virtually as long as you both have video on). If there's agreement, it can even happen over coffee, breakfast, or lunch in a quiet setting so that both of you can be more efficient with your time. (Everybody has to eat sometime!) Wherever it happens, it should have some structure, with an agenda.

Remember the Four Employee Needs, R-I-S-C (Resources, Information, Support, and Control)? The one-on-one meeting allows the boss a specific time to check in with each employee to see if they are getting what they need to be effective and successful. The meeting itself is a way to provide Support—that is, if you truly probe, listen, and respond.

If your employee has unmet needs, use this meeting to find out more and discuss those needs with them in more detail. As always, if and when it's appropriate, let them know *why* you can't give them what they need so that they aren't left guessing. Treat them like an adult.

In addition to determining what your employees may need, your objectives in the one-on-one should be to:

- Track the status of their Performance and Development Goals.

- Learn if there are obstacles to goal achievement that may need to be removed.

- Discuss specific issues—the employee's, yours, or even both— that may be affecting their work.

- Provide Value-Added Feedback.

- Provide targeted coaching.

- Share information with each other about the unit and the overall organization.

- Find out about their current level of morale, stress, and other related factors.

Timing

In most cases, one-on-one meetings should be scheduled every two weeks, ideally a year in advance, to ensure that the meetings get on and stay on the calendar. This allows for planned, frequent, individualized communication—by design. If a one-on-one meeting needs to be canceled due to an overriding commitment by either one of you, no more than about a month should go by between meetings.

Most one-on-one meetings should typically last about 30 minutes. Longer or more-frequent meetings can be scheduled as needed. A good rule of thumb is to spend about 10 minutes for their reports and updates; 10 minutes for your responses, feedback, or coaching; and 10 minutes for sharing information and wrap-up.

Approach

It's good to flip the responsibility and have your direct report lead the one-on-one meetings. Let them know that you expect them to bring the specific issues, challenges, opportunities, and ideas *they* want to discuss. When your team member feels directly involved by leading the meeting, they can have a greater sense of ownership (engagement). With this approach, you'll likely find more-active participation in these meetings that, with any luck, will lead to greater job satisfaction and better results over time— for everyone.

See the "One-on-One Meeting Template" (*Figure 11.11*) to help guide your direct reports to prepare the specific content or agenda for each meeting. You can always add your topics for a particular one-on-one as the need arises, either before or during the meeting.

One-on-One Meeting Template

Connection/Check-In

1. Performance and Development Goals - Status/Updates
High level description and detail, if necessary
- Are the goals on track? If not, why not?
- What are the challenges? Changes? Successes?

2. Other Action Items or Projects (If any)
High level description and detail, if necessary
- What important information needs to be communicated?
- What obstacles may be in the way?
- What control, support and/or resources may be needed?

3. Value-Added Feedback
What should continue or change?

4. Coaching Support
- What needs to be learned?
- What guidance or help is needed?
- What challenges or issues need to be addressed?
- What expectations need to be clarified?

5. Other Business
Two-way sharing of information
- What Unit, Departmental or Organizational information or updates should be shared (including rumors)?

6. Agreements/Next Steps
Who (employee or manager) is responsible for doing what by when?

Figure 11.11

Have your direct report bring two copies of the agenda to the meeting—one for each of you to review and follow. (They could also email your copy in advance.) This is an effective way to help your team member lead the meeting and keep both of you on track.

Consider using your copy of the agenda (paper or digital) to record notes, observations, next steps, and the like. I've found that this makes it very easy to track these meetings' takeaways without creating more paperwork or documents. Your agenda copy could be saved, scanned, and uploaded to your employee's digital file for future reference and follow-up after the meeting.

Connection

Start each meeting with the same opening question to allow the employee to share what's on their mind at the moment. Pay attention to how they respond, however insignificant their answer may sound. A simple, familiar question like "How's it going?" when asked the same way at each meeting may elicit an answer that can indicate any positive or negative patterns that may be developing that you should pay attention to. Even if they answer your standard opening question the same way (like with "Everything's fine, thanks"), actively listen and observe if they sound or appear more or less enthusiastic, concerned, attentive, focused, worried, satisfied, or whatever. Any differences in tone or delivery that you pick up on can be early and useful indicators of changes in their morale. Changes that you may be able to address before they become bigger issues!

Goal Status Reports and Updates

In these one-on-one meetings, you should expect brief, high-level status reports as well as updates for their goals, so that you get answers to questions like:

· Is the goal on track? If not, why not?

· What are the challenges to the goal achievement?

· What's changed, and why?

· What new priorities may affect the continued relevance or achievement of the goal?

· Which successes are related to the goal?

Learn what you need to stay informed about their goal progress, and use this meeting to offer help and support where needed.

Significant Action Items or Projects

When you think it's necessary, take time to drill down to discuss specifics. Reinforce the "no surprises" rule. This includes encouraging them to share any important information that you should know so you can be kept informed about issues or changes that may affect the completion of what your employees are working on. It's on you to make them feel *safe* to share the bad news along with the good news. If they don't feel safe to share failures or missteps with you, you may be unpleasantly surprised later by finding out about them from others—like your boss!

As with the Goal Updates, this agenda topic is another opportunity to offer help with what they may need (Resources, Information, Support, and Control). If more time is required to understand the situation, schedule another follow-up meeting to drill deeper if it can't wait until the next scheduled one-on-one meeting.

Value-Added Feedback

You can also use the one-on-one meetings to provide positive or negative feedback, as needed, to communicate or reinforce expectations, or discuss the quality of the work they recently performed. Remember that effective feedback is timely. You shouldn't wait for the scheduled one-one-meeting to deliver your Value-Added Feedback if you believe it would be more useful to deliver it to your team member sooner.

Coaching Support

The one-on-one meeting can also be a good opportunity to briefly coach your direct report by discussing other work-related problems, or even some personal challenges if appropriate. For coaching needs that require more time, schedule a separate meeting—just don't rush things. Your overall objective should be to focus on how you can help each team member succeed.

Here are the types of questions you might ask that may be useful as part of a one-on-one meeting:

- Tell me about your week.
- What have you been working on since we last met?
- Are you on track to meet the deadline...?
- How are you going to approach this?
- What can you (or we) do differently next time?
- What didn't go as well as you (or we) had hoped?
- What have you learned about this area of responsibility or project?
- What questions do you have about...?
- What suggestions do you have?
- What tasks are you ahead of (or behind on)?

You can always use this time to ask the three key questions that you ask "owners" to keep them engaged:

- What do you think?
- What do you need?
- How can I help?

Other Business

You and the employee should *both* share unit, departmental, or organizational information or updates. This information could include what's been heard informally through the "grapevine" and also what's been communicated through formal channels, like your management meetings. Examples of information could consist of "the buzz" about upcoming changes as well as other news about the latest policies or directives.

When people are kept up-to-date and informed about what's going on around them, their feeling of involvement increases. Effective bosses make an effort to keep all lines of communication open— both informal *and* formal. Remember, since your relationship with your team member should be a most important one, invest time to engage them in what's going on, and be sure to actively listen.

The one-on-one meeting might also be a chance for you to learn about more significant personal issues that may currently or potentially affect your direct report's job performance or work experience. Use your judgment when personal issues become part of the conversation. This may be a good opportunity to remind the employee to consider the benefits of your Employee Assistance Program (EAP) if you have one.

Agreements/Next Steps

At the end of the one-on-one meeting, your employee should briefly summarize what's been discussed and agreed to. This is a good developmental practice for the team member that will also let you know how effective the communication is between you. Before the one-on-meeting ends, there should be no misunderstandings—only clarity about who is responsible for doing what. This means that your direct report should know what they are expected to do, and by when.

Also, let the employee know what you will be following up with them on, and also what *you* will commit to doing, and when. Always have a deadline or due date for any action required, to ensure accountability—for both yourself and your direct report.

When you invest your time in maintaining scheduled one-on-one meetings with your team members, you'll find that you will consistently be in a good position to take any actions needed. You'll also be better informed and aware of all the factors and indicators associated with the Boss Triad—Trust, Needs, and Morale. And, in more ways than one, that means *everything*!

Part 7

Recognition and Loyalty

Recognition is a significant form of Support—one of the Four Employee Needs. Showing that you value someone should be standard operating procedure (S.O.P.) for a boss, regardless of what you do or where you do it. Most everyone appreciates getting an "attaboy!" or "attagirl!" acknowledgment, especially from their boss. It's a simple, straightforward form of recognition. Providing sincere recognition can be powerful because it helps your direct report feel valued—and supported. Feeling valued is also a core emotional need that for most people extends beyond work.

At work, most people desire to do their best. When you're the boss, giving recognition shows that you notice them and their work. It signals that you acknowledge the effort and the accomplishments of your team member.

For recognition to be effective, it must be authentic, genuine, and relevant.

———

Some useful recognition efforts can be program-oriented, like employee-of-the-year or team-of-the-month awards, bonuses, or other acknowledgments. Others can be more individualized, such as appreciation notes, shout-outs in company get-togethers, gift cards, and the like.

You can spend all sorts of time coming up with creative ways to show recognition and appreciation. However, don't forget the simplest method: say a sincere "thank you!" whenever you can. An honest, unrushed, and personal "thank you" can work better than anything else you might do.

Loyalty Starts with Recognition

Loyalty Cycle

Figure 11.12

When you consistently recognize your direct report's positive behavior or effective performance, it can start the Loyalty Cycle (*Figure 11.12*). A team member who feels noticed and acknowledged can begin to develop an ownership mentality linked to their job and, by extension, to their company or organization.

As was discussed earlier in this book, a team member who feels like an owner is more actively engaged and involved in what he is doing and how he is doing it. An active engagement level also contributes to high morale for your employee when they are recognized for their accomplishments and believe that what they are doing has meaning. An employee with high morale tends to produce consistently high-quality work or service because they care *and* feel cared for. High-quality work or service also leads to greater recognition from others, and so the Loyalty Cycle continues.

Have you ever felt really loyal to a boss or a company? How did you behave when you felt that way? As a leader, how important is it to you to have loyal followers? If you truly want your employees to be loyal, don't underestimate the importance of providing them with recognition when you are Leading from the Side.

Remember to be timely with recognition, just like with feedback. If you wait too long to acknowledge positive performance, the impact can be reduced, which won't keep the Loyalty Cycle moving forward. Investing time and energy in cultivating loyal employees pays off in multiple ways.

When your team member feels loyal, he or she becomes a positive force within your organization as well as a positive face to your clients and customers. Loyal employees can also help attract potential future talent to your team and organization by spreading the word to friends and colleagues about how they feel. Loyalty is positively contagious.

Whether or not you have loyal employees on board is probably the most meaningful metric for how successful your organization is— and how effective you are as the boss!

Leading from the Side (Summary)

Some tips to remember:

- Build a personal connection and rapport with people—one-on-one—so you can build trust and relationships more quickly and deeply.

- People are imperfect and complicated, as is communication itself. Therefore, be more mindful, deliberate, repetitive, and forgiving.

- Communication often goes sideways due to mistaken assumptions made about other people's intentions. Always check your assumptions when you're not clear, especially when the relationship matters.

- Active listening requires a deliberate focus—verbally, physically, and emotionally—on what the other person is communicating. Be sure they feel heard.

- When employees are engaged at work, they think and act like *owners*.

- Fun is an antidote for stress. Find ways to make work more fun when you can.

- Make people feel safe to share the information they have with you in a timely manner and openly.

- Stop delivering the "sandwich" when you want to give feedback—use the Value-Added Feedback model instead.

- If you cannot give someone roughly 80% positive to 20% negative feedback, you likely have a problem employee that you need to deal with.

- Think and act like a good coach if you want to be a good boss.

- Develop your emotional intelligence to increase your leadership and coaching skills.

- Your coaching approach should always be focused on the person being helped, not your own needs.

- Guide your coachee to develop, trust in, and apply their own knowledge, skills, insights, and judgment to their work.

- Determine if your coachee is genuinely ready to be coached before you invest too much time and effort.

- For delegation to be successful, both the delegator and the delegatee need to be ready.

- Use delegation to help your direct report learn and build their capacity to take on more responsibilities.

- The one-on-one is the most important meeting you have. Be sure to make it a regularly scheduled and structured meeting with each one of your employees.

- Consistently recognize and acknowledge your direct report's positive behavior or effective performance, to start the Loyalty Cycle.

Chapter | **12**

Leading from the Rear

The best leaders are agile and can readily shift from one leadership perspective to the other, as needed, to get and keep their followers moving forward. Let's quickly review the Three Perspectives for Leaders before I cover this last one in more detail.

When you're effective as a leader, you first *Lead from the Front* by inspiring your team to follow you. You use your skills and approaches to help your team members see and own the vision and to help them set goals to realize it. When you succeed here, a follower or two will likely also become a leader of others.

Then, as you *Lead from the Side*, you build personal relationships with your employees and focus on gaining their trust. Here, you do everything you can to give your direct reports what they need to be successful. Eventually, your efforts can result in more followers who become loyal.

After leading from the other two perspectives, you step back and try and stay out of the way to let your team do their jobs, which should lead to their accomplishing the chosen goals on their own while you mainly focus on the bigger picture. This is the third perspective, *Leading from the Rear*.

Leading from the Rear can require patience and discipline to periodically stop reacting to what's around you to see and assess what lies ahead. This perspective is proactive as well as strategic. It involves seeing the goals and path ahead and determining what's needed to ensure that your followers continue to follow and achieve the goals.

Nelson Mandela, in his 1994 autobiography, *Long Walk to Freedom*, labeled a leader who leads from behind a "shepherd." A shepherd looks ahead and stays aware as he or she guides "the flock." A shepherd protects and Leads from the Rear.

When you Lead from the Rear, you not only look all around to see the bigger picture, you also look to see opportunities for others to move up to the *front*, and become leaders as well. When possible, you help create those opportunities.

In my earlier example of the trail leader, if (or when) the group builds momentum and is moving along down the trail and over the mountain toward the fresh lake, the primary leader should now have the confidence in the team overall to be able to fall back even farther to the end of the line. From there, the leader can look ahead toward the team members and get an idea of the group's overall pace and progress as they move forward to the goal or goals.

It's usually a lot clearer from the rear than from the front or side to see who on the trail is falling behind and who may need some additional help to get in line or keep up. If you are truly paying attention, you can decide to move back up to the second perspective (Leading from the Side) and deal with whoever needs your help or support.

Leaders who always Lead from the Front (or even from the Side) may only see their committed followers, or those who may pretend to be following. Consequently, they can overlook others on the team who could be struggling to perform or to follow, for some reason or other. Such leaders may even develop an illusion or a blind spot that everyone is on board and following them, when in fact that isn't true.

A lousy boss with little interest in actually leading may not really care about the existence of "stragglers" or worry about whether or not they are following. I hope that's not you!

I once encountered a well-meaning midmanager early in his career, whom I'll call Stuart. He had two staff members, Jacob and Uma, who were not performing at the level they needed to in their roles. They were not clear about the unit's goals and what Stuart expected of them. Unfortunately, Stuart never really spent any meaningful time checking in with them or reviewing their progress. And they never felt safe enough to tell him about their struggles.

Stuart assumed that "no news was good news," so he continued to focus most of his attention on the work being done by those who were more vocal and whom he could more easily see from his position at the "front." What eventually happened? Discord within the team.

Two of his high performers, Sophia and Liam, eventually began to resent Jacob and Uma because they were not completing their work on time and meeting the team's deadlines. Stuart made things worse by overlooking Jacob and Uma's performance and assigning

Sophia and Liam additional work because he knew they could handle it. This wasn't a problem at first. However, day by day this created a significant issue (resentment) within the team—involving the Morale Factor of Justice/Fairness.

To the surprise of some, Sophia and Liam—the high performers—decided that they had better options and ended up leaving the company (they really left their boss, Stuart) to work for a competitor. This left Stuart with a significant and unexpected staff turnover problem that he could have prevented had he paid more attention to the entire team by operating within all three leadership perspectives. If he had, he would have been willing to step back and invest more time addressing Jacob and Uma's Information and Support needs early on. Reflecting on this experience, Stuart eventually learned a critical lesson about effective leadership, the importance of Leading from the Rear.

By stepping back and moving to the rear, you will be in a better position to see more and with more clarity. You have greater context with better vision that lets you focus on the goal ahead. You can also be more strategic, objective, and proactive with your decisions, because you are not too close to the goal—or too close to the others in your group. This Third Perspective puts you in a less-biased position to decide if changes are needed to respond to current circumstances. You've probably heard about being "in the weeds" more than once. Leading from the Rear can help keep you "out of the weeds."

Back to the trail leader example. You can see bad weather heading toward the lake area when you are at the rear, because you are far enough away from it. When you're at the front, you may be deep in the forest, or at least up against it, and can have more difficulty seeing what's ahead because of the trees!

Depending on your assessment of the situation, you might even decide to change the day's plan and head in another direction. In other words, you might choose to change the goal. From this Third Perspective, you can determine if you are best needed to move back to Leading from the Front so that you can communicate to the entire group that the goal has changed.

Here's an example of Leading from the Rear that doesn't take place in the woods!

Imagine a situation where your goal at the beginning of the year had been to achieve 15% growth in market share over the year. Each member of your team was focused on that goal and has been working on their action plans for achieving it. Now it's the end of the second quarter, and the information you're receiving from a very reliable industry contact points to a recession beginning in your business. This would be an opportune time to reconsider the goal and probably establish and communicate a new or revised one for the team to focus on. In other words, you go back to Leading from the Front. From that perspective, you can make any necessary adjustments required and can reset the vision and direction for your followers. And so on, leading through all Three Perspectives.

The activities associated with Leading from the Rear can have a critical impact on the execution of work, including the quality and quantity of what gets done. Remember what I described in an earlier chapter about the importance of simplifying? Effective bosses keep things simple and help their teams focus on finishing. "Finishing" means completing the tasks as expected, achieving the goals, and realizing the vision. Many of the activities needed for effectively Leading from the Rear also require good management skills to get positive results. And choosing and using the most appropriate style and approach for the person, team, and situation necessitates good leadership skills.

In short, better bosses practice Active Performance Management.

Part | 1

"Aim for performance results to occur by design, not by accident or luck."

Active Performance **Management**

The activities associated with the Three Perspectives for Leaders include all those commonly understood to be part of best-practice performance management. Performance management is generally considered to be a cyclical (typically annual) process involving goal setting, feedback, and coaching, along with tracking and evaluating performance outcomes.

Most of us humans follow cycles. Daily, weekly, monthly, and even annual cycles. By their very nature, cycles refresh. Adhering to a cycle enables us to begin again and to reset. It also brings an end to whatever has been started that may turn out to be ineffective. The Performance Management Cycle (see *Figure 12.1*) should *begin* with performance planning and goal setting—not end with it. Feedback and coaching are critical during this cycle. If handled appropriately, an annual performance review and evaluation/appraisal can provide real value to bringing a formal close and end to a performance cycle. If not, they can be a waste of time. You probably know that already.

Performance Management Cycle

Figure 12.1

Unfortunately, far too many annual reviews tend to be avoided, pushed off, or rushed. Consequently, they are perceived to have little value and are mostly dreaded by the direct report *and* the manager. In recent years, a trend has developed of dropping annual performance reviews entirely, in favor of an expectation for managers to provide continuous feedback to their direct reports with less structure and formality. If that actually happens consistently, it *might* be effective. However, as of now, I'm not convinced that completely eliminating the annual performance review is the best answer to a flawed performance management system or practice.

Although I appreciate the frustrations experienced by everyone involved, the annual review process doesn't have to "suck." I maintain that effective annual performance reviews can be useful in bringing performance management around full circle, with an informative end that leads to a more positive beginning of the new cycle.

Before deciding to scrap the review, I believe each organization should make a concerted effort to revise and update their performance review and evaluation process, forms, and training needs to improve their usefulness. Even though a lot of improvement may be needed, just be cautious about adopting too quickly what seems an "easier" solution. Consider working with your HR or People professionals to fix what you already have in place, so that you can try and leverage the value of the performance management cycle for *everyone's* benefit.

Although I have provided many recommendations for how to do this to my clients over the years, I won't be covering how to conduct an effective performance review and evaluation in this book. Each organization has to determine for itself how to handle it. Regardless of what the process is, I will emphasize the one iron-clad rule to follow: "no surprises!" You can do this by always providing regular, consistent feedback *and* coaching throughout the year.

Let's move on to other aspects of good management.

Effective performance management must be active, not passive. As a better boss, you should aim for performance results to occur by design, not by accident or luck.

I use the term "Active Performance Management" to reinforce your role as a boss in the overall process. Active Performance Management is a *proactive* focus on continually supporting in what ways and how well the work is to be done by your direct reports. Being able to move fluidly between the Three Perspectives, as needed, enables you as manager to be adept at Active Performance Management.

In earlier chapters, I've described the purpose, importance, and approaches for SMART goal setting, as well as value-added feedback and coaching. Those are Active Performance Management practices that should occur when you're Leading from the Front *and* Leading from the Side. What comes next are five critical activities that are part of Leading from the Rear when you're the boss:

1. Strategizing
2. Organizing Accountable Work

3. Supporting Action
4. Tracking and Adjusting Performance
5. Taking Corrective Action (when needed)

If you are effective and consistent, each of these activities also supports your ability to be effective when Leading from the Front and Leading from the Side.

1. Strategizing

A strategy is a broad plan that justifies and guides all actions (or tactics) linked to it. Strategizing is about seeing the big picture (goal) and determining how best to act on it. The strategies you choose should reflect your intent or purpose at a given time and should be changed as needed to respond to current circumstances.

Here's a simple example of a strategy with a related tactic or action to support it:

> **Strategy** — "Grow percentage of sales from new products."
>
> **Action (Tactic)** — "Train the salesforce to better understand the features and benefits of each new product."

When you Lead from the Rear, you have a better vantage point to see ahead and decide on the best strategy to keep everyone moving forward. Unlike Leading from the Front, this view is likely to be more focused on the immediate (here and now) tactical actions and urgent needs.

Big-picture thinking, as is needed in both management and leadership, is optimized by focusing on both efficiency and effectiveness when developing strategies (and tactics) for you and your team.

Efficiency vs. Effectiveness

Efficiency relates to how you make the best use of the available time, effort, and resources. Effectiveness, by contrast, is about what works to produce the result you want.

In most situations, management and leadership success is determined by decisions you make to strike the right balance between efficiency and effectiveness.

Sometimes you'll have to prioritize one over another. For example, you may correctly believe that the design of technology, as well as of many of its processes, is highly efficient. However, if your team members are not willing or able to *use* the technology or processes provided, they are mostly ineffective—no matter how beneficial (and efficient) you may think they are. Do you agree?

When you're the boss, occasionally you'll have to invest time to persuade and sell the benefits of your ideas. Sometimes you'll also have to provide training to your followers to help them realize the efficiency *and* effectiveness in how the work should be done.

For example, some people will need more training to understand how and why specific means and methods (processes) apply to their job. Others may need to be convinced of the value of using a particular tool or technology to overcome whatever resistance they may have to adopting it. As you select tools and technology or improve your processes, be sure to pay attention to the needs of the people who will be directly affected: the users.

To keep moving forward, here are some specific best practices you should apply with a strategic mind-set as you Lead from the Rear.

Information Gathering

Don't wait passively for information to magically pop up on your laptop or mobile device. Be proactive and find it yourself! Look, listen, and learn. The quality of your goals, plans, and actions will ultimately be determined by the value and timeliness of the information you notice, collect, and process. Effective leaders who have a strategic mind-set are consistently active information seekers and information consumers.

Here are some likely information sources:

· Feedback from customers and clients

· Existing (and previous) strategic plans for your organization

· Global and industry trends

· Industry data and opinions

- Media in all forms (for example, podcasts, periodicals, newsletters, videos)
- Opinions and insights of thought leaders—from any field
- Peer input
- Previous lessons learned
- Your boss's goals
- Your organization's existing measurements (including financial, performance, employee satisfaction, and others)

Become an expert at crafting and asking the right questions to elicit the information you need to make effective strategic decisions. (This is also required for effective coaching, as you have learned.) Try to be aware of and curious about what you don't know—and please do not allow your ego to get in the way. Be creative in finding the best sources of information for your particular need. And, of course, look to and listen to those people around you whom you trust.

At times you'll have to dig deeper and wider to find other reliable sources to get the information you need, when you need it. Of course, there's always Google and the like to satisfy your immediate and general curiosity. However, try to cast a wider net for a variety of viewpoints, because it's always better to have multiple sources to inform you. You may be surprised and pleased by what nuggets you can find when you make an effort to dig deeper.

Remember that information is an essential need for every employee. So be generous and regularly share useful information with your direct reports. Ensure that they always have what they need to know, as you help them strategize to meet their goals. Encourage them to also be discerning, and to filter the information they consume, as well.

With that said, know when you have sufficient information to move forward. Know when enough is enough. Otherwise, you and your team may fail to act quickly enough because of overthinking and become afflicted with "analysis paralysis."

Finding information will *not*, however, be your number-one challenge. Determining whether the information is actually useful—and how—will likely be a more significant concern. Use your judgment and critical thinking to filter and assess the information you gather. Since a lot of internet content is unvetted, take an extra step to check on sources, and use common sense before you accept data that purports to be "fact." When a leader succumbs to believing and acting on what turns out to be erroneous information, the team can get into real trouble.

Review

When you're strategizing, invest time to review what's already working—and what isn't. Do changes need to be made? If so, what are they, and what difference will they potentially make? The Start, Stop, and Continue process is a simple and highly effective method for reviewing performance and results at any level, whether individual, team, or larger organization. I have successfully used this straightforward approach countless times with many groups and teams.

Here's one example. When working with executive teams to help them prepare for their strategic planning processes, I tape three flip charts on the wall—labeled "Start," "Stop," and "Continue." I then have each team member write on a sticky note their responses in each of these categories. When they're done, the three flip charts contain the collective thoughts of everyone on the team—quickly gathered.

The team then does a "gallery walk" over to each chart to read what was written and decide what that data is telling them. An open discussion follows that's centered around things like the themes, the differences, the disconnects, the "aha!" moments, and so on. The team then references this shared information to begin their strategic planning.

Depending on your purpose and the time available, consider giving people a heads-up about the process so that they have more time to collect their thoughts before committing them to the sticky notes. You could describe the Start-Stop-Continue process on the meeting agenda, or even send the categories and questions to them as a pre-work exercise.

In addition to using what you gather by the Start-Stop-Continue approach, you will likely have other data points and metrics within your organization that you should review to measure progress. Help provide your direct reports with any information they can reasonably use for their individual reflection, especially client feedback.

Encourage your team to review their own performance periodically throughout the year. Why couldn't your direct reports also apply the Start-Stop-Continue approach? Whatever they do to reflect on their progress, don't have them wait until year-end when performance evaluations are due.

Use what works. However, don't make the review process or any other process you use too complicated. Simplify.

Planning

Good planning is an essential part of strategizing. It involves identifying the steps or path to take to reach the goal or goals. Action planning is an integral part of the SMART goal-setting process for both organizations and individual contributors. Effective plans identify the specific tasks that need to be completed, and by whom, with clear time lines and accurate resource requirements.

Effective planning also involves using good data after you've gathered it. Some data can be empirical or fact-based, and some will be subjective or anecdotal. The data you choose to use will impact your decisions, plans, and ultimately the direction in which you lead your unit. As I described above, a better boss determines what data to rely on and what to ignore or minimize.

With effective plans in place, a road map can then be followed by your team members, who are accountable for the performance results defined by the assigned goal or strategy. I'll cover this in the next section, "Accountable Work."

Although planning may not seem sexy, make it a regular, *strategizing* activity that you do when you Lead from the Rear. It can help to guide the modification (or development) of the Vision, Goals, and Actions when you need to go forward again to Lead from the Front.

Adjustment

As you continually gather information, you should review what's been done, plan your strategies, and make whatever adjustments you need to keep moving—even incrementally. Be willing to ask yourself, "Do the goals, priorities, plans, and expectations still apply as originally intended?" And if not, what needs to change—and why?

If an adjustment is needed, you don't necessarily need to give up on or change your goals and plans completely. Maybe you just need to go slower or go smaller. Your initial focus could be too broad or too general. Or you may need to be more targeted with your effort. Whatever adjustments you decide to make, what's most important is maintaining progress toward your desired results.

Apply the same thinking to support your team members as they are guided by their individual goals and strategies. Along with information gathering, planning, and reviewing, use coaching to help them to examine which adjustments they need to make to maintain or improve their progress.

It's extremely easy to get distracted or even derailed by urgent needs that aren't necessarily aligned with longer-term priorities and goals. Sometimes the most difficult decision you have to make is what to say "no" to. When you're an effective boss, you don't want your direct reports to be just *busy*. You want them to be busy doing the right things. Of course, the same objective should also be true for you.

Be flexible, and don't allow yourself to be rigidly locked into a strategy or plan without reconsidering it. Continue to look, listen, and learn. Making needed adjustments is how effective leaders stay on the appropriate course to successfully respond to the existing conditions and anticipated changes.

Be careful that your ego doesn't get in the way of what should be done to keep the team moving forward. An effective leader is not diminished by the willingness to make a change or an adjustment when needed—in fact, the opposite is true. The best bosses possess the courage and the confidence to make a change when necessary and don't allow themselves to get defensive as a way of avoiding "failures." Accept that every decision you make or solution you create will not be successful. Don't let your ego get you stuck. Keep moving forward!

To keep it simple: pay attention to the big picture, stay informed, adjust your strategy as needed, and always keep open lines of communication between you and your direct reports.

2. Organizing Accountable Work

Accountability means taking ownership for results and for the consequences (positive or negative) of the actions that produce the results. Accountable work means work that's "owned" by a specific person or team performing it. It should be clear by now that overall accountability starts and ends with you as the boss. To be a better boss, be ultimately accountable for your team's results, especially the negative ones. As you lead others through the Three Perspectives, do everything you can to support your team members to be accountable, as well.

Can we agree that much of the work expected to be performed in many jobs today involves interdependence? That means teamwork. We usually can't do it all ourselves, even though many of us prefer to! We often need others to get our work done successfully.

Ownership (alias "accountability") can be shared, and that requires reliance on other people to follow up or follow through with their part of the assignment or project. Have you ever worked on a significant project when two or more people were equally responsible for the overall results? Did you have any regrets about the outcome, despite your best efforts? Well, you're not alone.

Here's an example that may be familiar. Min and Belinda were the co-leads for their office relocation and shared accountability for that project's overall success. A significant task they were mutually responsible for was arranging the utility switchover, which they assigned to a lower-level staffer, Sandy. Both assumed that Sandy had followed up with the utility company. Unfortunately, she didn't. Min and Belinda also assumed that the other was checking in with Sandy. Neither person had. So the office was dark on the move-in day. Get it?

Here's an approach to take, especially when there is shared accountability.

Assign One Primary Owner

Unless you are willing to take risks, and are willing to rely on hope that your team members will not miss anything, it's best to assign one *primary* owner. The problem with shared accountability for significant goals, responsibilities, or tasks is that "things" can slip through "cracks."

With this approach the primary owner shouldn't necessarily perform all the actions related to the goal, responsibility, or task. Executing the actions can be delegated by the primary owner to others as needed, as long as you, the boss, are okay with it. However, the primary owner should ultimately be accountable for the results produced—or not.

Having a single go-to person with primary accountability for results reduces your odds for miscommunication and mistaken assumptions about who is doing what, by when. Assigning a primary owner helps to ensure that communication and follow-up are streamlined. Of course, anticipated and unanticipated problems may still occur, even when there is a primary owner.

Other team members can be supportive by double-checking what gets done by the primary owner, whenever it makes sense to minimize the occurrence of some potential problems. Otherwise, some important things may get overlooked. Remember 100/100 thinking (see Employee Engagement)?

When you've determined who has primary responsibility, here are three key steps for supporting accountable work.

1. Assign Appropriate Work

Begin by focusing your effort on assigning work that people are likely *capable* of doing. Everyone on the planet is capable of doing something, somewhere. Your job as a manager is to *determine if the work that you need to be done is appropriate for the person you have available to do it when you need it done.* Begin by considering some of the questions covered earlier in the Delegation Readiness section of chapter 11, as many of them may apply.

Here are some other questions:

· What are the goals or success criteria for the project or position (connect individual, departmental, and organizational goals)?

· What is the employee's current workload?

· What are their current priorities?

Your first step is to make sure that you address the needs of your direct reports. Do they have the Resources required to perform and complete their work? Do they have as much Information as you can reasonably provide? How will you Support them? Do they have adequate Control to effectively make an impact? Can they get the work done *and* not get burned out?

2. Set Clear Expectations

Be crystal-clear about what the expectations are, and how and why they are linked to achieving successful results. Clear expectations describe the "how much" or "how well" type of information for each of the most significant and impactful tasks assigned to a team member.

Here are more questions to consider as you choose the most significant and impactful tasks for which you will set your expectations:

· What results should your direct report's job produce?

· What impact should the work have on the project or organization overall?

· How should the person act with clients, coworkers, and other managers and colleagues while doing the assigned work?

· What are the core values the team member must accept?

· What standards must they follow or abide by?

· What specific processes, practices, means, or methods is the employee expected to use?

If you don't already have your expectations clearly defined for the team members you are managing, start by identifying the most important ones, and eventually add more to the list as needed.

3. Communicate the Expectations

Performance expectations need to be communicated early (and often!). Don't assume that they are known and understood just because they may seem obvious to you or you believe the team member should already know.

To successfully communicate expectations, a job description alone is inadequate. Job descriptions can be useful, but they usually don't describe specific expectations related to the performance of the many tasks and responsibilities listed on them.

What follows is an example of expectations for an administrative staff member (*Figure 12.2*). The Job Responsibilities on the left were taken from a job description and then were expanded to include the corresponding expectations.

Performance Expectations

Job Responsibility	Expectation
Manage supply inventory	Maintain methodology/process for tracking available inventory Inform appropriate staff when supplies are running low in order to replenish supplies before they are needed Monitor supply delivery to ensure timely ordering and receipt of supplies for events
Compile status reports every quarter	Ensure data contained in reports are 100% accurate Deliver reports no later than 2 weeks after each quarter ends
Monitor expenditures against budget	Update manager bi-weekly on expense activity versus budget Alert staff when their expenses are close to the budget levels

Figure 12.2

Use Checklists

I love checklists! They can be extremely handy because they save brainpower, reduce ambiguity in communication, can be followed repeatedly, and can almost guarantee that important items are not overlooked or forgotten. Checklists are also easy to share and regularly refer to. Professionals who perform the riskiest work—work that demands a high, if not perfect, success rate (like launching a rocket to Mars)—use checklists (so do pilots, surgeons, scientists, and so on). If the expectations for the successful completion or achievement of an assignment, especially one that is performed repeatedly, can be distilled down to a checklist, *make one*.

———

Determine how best to continually communicate your expectations to your direct report or team. Here again, adjust your communication style as needed to fit the other person's style. Remember to communicate your expectations clearly and firmly so that they don't sound like a vague "suggestion." By this I mean avoid giving direction that can sound like you are asking someone to do you a favor. You can do this without sounding like an a-hole. Consider using phrases that begin with:

"We need to..."

"Let's do it this way..."

"Think about trying this..."

However, if you're communicating with someone who responds better to even more-direct communication, then you could use more-directive language like:

"I need you to..."

"You'll need to..."

"I want you to..."

"This has to be done..."

The one-on-one meeting is always an appropriate time to have these conversations.

As with everything you do as a boss, it's critical that you communicate your expectations authentically. Just be yourself and *do you.*

Apply Consequences

Consequences should be associated with the results you expect whenever it's possible to link them. Without clear consequences, accountability for results can be haphazard and inconsistent. Consequences can involve either positive outcomes of completing the assignment (more interesting work and support for a promotion, and the like) or negative or adverse outcomes (such as less trust, and then less support when a new role or position is available). Consequences should also include the implicit (as in personal satisfaction) or explicit (as in financial compensation) incentives that may apply to each individual.

When your team members understand the *consequences* associated with doing their work, they can use that information to help focus their effort and motivation. If the consequences are vague or unknown, there may be less accountability for the work. You then may be left with wishing and hoping that your team members will produce desired results.

Lastly, continue to pay attention and be proactive. Make sure that the consequences are fair, consistent, tracked, and communicated to your people.

As the boss, remember that you also must be accountable for the results you are expected to produce. You're always "on," so be a good role model if you expect your team to follow you.

Don't Burn People Out!

Do you know why so many people are working at all hours of the day and night, with few breaks or downtime? It's because they *can,* not because they should. And too many bosses encourage it—intentionally or unintentionally, by their actions. Let's be clear: bosses are ultimately responsible for the burnout of their employees. If and when you're a boss, and your team members are burning out, please do your part to stop it!

As a boss, you too may be overworked and overstressed. If you are, how do you *feel?* Do you want to keep feeling this way for the rest of your career? Real leadership is needed in this area of overwork and overstress, and I doubt that your customers, shareholders, or stakeholders will provide it. The "bosses" will have to decide when enough is enough. Why not you?

Of course, the work has to get done, and you are ultimately accountable for producing results. Be assured that plenty of work was accomplished, with highly successful results, before we were endlessly tethered to our electronic devices 24/7. As you lead and manage, don't forget that human beings have limitations. If people work under great stress for long periods without actually disconnecting and recharging, they will be less productive, less creative, less engaged, less happy, and less healthy. They will burn out. This is not fake news. This is the truth. So it needs to stop. Only the better bosses can do it.

Start using your power and influence to discourage people from trying to keep up with endless work without ever disconnecting from it. Of course, do all that you can to make work enjoyable. As a better boss, try and encourage your team members to find meaning and joy in other parts of their life. You might begin with the person in the mirror. Since you're still reading this book, I'm counting on *you* to start designing a sustainable workplace for yourself and your team members. Time spent working is not separate from "living." For most of us, work is part of our life. That's why work shouldn't suck.

Remember, the world begins to change one room at a time.

3. Supporting Action

Can you remember anything you learned to do, including any skill you developed, that didn't require taking action? Of course, thinking and planning are critical to getting results. As a leader, you have to decide when enough thinking and planning has been done—and when you can support taking action. The time is right when you've developed a reasonable plan that you believe will lead to achieving a goal, with clear accountability. Then move toward action as quickly as possible so that you, and others, can learn from the experience as soon as you can.

Here's an example. Nia, a customer service manager, developed a new process for handling customer complaints that involved submitting a form to be included on the company's website. The intent was to streamline the process for everyone involved. She spent time designing the form, talking to her internal IT people about the functionality, and determining how to review the complaints as they were received. Nia decided to go "live" as soon as she had her plan in place.

Nia soon discovered that customers were not using the form and instead were going directly to the customer service reps with their complaints. It turned out that the problem was that the customers didn't want to take the time to fill out an online form, regardless of how useful she thought it would be. (In retrospect, Nia should have solicited more feedback from the customers before she moved ahead.) Ideally her intended plan would have worked. However, she learned quickly that it wasn't the right solution, because she was willing to *act*—and not overthink or overplan.

When you *act*, you move from the hypothetical "what if?" to the practical "what *is*." Without being impulsive, get into the "what is" mode thoughtfully and as quickly as you can so that you can truly determine what works and what doesn't—with actual data to review. When you act, you're able to learn by seeing and observing what's working—or what's not. You can then make adjustments as needed.

Some of your followers will be reluctant to take action because they may be afraid of failing. To keep them moving forward, acknowledge and address any fear that they have. Do everything you can to make each individual on your team feel safe to take action.

Here are some approaches for supporting action.

Promote Risk-taking

Learning and development typically involve changing thoughts or habits, or both, and that requires taking risks. To support action, support risk-taking. One of the potential consequences of taking risks is failure. Adults, in particular, don't like to fail. Encourage your direct reports to "fail safely" so that they can learn more quickly.

When I think about how poorly adults often deal with failure, I'm reminded of a child's opposite mind-set. When kids decide that they really want to do something, like ride a scooter or a skateboard, most focus on getting better at it despite how many times they may fall off, get scraped, or crash. They accept that risk-taking is part of the process of learning and improving. Of course, there is a limit to what is an acceptable risk—even for a skateboarder!

Good bosses are aware of the acceptable risks within the realm of the work assigned to their direct reports. No one should be asked or expected to do anything unreasonable or potentially catastrophic for themselves or the organization. Use your judgment and experience to guide people to take reasonable risks, and always support them if and when they fail. Sometimes the best approach is to remind your team members to "think like a kid" when they are reluctant to take a reasonable risk. Know whom you are dealing with, and don't be afraid to push someone out of their comfort zone if you believe they might respond positively.

Encourage Intelligent Mistakes

Successful risk-taking often leads to intelligent mistakes. An intelligent mistake is the opposite of a careless error. An intelligent mistake is what happens after someone does their best to think through a problem, thoughtfully plans ahead, considers the potential consequences of the decision, makes a decision, acts—and despite all this, something unforeseen then derails the plan and leads to "failure."

Naturally, nobody likes mistakes to happen. Because you are dealing with human beings, mistakes *will* happen regardless of how much you or your well-designed systems, policies, and procedures may intend to prevent them. Good coaching can help minimize unnecessary mistakes because you will have focused on developing better thinking and planning. As a better boss, you should encourage and challenge your direct reports to push themselves. Make it okay to try new approaches. Guide them to look for opportunities to apply innovative improvements to how they do their work.

As a leader, create a culture where it's acceptable to make intelligent mistakes. Support your team members to act—but smartly. And always support and encourage learning from every experience.

Focus on the "Why," not Just the "What" and "How"

In his insightful book *Start with Why,* Simon Sinek describes the importance of understanding why we do things or are asked to do them. He stresses the importance of understanding the purpose and the reason why we are doing, or why we are following, and so forth. It should be clear that effective actions can be planned and executed far more easily when your team members have their own compelling motivation—a "why" they can understand.

I believe that too many bosses are stingy with sharing information, especially the "why" variety. I wonder, *why* is that? Maybe it's because of the ancient belief that knowledge is power, and therefore one should be reluctant to give information (power) away. That ancient belief is current nonsense.

Provide your direct reports with "why" information early and often, to help them motivate themselves to solve problems and use their judgment. If you're worried that sharing information with your team members may diminish you in some way, you probably should have stopped reading this book several chapters ago.

When you're in coaching mode, help by starting with "why" questions to guide and develop your team member's ability to move toward action. You might discover that your direct report has a reason for inaction that needs to be addressed before they can move ahead. Find out what's stopping them. The earlier you figure that out, the better.

Remove Obstacles

If there are blocks or obstacles within the team member's control, then help them explore what they are, why they exist, and how to move through them. When you're the boss in a coaching mode, you're often in a position to help identify and help remove any organizational blocks that may stand in the way of their progress. Sometimes you'll need to use your power and influence within the organization to step in and help directly. This is an example of being an advocate for the employee. When needed, have the courage to use your impact to help your team member overcome what's preventing them from acting. Even if you fail on occasion, it will be worth your effort to try.

Be Curious and Open

Sometimes it's actually the boss who is the obstacle to the employee and prevents them from taking action. The phrase "lead, follow, or get out of the way" has been attributed to many people over the years. Some believe that General George Patton used it during World War II. Whoever said it first, I think it applies now more than ever!

When your direct report comes up with the most appropriate solution, don't allow your ego to get in the way of the best answers or the best ways of doing things. Unless you've been cut off from the mainstream, it should be evident to you that the pace of change and accumulation of knowledge continues to accelerate dramatically, almost daily. Always be on the lookout for and supportive of what works best—regardless of the source.

Keep an open mind and never stop learning. With all due respect to the wheel's incomparable design, most likely there will always be a new and improved way of doing something. If you want to support others to take action, make sure that you're not the one that's stuck. As you become more seasoned and experienced (meaning older!), you'll find that the value you can bring to your team will not necessarily be the direct discovery of new ideas. Instead, your real value will be in finding and developing the discoverers of those new ideas (your team members) and encouraging them to apply those new ideas by acting on them.

Be Positive and Optimistic

Remember, you set and signal the tone. When you are trying to lead someone to improve, change, or act, do everything you can to project and maintain a positive and optimistic attitude—especially when it's tough to do so.

As a boss, you're always "on," and your attitude (which is shaped by how you are thinking and feeling) seeps out of your pores. You may think you can hide or mask your attitude from others, but you can't do it for very long.

Finally, people want to follow *winners*. Winners think positively and act optimistically in almost all circumstances, especially the difficult ones. So be a good role model. If you're truly committed to supporting your team members to act, be biased toward action, and always think and act like a winner.

4. Tracking and Adjusting Performance

When you're Leading from the Rear, you can have an excellent perspective for effectively tracking and adjusting performance—*if* you pay attention. When you want to consistently reach your goals and achieve results with your team, of course, you need to focus on where you're going. You also need to know *where you are* along the way—and also to assess *where you've been*. With this information, you can ideally help everyone stay on course, get back on course, or chart a new one toward a new or revised goal.

Let's start with tracking. This should be done with each of your direct reports. Determine "how" and "how often," based on the capability and experience of those assigned the accountability.

Here are four reliable approaches for tracking performance.

1. See for yourself
2. Ask them
3. Ask others
4. Get more data

1. See for Yourself

In the section "Setting and Signaling the Tone" in chapter 6, I described the importance of managing by walking around (MBWA). The first step in tracking performance is to put yourself in a position to observe what's being done *directly*. Don't spy. Just look, listen, and learn from what you see.

When I meet with people at various companies, I hear how busy everyone is almost every day. A common complaint from staff at all levels is that they have too much work and not enough help to do it.

This may be true in your shop, and you may not be able to do much about hiring more people. Even if you have the authority and the resources, hiring more people isn't always the best solution, though it may have popular appeal.

As the boss, regularly ask yourself, "Is everyone busy doing what's important and productive most of the time?" Your answer to that question should guide any actions you take. Be sure that you're not fooling yourself by believing only what you *want* to see. Remember that it can be easy to fall into a "wishing and hoping" trap when you're the boss.

Some managers who deliberately choose to overlook what's really happening with their team can survive by being in denial for a while. However, if it's poor performance that's being overlooked, the team won't thrive. Eventually, the better team members leave, and the team sinks to some level of dysfunction.

Generally, here are some important things to look for.

- See how your people work alone at their desk, out in the field, or remotely. Do they seem organized or stressed? Are they productive, or do they just *look busy*?

- See how they typically relate to their coworkers. Do the conversations seem friendly and easy or sharp and curt?

- See how they deal with customers and clients. Do customers seem satisfied with the service they are receiving?

Anyone can have a bad day. So look for patterns of behavior. After you see for yourself what's happening with your team members, determine if what you're generally seeing reflects the type of behavior and activity that you think will produce the results that you want to see.

2. Ask Them

In the "One-on-Ones Are #1" section in chapter 11, I covered the importance of giving your employees an opportunity to share what's on their minds. This regular meeting is a chance for you to get *their* input on their performance. Listen carefully. Do *they* feel that their results are on track with your expectations? If not, why not? You don't have to wait for the scheduled one-on-one meeting to ask a direct report about their progress. Drop by periodically to do informal check-ins with your team.

As a boss, the difference between being successful and unsuccessful may be how quickly you recognize if your team members' results are tracking with your expectations. Regular and frequent check-ins with each direct report can be highly effective in helping you keep up-to-date with their performance as well as their level of engagement.

A formal or informal check-in is also a good opportunity to ask your team member the three questions that I covered in the "What Employee Engagement Means" section in chapter 11.

· What do you think?

· What do you need?

· How can I help?

Make an effort to ask these questions regularly so that they become part of your nature!

End-of-Day Check-Ins

Although anytime can be a good time to check in with your team members, I think the most useful time is at the end of the workday. When the "day" or shift is over, people are more apt to candidly reveal how they are thinking and feeling about the job than they might be at the beginning of the day when they feel fresh and maybe are more guarded. We tend to "let our hair down" later in the day, so this can be an opportune time to ask how things are going. If you pay attention to what you hear during these end-of-day check-ins and do them regularly, you'll likely pick up on patterns that may be developing for individual team members and possibly for your larger team as well. This end-of-day approach can be particularly effective when managing remote workers you don't "see" often.

These behavior patterns may indicate positive trends (as in people seem more energized and focused) or negative leanings (as in

"Stacey" appears to be distracted more). You can use this information to guide you in determining your next best steps to take for the entire team or for an individual direct report. Those next steps may be to keep doing what you're doing or to change or stop what you're doing as their boss. I'll share some ideas for adjusting performance later in this section.

3. Ask Others

Schedule intentional time to get out and look for ways to connect with other people whom your employee may work with or around. These people may be coworkers, clients, customers, vendors, or even other business partners. Look, listen, and learn. (I don't mean that you should look for spies!) Use what information you gather to help you keep track of your team members' performance as well as their impact on others so that you can help support them. Find people whom you trust who can be reliable sources of useful information about your employees, and, of course, filter it so that you can help your direct reports keep on track.

4. Get More Data

Look for other available and objective information that you can use to track progress being made (like workplans, reports, and other sources). For instance, customer satisfaction surveys can provide some performance insights that might apply to your team members. Another useful source of performance feedback for individuals can be from a more formal 360-degree Feedback Survey. (These types of surveys are typically conducted for mid-level to senior-level employees.) These surveys are best used to provide developmental information for the person being surveyed. This includes providing you, as the manager, with some insight into how others view your team member so that you can help coach them.

Be creative and look for relevant information, wherever you can find it, to help determine if your team member's performance is on track. You can decide how much attention and importance to give it, depending on the type of data and the sources' reliability. Don't wait until it's time for the annual performance review or evaluation—if you actually do one—to seek information. Always be on the lookout for what might be helpful. Be careful that you don't overreact to rumors, gossip, or innuendo. Again, filter the information you see and hear, and always use your judgment to determine what's most accurate, relevant, and useful.

Don't overlook the importance of regularly sharing the information you gather with your direct report, and use it to coach them as needed. Help them keep track of their performance throughout the year so that they can continually make any needed adjustments during their performance cycle. And don't surprise them with "new" information at the performance review meeting!

Approaches for Adjusting Performance

To get the results you want and expect from others often requires that you make adjustments. Adjusting is an *action*. As with so many actions I've described in this book, the adjustments should ideally be proactive, not reactive. When it comes to effectively adjusting individual performance, delivering value-added feedback should always be your most consistent go-to method. I recommend that you reread the feedback section until you are regularly practicing the approach. Being proficient at delivering feedback will make a significant difference for you as a boss, as you strive to adjust employee performance and work to ensure that you get desired results.

The need to adjust performance may arise for various reasons, including miscommunication, indifference, or some other form of a *problem*. If there are people who sincerely wake up each morning thinking, "I want to do a mediocre job today," I certainly hope they're in the minority. I choose to believe that most everyone wants to do good work. Sometimes, though, people don't—or won't—do a good job in producing desired results. Usually, it's because some sort of a problem exists.

Effective leaders are skilled at problem-solving. For there to be effective problem-solving between you and your direct report, or anyone else for that matter, you need to be on the same page. Unfortunately, we usually rush the problem-solving process. How often do you jump to offering solutions right away when you set out to resolve a problem or issue? Rushing to solutions is a common reason why many communication disconnects and performance breakdowns occur. Rushing can have a negative effect, whether we are trying to resolve an interpersonal problem or even a more tangible one. Remember: *go slow to go fast.*

Here are three steps to follow, sequentially, to become more effective at problem-solving or resolving issues that involve others.

Step 1. See and Understand the Problem

First, make every effort to get the other person to see that the problem exists *and* to understand what it is. If somebody doesn't truly recognize that there is a problem, it's rarely productive to invest any more time and effort to engage them in resolving it. The critical question to explore at this stage is "What's wrong (or needs to be fixed)?"

Here's an example that could apply to a situation you may encounter when you're a boss.

Ada is one of your key team members. She hasn't followed through with some of her recent commitments. You could start the conversation with her by saying, "Ada, the due date for progress updates is Friday. The last two weeks, you were late getting these to me." If Ada agrees or doesn't try to defend the action (or inaction), move on to step 2. If she has an excuse or denies that she was late, talk that through a bit more so that she can see and understand that a problem exists—for *you.*

Don't move forward to step 2 until you are confident that the other person *accepts* and *acknowledges* the existence of the problem.

Step 2. See and Understand the Impact of the Problem

Once somebody recognizes that a problem exists, they also need to acknowledge the impact or consequence of that problem. This is true whether or not the problem has any impact on them. If it does affect them personally—directly, or indirectly—then you'll most likely have a more open and willing person to resolve the problem with.

Even if the problem doesn't affect them personally, the objective is still to get them to see and understand its impact. If they're sincerely concerned about your interests or those of other people affected, they might be more motivated to move toward solutions. The logic for linking the problem *and* the impact is similar to what I described in the Value-Added Feedback model regarding *State the Impact* immediately after *State the Behavior*. The key question at this stage is, "Why does it matter that this problem is fixed or solved?" There needs to be a compelling answer to this question for those involved before effectively moving forward with problem-solving.

Continuing with the previous example, assume Ada acknowledges that she has been late with her progress reports. Now it's time to be clear about why it matters that the reports are received by Friday. So you say, "Ada, when I get the updates on Friday, I can then review them in time to share anything noteworthy in my Monday one-on-one meeting with Sandy" (the division manager).

If you're not sure that the other person understands why *they* should care about the problem's impact, go slower and invest more time trying to get them to understand it. Otherwise, you'll likely be wasting your time discussing potential solutions with a person who may be uninterested, dismissive, or possibly incapable. If you find that the latter is true, you'll need to consider another approach (that's more directive) to adjusting their performance.

Step 3. Explore and Find a Solution or Solutions

When a person can see and understand both the problem and the impact of the problem, they will be much better prepared and motivated toward finding an acceptable solution that will address the problem so that it stays fixed. No guarantee, of course! However, this approach increases the odds of being more effective and productive when you are in problem-solving mode.

Back to the example. Now, Ada sees and understands the problem *and* the impact. "Ada, what do you need from me to help you get those reports in on time?" Ideally, Ada will participate by coming up with workable solutions with you, her boss.

If your direct report still doesn't engage, keep exploring until you get the result you need. Disagreements are not always caused by the differences related to a solution's perceived merits or benefits. When one or all parties get stuck trying to solve a problem, it's often a result of not seeing and understanding the same problem and the related impacts at the beginning of problem-solving.

When you are Leading from the Rear, effectively tracking and adjusting performance is another way to ensure that results are produced by design, not by accident. Don't take it for granted that people are following along in the way that you need and expect them to. Consistently pay active attention to what's happening with each of your team members. Do you want to be surprised by a call from your boss about something that involves one of your direct reports? I didn't think so. Don't allow yourself to be surprised about *anything* concerning your direct reports—if you can help it.

Be Fair and Firm

When the tracking and adjusting of someone's performance is overdone, that's micromanagement. Don't overdo it. As with delegation, choose a style and approach to fit your direct reports' individual needs and capabilities. You should be empathetic, understanding, and fair. Recognize that sometimes you'll have to adjust *your* expectations instead of adjusting *their* performance.

Aim to be respected without being an a-hole. You don't have to be liked by everyone. Simply try to be *likable*, and remember to accept that your team members are human. Expect that mistakes will be made and that you'll have to step in to support your people at times. Effectively working with others and guiding them to produce results requires patience. Accept that we are all less than perfect, by design. With that said, know when to remain firm, especially with those people who may be inclined to take advantage of any perceived weakness of yours.

In deciding which approach to take, I've found that it's best to always assume positive intent—until you can't. This applies to being a boss or to any other role you may be in that involves interacting with people.

5. Taking Corrective Action

Not every team member will always perform successfully in their role, despite your best efforts as a boss. Even your best people will make mistakes and fail, hopefully not catastrophically. Your job is to help your team members learn from their experiences and continually improve their performance—if they can. That's what effective bosses do to build successful teams. If you make a serious, honest effort to apply the approaches described in this Active Performance Management section, you increase the odds that you'll get the desired results from your team members. Continue to pay attention to each of your direct reports by supporting and tracking their performance.

Most of us at various times in our lives may fall behind in our job performance as a result of a myriad of personal challenges. Finding the right balance between work and personal needs and commitments can be complicated, and sometimes the balance gets upended for a while. To get back on track, we need the support and help of others—often including our boss.

When you see that a team member's work performance may be suffering, start by being kind and empathetic. Show curiosity about what may be going on for the person that could be affecting their work, without getting overly personal. Be discreet and offer as much help as you can to them during a difficult period and see if they are able to manage their personal issues successfully. Sometimes you may want to recommend outside support that may be provided by your employee assistance program.

Some team members, however, have other reasons for why they are not performing to expectations and producing desired results. Their negative results could be conduct-related or job performance-related. The problem may even be that they don't really fit with the job they are in. They may lack what they *need* to do the job. Or they may lack the *will* to do the job. When you see a direct report consistently falling behind in their performance, it's time to assess what's going on and take action as you Lead from the Rear.

Don't wait too long, wishing and hoping that a significant underperformer will improve on their own without special attention (corrective action). They usually don't. Begin with this thought, "All you can do is all you can do." This quote from the motivational author Art Williams says it all about how you should approach being a better boss. Regardless of your personality and level of frustration, there's never any good reason to be an a-hole—so don't ever be one or allow others to talk you into being one.

When you've done everything you can to support your direct report, and their performance still hasn't risen to the level you expect, get help from your manager or your HR or People professionals or perhaps even an employment law attorney, especially if the situation is complicated. Effectively navigating through a corrective action process can be tricky, so don't handle it alone unless you have to. In that case, do your research and get the best advice you can.

When expected results aren't achieved, most medium to large organizations have a formal corrective action process (or should have one) as part of their employment policies and procedures. Follow your company's guidelines and work closely with your manager and HR professionals. Don't take any shortcuts here. Follow the process you have in place, despite how slow and bureaucratic it may seem. The process is intended to protect you *and* your organization, so be careful that you don't cut corners without trusted guidance.

Once you go down the formal path of corrective action, there should be one of two outcomes—they improve, or they don't. Of course, your Number 1 outcome should be that your employee will improve. Give your team member every reasonable opportunity to make a new start if necessary. If you must initiate corrective action with one of your direct reports, you will need to be willing to pay even closer attention to their performance. Be as supportive as you can.

Continue to be focused, firm, and fair once you begin a corrective action process, and be willing to check yourself too, because it's safe to assume that you're not perfect. Ask yourself the following objective questions:

· Have you made the goals and expectations clear?

· Do they know and understand what they need to do to improve their performance?

· Are they aware of the consequences if they don't improve?

· Are you giving them everything that they need to be successful, especially your support?

· Have you tried to sincerely coach them?

· Have you provided them with regular, Value-Added Feedback?

· Have you been fair and reasonable in the way you have treated them?

The primary objective of corrective action is to improve performance, not to punish the employee. If you want to be a better boss, have the courage and discipline to see your actions through. Your other team members, and your organization as well, should expect you to. Remember that you too have a job to perform, and you can't get the results you need if you don't have willing, able, and engaged team members. Accept that it's a fact that some people won't, or can't, change or improve. After you've done all that you can, be willing to see and accept the signals that your team member is not suitable for their job, then continue to take all required action following your organization's corrective action process.

An effective boss does the right thing for the rest of the team by having the courage to deal with an individual's conduct and performance issues in time so that they don't become a corrosive influence and negatively affect everyone else. If you don't make the tough decision to address poor performance, you will signal to the rest of the team (and your peers and manager) that you're willing to accept lower performance standards. When that becomes known, it can begin to negatively impact team morale (the Justice/Fairness Morale Factor), and probably also your reputation as a manager.

If you manage people long enough, I can practically guarantee that it will be necessary to take corrective action at some point. Unfortunately, I've worked with too many managers who allow themselves to get distracted and avoid acting on a team member's negative performance issues. They tend to wish and hope that things will get better. However, the team situation usually ends up getting worse. These bosses often lose their best people to other jobs, and most everyone else who sticks around has a lousy time at work.

I know that taking corrective action is, or likely will be, difficult. Remember that your role as a good boss is to support the *whole* team. Successful, engaged employees want to work alongside other team members who can carry their own weight. What you do and how you handle these situations with a non-performing team member will define your reputation as a boss.

Remember, each person on the planet can be successful doing something, somewhere. Your responsibility is to determine if that specific "something and somewhere" applies to the person you are managing. If your corrective action efforts fail, accept that the hardest decision you will make as the boss is deciding when to let someone go. If you handle these trying sitations well, meaning with fairness and compassion, you may find that some problematic team members may actually "fire themselves" before you have to. Even if you believe that someone "deserves" to be let go, it should never be an easy decision. "Be comfortable being uncomfortable."

Part | 2

"Find a way to see, acknowledge, and focus on the strengths that others bring."

Nurturing High-Performing Teamwork

I have worked with a few hundred teams at various stages of their development. That experience has taught me a great deal about how difficult it can be to create real teamwork. The fact is that true, effective, and winning teams are rare. Still, it's always worth it for a manager to try and nurture one.

You may be lucky enough to be on a high-performing team at least once in your career. However, the low odds shouldn't stop you from trying to build and nurture a high-performing team when you're the leader. Think of your favorite team sport. Can you imagine a respected professional on any team who doesn't want their team to be the champions in their sport? A true professional evinces a "winning" mentality. The best coaches and managers of these teams have the same winning mentality—maybe even more so. When managers and team members are all in synch, the highest performance usually occurs.

Based on what I've observed and learned, here are five key ingredients necessary to form a high-performing team.

Five Ingredients for High-Performing Teams

1. They Like Each Other

The high-performing teams I have seen develop and get to the performing stage truly *like* each other. They sincerely enjoy hanging out together, whether at work or outside of work. When people like each other, their communication becomes more open and fluid. Relationships become easier to maintain, especially when challenges arise. I know it may be rare to have *all* teammates like each other. That's the point—the highest-performing teams are rare.

2. They Respect Each Other

High-performing teams respect each other's skills, talents, *and* limitations. Each team member finds enough value in one another that a lack of perfection can be accepted without their feeling disdainful. When you respect someone, you admire them for who they are and what they offer, even when they are different and when you disagree with them. I know this may be hard to do!

It can take real effort to find reasons to respect certain team members. High-performing team members somehow find a way to see, acknowledge, and focus on the strengths that others bring. They also understand that these same strengths, when overdone, can be limitations that often have to be tolerated and mitigated.

3. They Trust Each Other

Trust is the key to all successful relationships. Of course, this is true for high-performing teams as well. High-performing team members don't wait for the manager, coach, or anyone else to prove that they are trustworthy. Rather, they start the cycle of trust themselves. When team members trust each other, 100/100 thinking and action occur more naturally. Read any article or research study, or listen to any story you want about the qualities of the best teams in any field, and you will see and hear the word "trust" applied.

4. They Make Time for Face Time

The best way for team members to reach a point where they like, respect, and trust each other is to spend time with each other outside of work situations, especially if the work itself is highly stressful. This could mean lunches together or time after work doing something together, something social, other than "working." High-performing teams develop when team members can see each other more personally as unique individuals. This may mean showing a more vulnerable side, which can lead to trusting each other.

Spending time with coworker team members may not be something you want to do, or feel able to do, depending on your situation. Just know that "face time"—meaning socializing—is a key ingredient for high-performing teams. The more time that team members spend socially together, the more opportunities they have to find reasons to like *something* about each other. When people begin to like each other, they become more open to finding personal and professional qualities to respect on both sides. When team members like and respect each other, trust appears and grows, and that solidifies the foundation for a high-performing team relationship.

The year 2020 began an accelerated adoption of remote working for many people, in many industries, across the world. Remote working will likely be a permanent option for some jobs. The average worker in the future may work remotely two days a week or more if they can. Fortunately, video conferencing technology has continued to improve and be utilized by all teams that are able to (or are required to) work virtually. The positive impact of remote work capability on individuals, and likely on the planet as well (less travel = fewer carbon emissions), is abundantly clear.

However, the negative consequences on team development include the lack of spontaneous personal encounters and connections in the office, hallway, or break room. Remotely connecting with people has to be more planned and deliberate. The connections can also feel more formal. A virtual meeting with someone does not look, feel, or sound the same as having them there in person. At least not yet.

I believe that less in-person face time can inhibit the social bonding time that's required for high-performing teamwork. To replace after-work socializing, some form of virtual "happy hours" have emerged as a second-best solution. These types of virtual connections are intended to be an effective alternative to help team members bond socially. However, they can be less effective and efficient, because participants may be much more self-conscious than they might be in an in-person setting. This can be true for both the introverts and extroverts in the group.

No doubt, there is still more to learn about successful team development as the remote-working world continues to be commonplace. Right now, I'm confident that high-performing teams can still be formed with remote workers, though it will probably require even more deliberate attention and effort to do so. It will take enlightened bosses with a 21st century mind-set and approach to do it!

5. They Practice

High-performing teams don't get to that high level without practice. Practice requires focus and commitment. High-performing team members continually focus on the goals (results) and support each other to achieve those goals. They remain committed to each other regardless of the challenges, obstacles, mistakes—and even the failures. Every meaningful relationship requires effort, along with a willingness to reset and start again without giving up on each other. That's what "practice" means in this context. For a high-performing team, it involves applying what's been learned about completing the assigned tasks and continuing to practice. It also includes learning how best to interact with other team members—and practicing new approaches to improve relationships.

When you are Leading from the Rear, you're in a good position to nurture high-performing teamwork by creating and planning opportunities for these ingredients to develop. You can start by recognizing what it takes to get to the high-performing level. Then you can assess your team to determine if you have the right "players" in the right roles. If and when you do, you'll be much more successful in getting the team to a high level. If you don't have the team members you may need, for whatever reason, don't give up trying to get the ones you *have* to be the best they can be. Just be realistic about what's possible, without getting discouraged.

As the boss, you'll have to honestly decide for yourself if you are willing to invest in nurturing a high-performing team. As you can see, it's not easy. On rare occasions, a high-performing team can form without a committed leader, but it's much harder. Virtually every team needs a good leader. I sincerely hope that you'll make the right decision to be one.

Highest-Performing Teams

I've identified 21 characteristics for the *highest-performing teams* and have developed a team self-assessment based on them. I share this assessment with many of the teams I've coached. I typically discuss each characteristic with them when they are forming so that each team member has a good idea of how high the bar is. I then administer the assessment with the same team at various points throughout the project or work year.

Here are some brief descriptions for each characteristic so that you can have a better sense of the meaning and intent of each.

1. High Level of Interdependence
Team members have a strong reliance on each other's performance in order to achieve the team's goals and results.

2. Clear, Incremental Goals
The goals are not ambiguous, abstract, or too fuzzy. Milestone wins are clear so that progress can be measured and celebrated.

3. Well-Defined (and Flexible) Roles and Responsibilities
Everyone knows what everyone else is supposed to be doing so that no task slips through the cracks. Team members can see and understand how they can offer help when needed.

4. Complementary and Competent Skills
The team overall has the shared ability to perform what is needed to produce desired results.

5. 100/100 Mind-set and Commitment to Team and Each Other

Each team member has an ownership mentality and is highly loyal to each other.

6. Celebrate All Meaningful Accomplishments

The team looks for opportunities to recognize achievements, both large and small, by individuals and by the team collectively. Sincere recognition encourages progress and more recognition.

7. High Level of Trust in Each Other

Team members feel extreme confidence in each other and believe that someone always has their back.

8. Share Sense of Urgency to Act

The team is biased toward action.

9. Clear Speaking and Listening

Team members are effective communicators and make a deliberate effort to ensure that messages are understood as they are intended.

10. Honest and Unobstructed Communication of Needs

No one waits and assumes that their needs are known and will be met. Instead, they let other team members know what they need to perform their job on a timely basis, and accept when some needs may not be met.

11. Clear and Collaborative Working Approach/Plan

There is neither chaos nor resistance. The team members understand and buy into how the work will get done.

12. Well-Defined and Universally Accepted Decision Methods

The team anticipates the types of decisions that will need to be made, how they will be made, and by whom.

13. Smoothly Follow and Share Leadership as Needed

Each team member understands and accepts that they may need to pivot between being a follower and a leader, depending on the circumstances.

14. Consistently Focus Mutual Effort on the Right Things

The team works together to stay busy doing what's needed in the moment without giving in to distractions that can slow them down.

15. Like and Respect Each Other
Team members get along well and want to work together, especially when ideas and opinions conflict.

16. Feel Safe Sharing Ideas, Feedback, and Differences
There is no fear of being vulnerable to ridicule, attack, or alienation when speaking out.

17. Are Consistently Optimistic and Positively Motivated
Team members are believers in what's possible and are not held back by negative thoughts or outside naysayers.

18. Members Are Emotionally Stable and Agreeable
They are self-aware and exercise an appropriate level of maturity and self-control in their interactions with each other as they respond to challenges and setbacks.

19. Members Are Patient with Process
They accept that consistent results are produced successfully when the team follows an agreed-on method for getting things done.

20. Accountable for High Standards
Each team member owns the team's work and their part of it and expects the best results from themselves and others.

21. Consistently Perform at a High Level
Each team member performs at the highest level they are capable of without compromise or the need for others to notice.

If you want to be a better boss, why not actually aim for being a highest-performing team each time you assemble a new group?

Winning Organizations

An organization should be viewed and treated *as one team* if it's going to be successful over the long term. This absolutely becomes more challenging for leaders in larger, more-complex organizations. For a high level of organizational success, the definition of what a "win" is and what a "team" is may need to be redefined and reinforced until it becomes part of the cultural fabric of your company or agency.

Moving forward, the objective of future leaders should be the creation of more winners among their followers. This can happen by providing more avenues and opportunities for people to follow along so they can personally experience a *win* and feel the motivating effect that flows from it. When that happens, your organization will also be a winner—and, with any luck, will stay that way.

Here's an example. While working with several large commercial construction companies, I have seen the desire to achieve a "one-team focus" be an ongoing challenge. One very successful company I know well built its reputation around its capability to run complex projects as the general contractor. This same company has also increased its competitive advantages over time by adding "self-perform" services like concrete and drywall installation that other general contracting firms often subcontract. On their projects where all the construction services are included as part of the package, the company had preached to their employees that they are "One Company."

Despite the best efforts of their senior leadership, however, this mind-set has proven to be difficult for the various "teams" to adopt while operating within the larger team. One reason is old habits. Even though the "One Company" mind-set and approach to doing business can provide a "win" that benefits everybody in all divisions, many of the leaders of the various divisions have had difficulty thinking beyond getting a "win" for their primary team. They have been conditioned to focus on "their" team first, rather than on the company overall.

When these self-perform units began to operate as one team, some decisions needed to be made that created more challenges for some but still contributed to a greater benefit for the larger team (the company). Still, old habits have prevented some team leaders and team members from expanding their focus to the larger team's win. In some instances, the concrete group in my example had to work overtime to accommodate a need that the general contracting group had that was necessary to accelerate the project's ability to meet the finish schedule. The bottom line for the concrete group was that they had to sacrifice the group's production costs to do it.

The difference here is that the actual bottom line was different and expanded with a "One Company" mind-set. The new win for all the team members in this company was measured by the results produced by "cooperation" and "collaboration." It wasn't easy for them to adopt this shared-win thinking when they were used to operating as more-independent units. The good news for my client was that the limitations created by the old views of some were gradually becoming mitigated by the more progressive thinking of their new leaders.

We're often more familiar with individual or smaller team competition that's focused on narrow sales, revenue, production, or service targets. Although short-term benefits may accrue for some in this type of motivational approach, over the longer term, siloed thinking within more-complex companies can lead to a negative result. This is the main reason why emphasizing internal competition within organizations can often be counterproductive if it's not linked to achieving the larger company's objectives. Traditional competition creates more losers than winners and often discourages cross-team cooperation and collaboration. This can eventually result in organizational dysfunction, despite the positive intent of the leadership.

As you are nurturing high-performing teams, encourage your team members to participate in healthy, positive, collective competition by being inclusive, sharing information, and helping each other learn and develop skills. Rather than pit one team member or team against another, create the conditions that primarily reward cooperation and collaboration. Focus the actual competition on beating a shared goal, not beating each other! This approach can increase the chances that more individuals across your organization will find greater reasons to feel motivated—and stay motivated to produce better collective results.

As your team understands and learns how to become their best, you will eventually attract and retain others who also want to be *their* best. And you will likely see more high-performing teams.

How to Hire the Right People

The most important decision a manager makes is whom to hire. It's the most significant and positive impact you can have as a leader.

So make it a priority to develop your ability to choose competent people with the right character traits for the team. This is a core tenet of Leading from the Rear. It involves investing the time and energy required to be both thoughtful and strategic in making the right hiring decisions that can enable your team to perform at a high level. As a team leader, identifying talent—and potential talent—is vital in building sustainable, successful teams. It's always advisable to get help and support in this effort, but don't outsource this *responsibility* to anyone else.

A successful hiring decision is best informed by the answers to two questions: "Can they do the job?" and "Will they fit—really fit into the culture you have or the culture you want to create?" A verifiable résumé can provide you with a great deal of information about the "can-do" question. However, determining a reliable answer to the "really fit" question is more complicated and tricky.

Far too often, a good résumé or a good interview performance, overflowing with competence, can seduce leaders into making the absolutely wrong hiring decision. A job candidate you think is a *perfect* fit because of their accomplished skills and experience (competence) eventually can bring more harm than good if they lack the other necessary qualities (character) needed to work well with you and the rest of the team.

Every employer wants superstars on their team who are highly skilled at performing their job *and* who "play well with others." As you've probably discovered, finding a potential team member who possesses both high competence and high character is not easy—regardless of the "sport." There really aren't that many superstars like that to choose from. It takes a lot of effort, patience, and discipline to make the right hiring choices. And even then, you won't always succeed.

I saw a tweet from Jonathan Reichental, a technology leader in Silicon Valley, that read: "The culture of an organization is built one hire at time." I completely agree. And the higher up you are in the leadership chain, the more responsible you are for nurturing your organization's culture, beginning with whom you hire.

Consider your most difficult team members—those who are negatively affecting the team's performance. Take a few minutes and identify the reasons they are "difficult." Do they mostly lack the skills, experience, or potential to perform, or do they perhaps lack the necessary character traits to become valued team members?

Competency alone should not be the only factor that defines "talent" for a team member. Too often, the belief that the team will be better with the new addition of a highly competent team member is followed by the hope that any remaining character questions, doubts, or concerns will not become a problem. This approach might be fine if you're hiring someone who is more of a solo actor—an individual contributor rather than an interdependent team member. Otherwise, it can be a huge mistake for you *and* your team.

Character issues are too often overlooked by hiring managers and can be overshadowed by a candidate's seeming impressive ability or experience. Be careful that you don't fall into this common trap when you're the boss responsible for selecting a new team member. Tolerating team members with low character most often limits team performance over the longer term. It can also restrict your ability to recruit new talent who might otherwise be attracted to your organization.

Once you've determined that your potential candidate can do the job at least at an acceptable level, all things being equal, it's usually better to choose someone you believe has the desirable character traits you want over someone who may possess more skills and experience. When it comes to improving individual performance, you can help a team member grow and develop skills and abilities more easily than you can change their personality and work ethic (their character).

Here are some questions you should consider to help you choose team members that will fit the culture you are building or maintaining:

Prepare—Who are you looking for?

· What is the requisite or acceptable level of competence for the job, and how can you best determine if the candidate has it (for example, skills, abilities, experience)?

· What are the character traits of your strongest team members (*not* including their skills or abilities)?

· What do your top performers do that makes others want to work with them?

· Why have people failed (or why are they currently failing) on the team? Which personal qualities got in the way and prevented them from being valued team members?

· What are the positive character traits that are shared across the team?

· How do these positive traits benefit the team? Why are they important to the team's performance?

Recruitment

Many available resources can help you to recruit talent. I encourage you to tap into them and build your knowledge and expertise on how it's done. I can add a few tried-and-true best practices that I have found to be fruitful:

· Cast a wide net to attract the unexpected job seeker. Online tools make this really easy. Be creative and don't only look in the usual places.

· Don't focus on job titles alone; look for relevant non-professional experience.

· Encourage and incentivize your employees to spread the word to their friends and colleagues.

· Use your professional and informal networks. Ask suppliers, vendors, and other contacts for leads to potential candidates.

· Ask your company alumni (those who left on good terms!) for help sourcing candidates. Be sure to acknowledge their effort in some tangible way.

Finally, this last one requires that you start *early* before you have a need to fill a position.

· Be visible and create a positive and attractive buzz in your professional community through appearances, speaking engagements, written pieces in journals or social media, and so on. Remember the adages "Success breeds success" and "Game knows game." Associate with other winners if you want to attract more winners.

Here's one more: develop a successful team, then talent will usually find you.

Four-Part Selection Process

It's likely that you already have Human Resources or People support in your company or agency that can help plan, design, and coordinate your recruitment and selection processes. Work closely with them as you consider how and when to apply the Four-Part Selection process outlined below. Most experienced talent professionals will be well aware of what I've listed, and should be open to partnering with you during the process. Still, be sure that you maintain responsibility and accountability for the outcomes throughout. In most cases, the final decision for whom to hire will be yours.

1. Leader/Manager Interviews

· In addition to competency-related questions, develop behavior-based interview questions that include the most important character traits you are looking for.

· Some good questions to ask are:

  ‣ Tell me about a time you helped a coworker when they were falling behind in completing an important assignment. What did you do and what was the outcome?

  ‣ What significant skill or quality do you have that makes you qualified for the position?

  ‣ Tell me about a time when you overcame a challenge in your life. What did you learn?

2. Team Interviews

- Have your team members participate in the interview process. Schedule one-on-one interviews with the candidate and each of your team members if logistically possible. Otherwise, have the team as a group interview the candidates. Provide the team with appropriate interview questions beforehand, and encourage them to develop a few of their own. Work with HR or your People professionals to be sure that the questions are relevant—and legal.

- Some useful questions to ask are:

    - What does being a "team player" mean to you?

    - Describe a time when you had a disagreement with your manager or a colleague. What happened? What did you do? What was the outcome?

    - What type of work environment do you prefer and why?

    - What do you do to keep learning?

- Schedule some informal, structured group time with at least a few of your team members and the candidate. Discreetly observe the interaction between them—if you can without "spying."

- Follow up with each team member to get their assessment on the candidate's qualifications and "fit."

- Be sure to get their individual assessments first before they share them with other team members or coworkers. This will minimize bias and groupthink.

- Find out if there are any concerns, questions to follow up on, or any additional information needed to make a good decision.

3. Psychometric Testing

- Consider identifying a personality questionnaire (dozens are available online) designed to measure the essential character traits you are looking for. Have your team members complete it first, then establish a benchmark representing the desired score for the new candidate.

- Administer the instrument to the candidate and compare their score to your benchmark. Be sure to consider their score as only one part of the process. *Don't* make a hiring decision based on the "test" alone.

4. Reference Checking

- Try to get the most relevant references you can.

- Don't fish around for general impressions that may be too subjective. Stick to the facts, and ask specific questions related to the job you're trying to fill. With any luck, you'll get some helpful responses.

- Listen for what's being said and what's *unsaid*.

- Some useful questions to ask a reference are:

  - What was the candidate's most memorable accomplishment, and what impact did it have?

  - How do you think the candidate could improve?

  - Would you hire or like to work with the candidate again, and why?

In both "up" and "down" economies, there will always be competition for talent. Talented people are positive and trustworthy; can handle stress; can organize their time and workload; can learn and adapt; can work well with coworkers; can communicate clearly; can make smart decisions; and can consistently treat customers so that they feel valued. Coupled with technical competence, these qualities are a sound basis for what talent looks like.

Sometimes hiring managers get too narrow or conservative in their thinking and approach. They can get caught up in the "similar-to-me" effect and favor candidates who remind them of themselves. Or they place a rigid emphasis on the completion of a specific academic degree, or make it a requirement for the candidate to have performed the same work done by someone who was previously in the position. This kind of rigidity can lead to your losing out on acquiring potential talent.

Be Sure to Focus on What Matters Most

The next time you review a résumé or actively recruit new talent, particularly at the entry levels, be open and creative in how you consider and evaluate the relevancy of previous experience and transferable skills. Some innate skills and qualities are more critical to an employee's success than the technical skills you can provide through training and experience.

I believe that throughout my life I've benefited greatly from a well-rounded, liberal arts course of study. However, I also think that the most applicable and relevant education I received relating to my profession was gained, oddly enough, by working in the restaurant business while I was a student. During those college years, I learned countless lessons while working as a host, a waiter, and especially as a bartender. And most of these lessons that I learned about the world of work occurred with live music blaring, cocktail servers lined up with armloads of drink orders, usually friendly but often aggressive customers leaning over the bar demanding a drink or conversation, and a hovering manager in the wings.

In my various roles in this restaurant and bar, I could see how people were both similar and different. I learned how important it was to be aware of my surroundings and the people within them and still stay organized and focused on what I was doing and what needed to be done next.

I learned that it was always important to treat customers as individuals whenever I dealt with them, however brief it was. I also learned from observing my coworkers that if you really don't like people at a core level, working with them will not be easy or effective.

Truth be told, I acknowledge having some "similar-to-me" bias toward people with work experience in the hospitality business for any work involving client or customer contact. I've found that people who successfully create a positive experience for customers in that industry typically understand what "service" means and looks like. I've seen many bright people with meaningful hospitality backgrounds go on to receive technical training in other industries and become superstars in their new jobs due to their character and competence. Pay closer attention, and you may discover that you have an excellent candidate serving you lunch today!

My point here is to be open and flexible when thinking about who might be the best fit for your open position and where to find them. Unfortunately, résumés can be one-dimensional and don't always allow for a well-rounded representation of the person *or* their potential. I know that résumés are not going away. Just don't limit yourself or your options, and be willing to see more than what's on the page when you have the opportunity.

Diversity, Equity, and Inclusion

As much as cultural fit should be a significant focus in your hiring process, so too should Diversity, Equity, and Inclusion—*if* you want to take a 21st century approach to managing and leading.

Diversity means having team members of different ethnicities, genders, ages, socioeconomic statuses, identities, and the like. *Equity* means providing equal opportunities and support to team members for them to succeed and get their individual needs met. *Inclusion* means that each member feels valued, regardless of their role in the organization.

The millennial and Gen Z generations are the most diverse in American history. If you want your organization to thrive, to perform at a high level, and to be highly competitive, then make diversity a sincere priority in your hiring processes from this day forward. If your HR or People function is competent, work closely with those professionals to ensure that you are casting a wide net. Be proactive and get out of your comfort zone when it comes to hiring. "Similar-to-Me" is the most common bias to avoid. It's usually unconscious, so recognize it in yourself and work to remain aware of how it might be limiting your willingness to increase diversity in your organization.

Take equity seriously. If you don't promote fairness and truly walk the talk in the way you manage and lead, you will eventually lose talent. This will likely have a negative impact on your organization's reputation and ability to attract new talent, which can accelerate a downward spiral. If you treat people equitability, they should feel included and valued. Again, walk the talk.

Don't wait for others to act. Take an active lead in Diversity, Equity, and Inclusion efforts so that you don't miss important and significant opportunities to positively impact the future on many levels—organizational, local community, and even national.

When you are successful at hiring talent, you'll find that almost all the leadership and management approaches I've covered in this book will be more easily applied and acted on. That's why *hiring is the most important decision you can make*. Having the right people in place on your team will help you to be a better boss.

Leading from the Rear (Summary)

Here are some tips to remember:

- For performance management to be effective, it must be active, not passive. As a good boss, aim for performance results to happen by design, not by accident or luck.

- When you Lead from the Rear, you have a better vantage point to see ahead and decide on the best strategies. Track your team members' individual performance by continuing to look, listen, and learn. Make needed adjustments to stay on the appropriate course for the existing conditions.

- Having a single "go-to" person with primary accountability for results improves your odds for less miscommunication and fewer mistaken assumptions about who is doing what and by when.

- Everyone on the planet is capable of doing something, somewhere. Your job as a manager is to determine if the work that you need doing is appropriate for the person you have available to do it.

- Be clear about what the expectations are and how and why they are linked to achieving successful results.

- Consequences should be associated with the results you expect, whenever it's possible to link them.

- Move toward action as quickly as possible. Get into the "what is" mode as soon as you can so that you can truly determine what works and what doesn't—with actual data.

- Promote risk-taking.

- Encourage intelligent mistakes.

- Focus on the "why," not just the "what" and "how."

- Remove obstacles.

- Be curious and open to other solutions and ways of doing things.

- Be positive and optimistic.

- Be creative and look for relevant information, wherever you can find it, to help determine if your team member's performance is on track.

- Choose a style and approach for tracking and adjusting performance to fit your direct reports' individual needs and capabilities without micromanaging.

- Don't wait too long and simply wish and hope that a significant underperformer will improve on their own without special attention (corrective action).

- Continue to be focused, firm, and fair once you begin a corrective action process. See it through.

- Nurture high-performing teamwork by creating and planning opportunities for team members to get to a place where they like, respect, and trust each other.

- Use the Highest-Performing Teams assessment questions to challenge team members and remind them how high the bar is.

- You can help a team member to grow and to develop skills and abilities more easily than you can change their personality and work ethic (their character).

- Be open and flexible when thinking about who might be the best fit for your open position as well as where to find them.

- Focus on creating a culture within your organization where Diversity, Equity, and Inclusion will continue to thrive naturally.

- Whom you hire is the most important decision you make as a better boss.

Chapter | **13**

Be a Good Gardener

Do you remember the last time you saw a beautiful garden? It may have been a flower garden or even a vegetable garden. Do you think that beautiful garden became that way by accident? Not likely.

When I was a kid, a neighbor had a flower garden that every grownup on the block admired. I can remember playing with my friends in a yard next to his house and noticing him throughout the spring and summer tilling the soil, planting seeds, and enthusiastically working that garden of his—when he wasn't throwing back errant baseballs! When he began gardening, there was only dirt, but in time there would be lots of colorful, healthy flowers thanks to his effort.

Like my childhood neighbor, a really good gardener takes responsibility for the entire garden, then patiently and purposefully follows a process for cultivating and nurturing it without ignoring or avoiding any step. The steps in that process involve all four of these activities: seeding, feeding, caring, and weeding.

Seeding

A good gardener first begins by installing the right plants—by seeding or by transplanting. The plants chosen need to be suitable for the season and location. They also need to complement the other plants in the garden.

Feeding

Once the right plants are in the right place, a good gardener makes sure that each of them is continually watered and fed the nutrients they need to grow and flourish. The amount, type, and frequency of the water and nutrients needed will depend on the particular plant and the stage of growth the plant is in. A good gardener attends to each type of plant, recognizing that each one may have different needs at different times.

Caring

When the plants are well-watered and fed, a good gardener doesn't hang back and wait for the blooms to appear. The good gardener actively pays attention to the plants by spending time in the garden observing how they are growing—or not. They know when to roll up their sleeves and trim and prune as needed so that the plants can coexist and flourish within the garden. A good gardener stays involved with their garden.

Weeding

Despite proper (even excellent) caring and feeding, some plants will wither for various reasons and have to be removed. Additionally, weeds have a way of getting into almost every garden regardless of what may be done to prevent them. A good gardener understands that weeding is necessary to successfully develop, cultivate, and maintain a garden that can thrive. Nobody really likes weeding—not even most gardeners. However, good gardeners know that weeds are "takers." They take what the good plants need to thrive and can inhibit the growth of other plants. Good gardeners keep a sharp eye out for weeds and deal with them when they appear; they don't wait and wish and hope that they'll go away on their own. Because they won't.

If you haven't already made the connection, leading and managing are similar to gardening.

Seed

Look for and hire the best people you can find and put them in the right roles so that they can succeed. Be patient and don't try to force-fit the wrong people into your organization.

Feed

Be sure to clarify roles and responsibilities for your team members and help them identify meaningful goals that align with yours and the organization's. Provide regular Value-Added Feedback and acknowledgment so that people can motivate themselves.

Care

Don't just be a boss—be a coach and encourage learning and development. Guide your direct reports to think and act like owners. Actively help them to improve or to correct their performance when they are struggling.

Weed

Pay close attention when you have new hires to ensure that they are the right fit for the job you have for them. Also, be willing to see if some of your more-seasoned team members have retired on the job. If you're a boss long enough, you'll inevitably encounter performance or conduct issues with some team members that will need to be addressed to support the rest of your team. When significant problems occur, respond quickly and follow through with corrective actions. Once you've done all that you can do, remember this: *"Don't water your weeds."*

Accept Help

Good gardeners also know when they need help, and they use it when it's offered and available. Leading and managing people can be an extremely challenging art *and* science if you take the responsibility seriously. If you want to be a better boss, don't allow your ego to prevent you from looking for and accepting outside support—from a peer, your manager, or your HR or People professionals. Even the best-of-the-best need help sometimes.

Chapter | **14**

Transition to Boss

When you decide to become a boss for the right reasons, transitioning to being a manager and a leader of people can be an exciting, rewarding time in your career. You can expect lots of shifts and changes in how you experience others at work, as well as in how you experience yourself. It can be very different—to say the least. Are you sure you really want to do this?!

I hope you've figured out by now that I don't want people to have a lousy time at work. With that said, I believe it's vitally important that new managers or supervisors transition to the boss role starting on the right foot and avoid having a lousy time at work themselves.

Let's start with some common mistakes that people make when they first become a boss.

1. When getting that first taste of additional power, some new managers focus on their new power rather than on their direct reports' needs.

2. Some fail to solicit feedback early and often about how they're doing from trusted sources, including from, but not limited to, their manager.

3. When first becoming a manager (boss), some delegate assignments without being clear. This can create confusion and frustration with and from direct reports.

4. Some new managers can overlook the importance of being discreet, especially when it comes to understanding the need to deliver negative feedback privately to their team members.

5. Some new managers, and even seasoned ones, can fall into the trap of supervising everyone the same way without accounting for individual needs and differences.

6. New managers are human, and some humans can't help but be selfish and keep the interesting work for themselves, especially when they have the power to do so.

7. Some allow their team members to put them in a position where they feel they *must* take a side with one person or another, rather than maintain appropriate objectivity and neutrality.

8. In the early stages of transitioning to the role, new managers can put too much distance between themselves and their team members, without striking a balance. I think John Maxwell, a noted leadership author, said it best: "Leaders must be close enough to relate to others, but far enough ahead to motivate them."

9. There can be a reluctance to let go of former duties and responsibilities that were part of the manager's previous individual contributor role. It's understandable because there is comfort in knowing what you already know how to do. (Remember the importance of "being comfortable being uncomfortable.")

10. A prevalent mistake for new managers is not managing time effectively. People who are already challenged with time management as individual contributors can quickly feel overwhelmed when taking on the expanded responsibility of being a boss.

———

I've witnessed many other mistakes by well-intentioned new managers as they have navigated through their early experiences in the role. However, the 10 common mistakes listed above should give you a clear idea of what to avoid if you are not yet in the position.

Meanwhile, here are some additional helpful tips for when you are transitioning to the boss role.

First, manage yourself. Make sure that you stay organized and prioritized so that you manage your time as well as you can. It's critically important that you allow time in your schedule for the unexpected—because there will be *lots* of "unexpected."

Find out what your manager's goals are—for you and for your team or unit. But don't assume that they necessarily know or will tell you without being prompted. Your willingness to ask the question about their goals may be helpful to both of you in the long run. What's most important is that what you focus on, particularly when you are starting as a new boss, aligns with your own manager's expectations.

One of the themes of this book is "go slow to go fast." That mantra definitely applies when you are transitioning to a manager role. Even though you may have generated lots of ideas about what to change while you've been waiting to become the boss, don't rush in too quickly and risk doing too much, too soon. Keep in mind that your team will first have to adjust to one significant change—that is, accepting you as the boss!

When you begin in a boss role, communicate to your team:

· What they can expect from you

· What you expect from them

· Your leadership and communication style

· Your vision for the unit and how it aligns with your manager's goals

Be ready to communicate this information to your team continually. Remember the power of repetition.

Never compare your approach to that of your predecessor. What that person did, and how they did it, is no longer relevant. *You* are now the boss, and you'll do things your way. It's best to move on and focus on the future, whether or not what the previous boss did was perceived to be positive or negative. It doesn't matter much at this point.

Dealing with former peers can definitely be a challenge. You can still be friends with someone as their boss—*if* you set clear boundaries. Be transparent with everyone about what information you can and can't share, and emphasize that what you can't share is a matter of professional ethics and does not involve whether you trust them personally.

Make clear in your conversations when you are in "friend" mode or in "work" mode. Be sure there is a shared understanding of the mode you are in. It's usually best to start with a wider boundary with your work friends and then see how things go. It's easier to become more friendly as you, and they, successfully adjust to your new relationship as the boss. It can be much harder and more awkward to create greater distance with friends when things are not going well for you, or them, in this new role.

Be careful that you never play favorites. It's human nature to want to associate with people whom we like. As a boss, you may not *like* everyone on your team. However, your job is to treat everyone fairly and to be *likable* to each team member.

Unfortunately, some former peers who may not have been your friends will not readily accept you as their new boss. It's a good idea to know your policies and procedures and any related labor agreements that may affect the people you are managing. When you are a new boss, you will likely be tested by some of your direct reports. Those with more experience than you might challenge you just because they can. Others who were passed over for your position may try to prove that they should have been promoted, rather than you. Depending on the personalities you're dealing with, former peers can be a real pain that may cause you to question why you ever accepted the promotion. Don't be discouraged, as it's often part of the transition to being a boss. I do hope that you don't have to deal with too many of these thorny issues. However, I want you to be prepared in case you have to.

Don't be isolated. Reach out to other managers and new peers whom you find you can trust. Find people whom you can lean on and learn from. Be there for them when they need you. Look for and listen to feedback from trusted sources. Continue to manage your ego. And don't feel that you have to be perfect. You *will* make mistakes—it's part of the learning process.

Sometimes when you start out in a new role it can be easy to forget the progress you are making. So, acknowledge to yourself your accomplishments and the growth you experience in your new role. You might find it helpful to keep a weekly "learning journal" that you can refer to later to track your progress. And don't forget to look at the two column lists I told you about early in chapter 6.

It's vitally important that you start off being positive and intentional and avoid becoming cynical and detached. Time at work shouldn't be treated like a prison sentence. Remember to be flexible, authentic, and forgiving—of others *and* yourself.

Be aware of your stress levels. Remember: how you think and feel "comes out of your pores." Expect to be overwhelmed at times—maybe even often—and be sure that you prioritize your mental as well as physical health. You're not a machine, so don't pretend to be. Set reasonable limits on your work hours and have the discipline to turn off your devices whenever you can and enjoy the other parts of your life. Give yourself permission to de-stress daily—for your sake, as well as your team members'.

After you begin in the new role of manager, it might be helpful to reread some of the previous chapters in this book. Be ready for a most challenging job when you're the boss.

Hopefully, you decided to take on this new role for the right reasons. The world needs better bosses. I respect each of you who has the courage to be willing to step up and be one.

Chapter | **15**

Managing Up

To be an effective boss, you can't do it all alone. You'll need the support and backing of *your* boss at times along the way, especially when you're advocating for your team members. I've encountered more than a few managers who found that their advancement plateaued at various levels, mainly because they weren't successful at building positive and productive relationships with their bosses. Despite their considerable skills and talent, these otherwise successful managers didn't factor in the importance of "managing up," and it limited them. The need for managing up may be even more critical when you're part of a complex, politically sensitive, and competitive organization.

When you consider managing up, start by remembering the golden rule: "Treat others as you would like others to treat you." In other words, treat your manager the way you would like to be treated by your team members.

Here are a few approaches that can be very useful as you navigate your management career and, I hope, develop positive relationships with your bosses. (By the way, these tips can be helpful to anyone with a boss!)

Build Trust

A critical factor in managing your boss is building trust with them. This shouldn't surprise you. Always start by being trustworthy first. *Demonstrate* to your boss that you can be trusted by being well-aware of the Four Elements of Trust (Integrity, Concern, Competence, and Reliability). And if your boss is mistrusting by nature, understand that it may take a while to get your positive intentions through to her or him. Accept that some people may be guarded and jaded by their experiences with others. Just don't give up trying to show your boss that you are trustworthy.

Anticipate Their Needs

Your boss has the same types of needs that everyone else has (Resources, Information, Support, and Control). So, observe and get to know them *and* their style and favorite approaches. Their specific needs will eventually be evident. When you sense that they lack something that you can provide, be proactive and deliver. Don't wait to be asked.

Provide Information Generously

You can bet that information will always be a need for your boss. Share what you know, and keep your boss regularly informed in a way that fits his or her work style. A poorly informed manager can't effectively advocate for your needs *or* your team's needs *or* make the best decisions for your organization. Recognize that some leaders tend to spend too much time Leading from the Front and can easily become disconnected from knowing what's happening at the place where the work actually gets done. Help your boss by illuminating any blind spots you can see that they may have about what's really going on.

Be a Good Communicator

Don't expect your boss to be a mind reader. Present your ideas, problems, issues, and opportunities as clearly as you can and in whatever format is most appropriate for them and the content (as in verbal or written). If your boss doesn't schedule one-on-one meetings with you, suggest that they do.

Sometimes you may need to "sell" your ideas, especially when you are in an advocate mode. So, develop the courage and confidence to express yourself in a compelling way. And remember: timing is everything. For example, if you know your boss's schedule is tight, don't rush and try to sell all your ideas at one time—instead, be organized and strategic. Choose your moments wisely, and always be prepared.

Relay Both the Good and the Bad News

Sharing *good* news is easy, so be sure to do it, early and often. Don't allow your boss to be surprised by *bad* news. Always be the first person to tell your boss about things that went wrong, especially if it involves you or your team. Do you really want your boss to come to you about a mistake you made that they learned about from *their* boss? Yes, timing is everything; just get out in front of sharing the bad news as quickly as possible, because this type of information won't get any easier to deliver by waiting.

Use Their Time Efficiently

Everyone is pressed for time, and I'm sure your boss is no exception. Think twice before using their valuable time. Double-check and determine if you can handle a problem or issue, or answer a question, on your own. When you do go to your boss, always bring two possible solutions to your problem or situation, just as you would expect your direct reports to do when they come to you for help. Right?

Be a Role Model

If you get frustrated by your boss's behavior or way of doing things, don't tell them what you would like changed—instead, *show* them. For example, if they don't listen well, practice active listening in your interactions with them and others. Remember that we train people how to treat us. Modeling good behavior is usually the best way to help your boss make changes to theirs.

Keep It Together

When you're feeling under pressure or face significant conflict and change, do everything you can to maintain control of your reactions, especially when there is a complete screw-up. If you overreact or allow yourself to get in and stay in an emotional state for too long, you may become another problem for your boss to deal with.

Start by being open to receiving feedback from your boss. Manage your ego and keep a check on your defensiveness. Don't allow your "hair to catch fire." Develop your coping skills and resiliency so that you can become the "go-to" person for your boss when things around you begin to heat up—as they likely will!

Chapter | **16**

Managing Yourself

One of the most important things you can do to remain effective in any part of your life is to continually manage yourself. This ability may determine your future success and the kind of results you can achieve.

"Self-help" is probably the most popular topic there is. The "best of the best" make sure that they focus on the complete self—mind, body, and spirit. Many beneficial and thoughtful books, articles, videos, blogs, and podcasts cover this subject well and are readily available. It would benefit you to pay attention to those sources of information that most resonate as you consider self-improvement.

Meanwhile, I do have my own top ten list for you to also consider:

1. Try Hard to Stay Out of Your Own Way.

Too often, we let our ego, drive, and even our best intentions form a cloud or shadow that becomes an obstacle that can keep us from thinking and doing what we should—especially at work. Be humble, especially if you're a standout in your field.

2. Feed Your Head.

Always be curious. Read, look, listen—and learn.

3. Feed Your Body.

Remember that you're not a machine, even if you're often tethered to one. Get a balanced diet. Sleep. Exercise. Repeat. Invest in your body as if you were a professional athlete. Even if you rely primarily on your brain rather than on your throwing arm, don't you need your body to be healthy, as well?

4. Feed Your Spirit.

Seek out positive relationships and allow yourself to be inspired. If you are getting weighed down or slowed down by others who are negative, commit to shedding these relationships or at least minimizing the time you spend in them. Make and build connections with others in both your personal and professional life.

Positive relationships can be found with other people (like close friends and family and also casual acquaintances), your pets, and of course with a higher being if that is meaningful to you. Even if you're not religious or spiritual, have faith in others, and believe that help and support will eventually be there for you when you need it—especially if you commit to helping others when you can.

5. Find Your Balance.

Look for the right balance in your life between your work and your personal time. Over time your life's priorities will change, and then you'll need to adjust the balance. Don't aim for a perfect 50/50 balance because it isn't possible. The key is to manage your stress, avoid burnout, and invest your time in what's truly important to you—your priorities! If you struggle with your use of time, invest in a book, class, podcast, or video that can help you improve your time-management skills. Recreate, party, let loose when you can in the way that you like to do. Just know your limits!

6. Keep Track of Your Learning and Accomplishments.

Invest a few minutes each week, maybe on Friday if it ends your week, looking back on the previous week. Keep notes someplace that is easily accessible—on your digital device or on paper. What were your successes? What would you change if you could? What happened that made you feel good? What lesson did you learn that you might apply next week or sometime in the future?

7. It's About the Small Stuff.

Richard Carlson wrote a best-selling book some years ago titled *Don't Sweat the Small Stuff…and It's All Small Stuff: Simple Ways to Keep the Little Things from Taking Over Your Life*. A core message of this still-relevant work includes the admonition to notice and appreciate the "small stuff." Such stuff can be as simple as finding time to laugh. A good sense of humor can help to keep you centered, stable—and sane. As you've probably figured out, humor is also contagious. Spread it around.

8. Practice Positive Thinking and Being Grateful.

Do whatever you need to do, as often as you need, to remind yourself that being positive and grateful attracts more positivity to you.

Being optimistic, especially when you're feeling low or have had a setback, helps with managing stress and overall health.

9. Use the Personal Effectiveness Wheel.

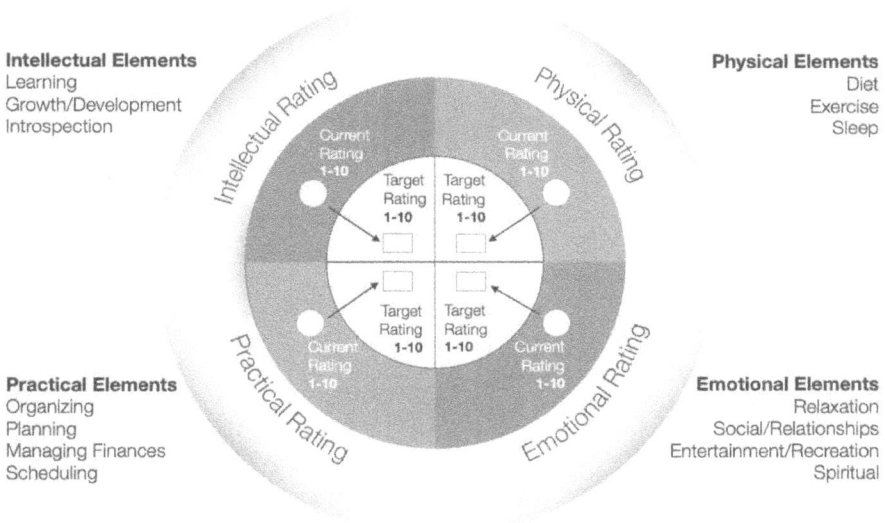

The "Personal Effectiveness Wheel" (*Figure 16.1*) can help you determine the areas of your life on which you want to focus more of your valuable time and energy.

Personal Effectiveness Wheel

Intellectual Elements
Learning
Growth/Development
Introspection

Intellectual Rating

Current Rating 1-10

Target Rating 1-10

Physical Elements
Diet
Exercise
Sleep

Physical Rating

Current Rating 1-10

Target Rating 1-10

Practical Elements
Organizing
Planning
Managing Finances
Scheduling

Practical Rating

Current Rating 1-10

Target Rating 1-10

Emotional Elements
Relaxation
Social/Relationships
Entertainment/Recreation
Spiritual

Emotional Rating

Current Rating 1-10

Target Rating 1-10

Instructions: Consider each of the four dimensions of your being. In the outer circle, rate your current effectiveness in each dimension based on your perception of your current results and satisfaction levels. In the inner circle choose a target rating for each dimension that indicates what level you would like to improve or maintain. The target levels do not have to be equal for each dimension unless you want them to be. Choose the right balance for how you want to be effective.

Figure 16.1

10. Focus on What You can Control and Influence.

Let go of the things you can't change or don't have the energy to deal with. Always start with managing yourself.

Chapter | **17**

Maintaining
Your Momentum

Learning about how to be a better boss takes more than merely absorbing information. It first requires thinking about the content, then understanding how it fits with what you already know, subsequently changing some of your thoughts about "what is," and finally determining how to apply the information. Then the hard part—*practice!* If you really want to change or improve any personal behavior, you have to change your habits and practice. The insightful author and journalist Malcolm Gladwell offers some appropriate wisdom, "Practice isn't the thing you do once you're good. It's the thing you do that makes you good." I would add, make every effort to "Get *out* of the habit of being *in* the wrong habit."

Since you have evidently managed to work your way through this book, keep your momentum going by investing a bit more time considering these questions to help you plan how to realize your future of being a better boss.

1. What concepts or approaches have you learned that are the most significant for you?

2. What are you willing to change as a result?

3. Over the next month, what's ONE commitment you're willing to make as a result of what you learned? What results do you expect?

4. What obstacles do you anticipate, and how will you overcome them?

5. What support do you need to follow through on your commitment?

6. How will you hold yourself accountable?

7. What will you need to do differently (habits) to meet your commitment?

8. What is your next "best step" or action to take?

———

Adopting changes usually occurs incrementally for most humans. Take one steady step at a time, just like on a walking path, even though you may think you can take more than one. It can be easy to trip or get overwhelmed if you try to change too many habits at once. "Focus on one peanut at a time. Then eat one peanut at a time. Repeat."

When you focus your effort on a single commitment that leads you to improve your approach (*and* then you actually see a positive result), you'll feel more inclined to do more. Again, be willing to practice what you've learned. Never allow failures or setbacks to deter you—they are simply part of the learning process. Begin again, make adjustments, and keep at it. It's okay to start small—and to seek help when needed.

If you stay ruthlessly focused on what it means and feels like to be the best version of yourself, positive momentum *and* positive results will surely follow.

The **Conclusion**

Sooner or later, most of us realize that the time we're given in this life is the one thing that we can't replace or get more of when it's gone—regardless of our power or wealth. Between life's ups and downs, I try to be grateful for every fleeting minute that I have. When I feel gratitude, the beginning and end of each day is a success. Over time I've learned that people define success differently, depending on their circumstances and their current stage of life.

One piece of advice I received that most impacted my professional success occurred when I was deciding whether to start my consulting practice. The advice was: "Leap and the net will appear." It was a valuable message given by a generous and wise family friend. And I needed to hear it at a time when I was making a critical mid-career life decision.

Regardless of your age, if you ever feel a strong calling to switch gears, or to go in a different direction, consider my friend's words and decide if they resonate with you, too. As you move on with your life and career, decide for yourself how you want to measure success. And then do everything you can to achieve it by design—*your way.*

A few years back, a group of young professionals I was consulting for asked me what thoughts I had about pursuing success in general. I thought it might be helpful to end this book with what I shared with them then. I believe you'll find that these tips have been universally relevant for a very long time.

1. Listen to everyone's advice and insight, and always encourage people to share more of what they think. Just be sure to rely on your own filter. Be open and true to yourself, determine what should stick with you, and leave the rest aside.

2. Always be grateful for what you have—and for what you *don't* have.

3. Don't worry too much about what's in front of you. Make your own way at your own pace, and try to relax. Find the flow. When you look back on your life, every decision and every turn you've made will somehow make sense.

4. Be curious. It will help you be a better listener, and that will lead to stronger, more meaningful connections with people.

5. Start early and stay late (but not too late!). Work hard and recognize that hard work alone doesn't always to lead to success. Luck also plays a part in being successful—at anything. You've probably heard that "Luck is when preparation meets opportunity." So be prepared by working hard, and opportunities will appear.

6. Manage your time and your workload. Know what to say "no" to. Be able to ask other people, "How can I help?"

7. Life is about relationships—with family, friends, and colleagues. Be a "giver" and not a "taker." Always make "deposits" and actively invest in relationships if you want to have people around when you need them.

8. Develop the qualities of the most successful people: Always be learning, and connect with others in an authentic way that makes them feel individually valued.

9. Spend part of your day dreaming, and be bold enough to follow your dreams. Life is a gift—an incredible opportunity to write, direct, and star in your own "movie." You don't have to be a supporting actor following someone else's script. When you're clear about what you want to bring into your life, "act as if" it's already there.

10. Be willing to discover—and rediscover—who you are as you grow, change, and move through the different stages in life. Always respect and like yourself first. That will attract others to you.

Whoever you are and whatever you do to make a living, I hope you will appreciate and generously share the talents and strengths you've developed, and are developing, along with the privileges you've been given as you pursue and define success.

Remember that most of us spend a considerable amount of our waking hours at work. If you've chosen to be a boss, don't ever forget that your positive or negative actions can significantly affect how others feel about their lives while working for you. Your treatment of people can linger and have a carry-over effect when they're at home by themselves or with their families, and even beyond. Your behavior can have a profound influence on others—directly and indirectly. What you do as a boss matters a great deal.

I've heard it said that a good leader is like a good music conductor. A talented conductor energetically guides and inspires skilled musicians playing various instruments to perform together by setting the tone and tempo, and clearly communicating with them throughout the piece as they produce a collective result—enjoyable music! As you lead from the Three Perspectives, why not bring similar enthusiasm and commitment to your role? If you did, what might be the result?

Accept that you'll make mistakes and learn from them without losing your self-confidence. This book is not about how to be a *perfect* boss. It's about how to be better *as* a boss. Being a better boss happens naturally when what you do genuinely matters to you, and when you pay close attention to ensure that *no one* has a lousy time at work.

I'm sure that if you consistently *care* about the people you work with, you'll figure out the right thing to do most of the time. Believe that, believe in people, and believe in yourself.

Acknowledgments

I'm grateful to have valued family, friends, and colleagues who have helped support, encourage, and advise me at various points as I wrote each section of this book. When the book was barely an outline, these special people included Steve Lamont and Rusty Rueff. As the book developed and began to take shape, David Rzepinski, Dick Gregory, Ross Edwards, and Paul Vagadori provided valuable guidance and inspiration that helped me to push forward to completion.

I'm very thankful for my editor Mark Woodworth who added broad insight, expertise, and professional touches to my writing. Mark's positivity and encouragement throughout the editing process was a needed source of inspiration. I'm also very grateful for Deborah Heimann, who contributed her proofreading patience, skill, and overall attention to detail to give the book the finishing touch it needed.

Thanks to Alan Dino Hebel and Ian Koviak of The Book Designers for their professional polish of the book design. For a newbie author, they made the process easy.

What people see in my printed and digital work, including this book, reflects my wife Michele's taste, judgment, and many graphic and artistic talents. She is not only my great love and life partner through thick and thin but is my number one associate! Her unwavering support and commitment helped me get this project over the finish line.

As this book has slowly progressed from inception, my son and daughter Nick and Grace have also grown, entered the work world, and have recently become new bosses themselves. Thinking of them and their work challenges helped me focus my thoughts and ideas to try and help them and others like them, particularly during the final stages of writing. Among my many roles, being their dad brings me the most joy. I value and appreciate the love and pride they have for who I am and for what I do more than they will ever know.

If I have worked or connected with you at any point, I'm also grateful to you because I'm sure that each one of you has somehow influenced me in one way or another. The concepts, approaches, and tools I've described on these pages are somehow the result of my experiences that included you.

The **Index**

About the **Author**

Jim Delia is an organizational development consultant, trainer, facilitator, and primarily a coach helping leaders at all levels in the private, public, and not-for-profit sectors plan and implement strategic, organizational, and personal changes to achieve better results. He is also a presenter at various in-person and virtual events and conferences throughout the year. Jim lives in the San Francisco Bay Area.

For more information about Jim's customized services, visit:
Deliaconsulting.com

www.ingramcontent.com/pod-product-compliance
Lightning Source LLC
Chambersburg PA
CBHW050238270326
41914CB00041BA/2038/J